Southeastern Indians
since the Removal Era

SOUTHEASTERN INDIANS

Since the Removal Era

edited by
WALTER L. WILLIAMS

Athens • The University of Georgia Press

Set in 10 on 13 point Trump Medieval type
Printed in the United States of America

Library of Congress Cataloging in Publication Data

Main entry under title:
Southeastern Indians since the Removal Era.

  Bibliography.
    1. Indians of North America—Southern States—His-
tory. 2. Indians of North America—Southern States
—Social conditions. 3. Southern States—Race rela-
tions. I. Williams, Walter L., 1948–
E78.S65S67   975'.004'97   78-10490
ISBN 0–8203–0464–6

Contents

Illustrations

Maps

Foreword

When the average American speaks of Native Americans of today, he usually means those American Indians living in the West who reside on reservation lands. Most people are misinformed about the fact that more than 100,000 Native Americans live on the Atlantic Coast. They are also astonished to learn that more than 75,000 American Indians live in the Southeast.

From the Big Cypress Reservation in Florida to the federal lands of the Choctaw in Mississippi, there are several official reservations in the South. But there are also Indians who are greater in number than those who reside on trust lands. For various reasons, some Indians did not "dance" to the music of Andrew Jackson's Removal Act of 1830. The Lumbees who stayed in North Carolina, for example, fought for their identity in the courts and later used their guns against the whites in a decade of terror during the 1860s.

Even the present-day federal reservation Indians began their post-removal history as unrecognized groups. Four thousand Cherokees died on the Trail of Tears, yet a remnant remained in the Great Smoky Mountains. When the Seminoles saw they could not win their war of independence against the United States, they chose to hide rather than fight and lose.

Today, it appears that Indians of the Southeast are entering a new era. Those on the reservations are fighting for self-determination, while those who are not on reservations are seeking federal recognition through congressional legislation.

Professor Walter L. Williams has made a great contribution to southeastern Indian history by bringing together a collection of essays written by authors who have expertise in a people who were almost forgotten but now seek a place under a new rising sun. Readers will find *Southeastern Indians since the Removal Era* most informative and enjoyable.

ADOLPH L. DIAL

Pembroke, N.C.

Preface

The purpose of this collection is to bring together in one volume an overview history of the Native American groups remaining in the southeastern United States. Each of these essays was written especially for this study, which brings together for the first time research that is being done separately on each remnant group of native people in the South. In addition to expertise in the documentary sources, the criteria for including each author in this volume was that he or she had extensive personal contact with the Indians about whom they were writing. Too much inferior writing has been done in American Indian history by scholars who have not had the perspectives gained by such personal contacts.

Although this study is primarily historical, aimed at analyzing a largely ignored group of people in the South since the 1840s, it is also interdisciplinary. It is directed toward those who are interested not only in the history, anthropology, and sociology of the South, but of Native American studies as well. There is much literature on the archeology, ethnography, and early history of southeastern Indians up to the 1830s, but very little has been written on those Indians who remained behind after the removals. In studies of the New South, Indians are hardly ever mentioned, even though they offer a different perspective for understanding race relations in the region. Likewise, the history of Native Americans after the passing of the frontier has also been neglected. In both of these fields, this collection can make a contribution. As Indians and as Southerners, these peoples are increasing their ethnic awareness and can no longer be ignored.

Gratitude is expressed to the Taft Fund, at the University of Cincinnati, for financial aid to this project, and to David Lawson for the maps.

In an edited collection of essays, the primary effort is made by the contributors themselves. All of these authors are published scholars who have taken time from their current research projects to write a chapter on the group of Native Americans with which they are most familiar. I think the effort to gather the most prominent specialists has "paid off," and they have been exceptionally cooperative in this collaborative venture.

The reader might be surprised to find, in an avowedly historical work, that the majority of the authors are anthropologists. But, if we consider the topic, it is not so surprising. While Indians in the South have been a classic concern of anthropologists, going back to James Mooney in the 1880s, historians have only recently begun to turn their attention to these peoples. The state of historical studies on southern Indians after 1840 is still, unfortunately, somewhat like the situation a few decades ago, when historians deferred to sociologists in the study of Afro-Americans.

Recently, however, historians and anthropologists have begun moving closer together in subject interests and patterns of thought. Historians are moving away from a concentration on "great men" and more toward the total cultural framework in which the mass of people in a society live. Anthropologists, on the other hand, are deemphasizing a static view of cultures, divorced from their time period, and are now looking at the historical processes of continuity and change through time. Perhaps this merger of perspectives, along the lines of cultural or social history, can best be summarized as "ethnography in time perspective."

There are other ways the two disciplines are moving together. Historians, partly under the pressure of non-Western intellectuals, have abandoned that old ethnocentric concept that "history" is confined to the Western cultural tradition, with other ways of life being seen as unchanging. In analyzing the historical process in that non-Western *majority* of the world, historians have been forced to borrow many of the techniques and insights of anthropologists. Concurrently, anthropologists have discovered the value of historical documents as sources for their analyses. Both disciplines, based on intimate personal contacts with human subjects or those people's writings, probably also share a more humanistic viewpoint than some of the other social sciences. While justifiably utilizing modern quantitative techniques as a method of inquiry, historians and anthropologists feel a humanistic concern, of a special personal relationship with another group of people, that questionnaires and statistical analysis alone cannot provide.

These essays attempt to provide a total picture of the ways of life of these remnant peoples. Because each Native group was a separated small community, isolated from other Indians (as well as non-Indians) for much of their post-removal history, the study of remnant Indians must necessarily be localized. Their history was distinct from that of western Indians, and is not understood by a general reference to Native American studies. In this aspect of localized isolation, the anthropological approach can make the greatest contribution because of dependence upon direct field-work involvement with the Native people. The result, based on interviews with older individuals of the group, by scholars living amongst the community, makes for an "inside" viewpoint. We can begin to see the past as the Indians themselves see it, and to define it in their terms.

Another focus of these essays concerns white attitudes toward these remnant Indians and the resulting policies. Historians, with their training in searching documentary evidence of the past and in knowing the general "temper of the times," can make their most significant contributions in this area. The only trouble is that historians sometimes *claim* to be doing Indian history when, in fact, they are really doing the history of *white* attitudes *toward* Indians. This approach is comparable to defining United States history in terms of European attitudes and actions about the United States, and American historians have been continually proclaiming their independence of such an approach since Frederick Jackson Turner.

Nevertheless, understanding white attitudes is crucial, simply because the way of life of these Indian remnants (often in ways that the people themselves did not recognize) was to a great extent determined by the non-Indian majority. *The* major problem for all southern Indians of the last century and a third has been to define their ethnic status as a third group within a biracial society. Thus southern Indian history will be incomplete until these inside *and* outside approaches are integrated into an understanding of their changing lifestyles and positions within southern society.

Interdisciplinary teams of historians and anthropologists, as represented in this collection, offer the best chance to reach this understanding. Anthropologists can keep historians from looking at

Indians as just one of a number of irritating challenges in the gloriously expanding frontier, and constantly remind them that there are other sources for understanding the Indian past besides government reports. Historians, on the other hand, can acquaint anthropologists with the complex relationships of occurrences in a certain time period and expose them to the "mysteries" of primary source documentation.

One scholar who has worked long and hard to unite these two approaches in the study of southern Indians is Samuel Proctor. Professor Proctor has provided encouragement for this project since its inception, and he chaired a session on this topic at the 1975 Annual Meeting of the Southern Historical Association. His work at the University of Florida, in collecting oral-history interviews from numerous tribal groups, has aided immeasurably in the preservation of the Native peoples' past.

All these scholars owe their greatest debt of gratitude to the Indian people with whom they have worked. Many of the data that are presented here would not have been known if it were not for the generosity of these original Americans. It is hoped that they will continue to be involved with, and encourage, the writing of their histories so that their story, at long last, will be known.

WALTER L. WILLIAMS

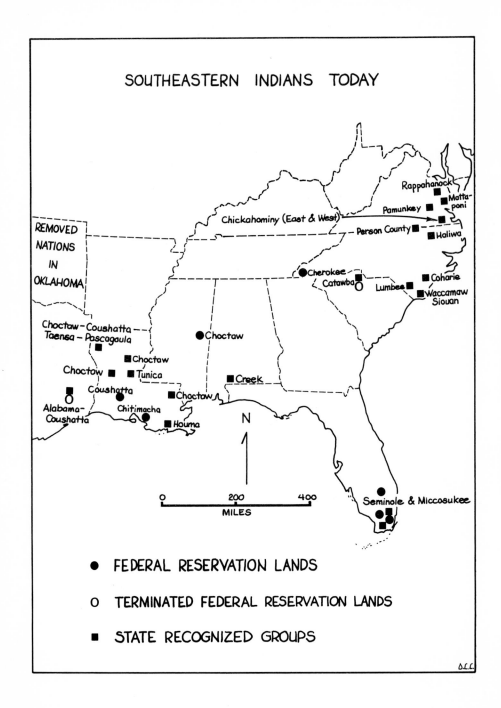

SOUTHEASTERN INDIANS TODAY

REMOVED
NATIONS
IN
OKLAHOMA

Chickahominy (East & West)

Rappahanock
Matta-
poni
Pamunkey
Person County
Haliwa

Cherokee
Catawba
Lumbee
Coharie
Waccamaw
Siouan

Choctaw—Coushatta—
Taensa—Pascagoula
Choctaw

Choctaw
Choctaw
Tunica
Creek

Coushatta
Chitimacha
Choctaw
Alabama—
Coushatta
Houma

N

0   200   400
MILES

Seminole & Miccosukee

● FEDERAL RESERVATION LANDS

O TERMINATED FEDERAL RESERVATION LANDS

■ STATE RECOGNIZED GROUPS

D.L.C.

Introduction

1

Southeastern Indians before Removal
Prehistory, Contact, Decline

WALTER L. WILLIAMS

W hen American Indians of today are discussed, it is usually in reference to the large reservations of the western
United States or the growing numbers of urbanized Indians in the big cities. Few people think of the South as the home of
modern-day Native Americans. If non-Indian Southerners are pressed,
they might recall visiting Indian lands as tourists, usually among
the mountain Cherokees or the Everglades Seminoles. Yet the
South, probably more than any other section of the United States,
is generally perceived as a purely biracial society, defined in black
and white terms.

Most Americans would probably be surprised to discover that the
fifth-ranking state in Indian population is North Carolina. Moreover, every southern state has some resident Indians among its
population. The 1970 census lists 75,644 Indians in the South, most
of whom are descended from Native peoples indigenous to the area.
Over half of that number (44,195) resides in North Carolina, but
the other states, in order of Indian population, are Florida (6,392),
Virginia (4,862), Louisiana (4,519), Mississippi (3,791), Georgia
(2,271), Alabama (2,163), South Carolina (2,091), Arkansas (2,088),
Tennessee (1,432), Kentucky (1,322), and West Virginia (518).[1]

These numbers are admittedly small, yet the Indian peoples of the
South are important beyond their numbers. Their experiences can
offer valuable insight into interethnic relations because of their long
period of survival *within* the white-dominated society. With the ex-

ception of the Iroquois of New York and Pennsylvania and scattered small groups of New England, Indians who have remained in the South have had a much longer time to deal with the absorption of their lands by the Anglo-American system. Their methods of adaptation, experienced by most surviving Native American groups for not much more than a century, are crucial to understanding Indian history "behind the frontier." While much scholarly and popular attention has been devoted to the Indian as an opponent in the struggle for western expansion, little consideration has been given to those Native peoples who survived within the confines of the legal and social networks of Euro-American culture.

The remnant groups of Indians in the South are also important because they have not only managed to survive as a distinct ethnic group, they have retained an Indian identity within a society in which ethnicity has been defined as a black versus white dichotomy. In doing so, they provide a different perspective for analyzing southern race relations outside its usual biracial context. Their ethnic persistence provides an excellent case study for analysis of the whole problem of ethnicity.

To understand the situation of Native American peoples of the South today, it is necessary to have some knowledge of their past. Indians, probably more than any other group of Americans, have had their present status determined by what has happened to them in the past. The Native American past did not, of course, begin with the coming of the Europeans. Even though historians have a tendency to see the "prehistoric" times as one era, those eons were anything but static. Like other peoples of the world, the original occupants of America experienced vast changes in their ways of life through time. Their cultural development refutes the stereotype of the "unchanging primitive" that is somehow conceived as being ahistorical.

Most archeologists agree that the first humans to people the New World migrated from Asia by way of a bridge of connecting land between Siberia and Alaska. Geological, biological, and archeological evidence indicates that such crossings probably began about 30,000 years ago, when the level of the Pacific Ocean was lower. Although these dates are currently under debate, and may be revised even further back in time, there is no doubt that there was fairly widespread occupation of North America by 10,000 B.C.

These earliest people have been called, by archeologists, Paleo-Indians. The scant surviving evidence suggests that they lived in small groups of about twenty people each, probably organized on an informal basis through kinship ties. These earliest Americans survived by hunting big-game animals, which meant that they were nomadic. They hunted with spears and had no help besides their domesticated dogs, so they had to travel lightly with minimum materials.

About 8000 B.C. a warming of the climate, with the end of the Pleistocene Ice Age, caused the extinction of many of the large mammals upon which the Paleo-Indians depended for food. The ecological change meant that these hunters had to turn to other sources for survival, as new local environments began to form. After this time, North America became much more diversified in its geography and climate, and the Paleo-cultural unity dissolved into many local adaptations. Although there was much diversity from one area to another, it is possible to designate the Great Plains as a transition zone between eastern and western adaptations.

The peoples in eastern North America, from the Great Lakes region to Florida, evolved a new way of life that is referred to as the Archaic. After 8000 B.C. these peoples began to rely much more heavily on fishing and small-game hunting and on collecting shellfish and wild plants. Such utilization of new, localized sources of food meant that people did not have to move as often, so they could afford to make more tools. Stone, bone, and wood were the major tool materials, and the Archaic Indians were beginning consciously to change their forest environment.

By about 2000 B.C. a new invention appeared that would have far-reaching effects on their way of life: pottery. Although pottery was also being developed by Indians in Mexico and South America, it was probably invented independently by southeastern Indians of the coastal Georgia area. The development of an easily constructed, lightweight, waterproof vessel allowed storage of food year round. Such advances brought about increases of population and corresponding cultural changes that produced a new stage known as the Woodland Era.

By the beginning of the Woodland period (about 1000 B.C.), plant collection had evolved into agriculture. The new Woodland culture spread south from such agriculturally rich areas as the Ohio River Valley, and was marked by a new ceremonialism associated with funeral rites. The dead were buried in earthen mounds and provided with food and tools to take with them into the afterlife. Objects of value were traded over an extensive territory, from as far away as the Rocky Mountain and Great Lakes regions. This cultural explosion gradually diffused over the entire Southeast, and continued in coastal areas until the coming of the Europeans.

The next great emergence of a new way of life developed in the Mississippi River Valley after about A.D. 700. This Mississippian stage represented not only the evolution of Woodland forms but a strong cultural influence from the Indians of Mexico. By some means—trade, land migration, or water-travel contact along the coast of the Gulf of Mexico—elements of the great civilizations of Meso-America reached the Mississippi. There, in the fertile farmlands of large river valleys, this new culture arose. The Mississippians developed towns around a ceremonial center consisting of huge mounds. These mounds were not used primarily for burials but as high platforms for their religious temples. Major temple mounds still survive today, especially in the Mississippi Valley from Louisiana to Wisconsin, and spread eastward into Alabama and Georgia and westward into Texas and Oklahoma.

The various Mississippian political units (more accurately described as city-states than tribes) developed a high standard of living, based upon intensive agriculture of corn, beans, and squash. This prosperity allowed the rise of an artistic and craftsman class, as well as a high class of religious leaders. Such social complexity and stratification of people into separate classes meant further growth. Ironically, the increase of population meant that competition for the best valley farmlands increased, to the point that organized warfare arose. Moats and palisades were built around the towns, and people lived in rectangular wood and mud-plastered houses either inside or near the defenses.

Mississippian culture reached its height between A.D. 1200 and 1600, but several Indian states followed this lifestyle into the historic era. French explorers wrote detailed descriptions of the Natchez

Indians of Mississippi and Louisiana, who probably best exemplified Mississippian culture.

During the 1500s and 1600s, the complex development of Mississippian culture declined drastically, partly because of the impact of warfare on their long-distance trade patterns. The major reason for this decline, however, was tremendous population decreases brought about by the introduction of Old World diseases. Probably the most important factor in European success over the Native Americans was disease. Europeans of the Age of Discovery, whose immediate ancestors were people who had survived the ravages of the Black Death, were likely among the most disease-resistant humans who ever lived; but the disease organisms also had survived, and when Europeans brought these foreign germs with them, the Indians had no immunity. Almost from the very beginnings of European contact, epidemics of smallpox, diphtheria, scarlet fever, measles, yellow fever, and other Old World diseases broke out among coastal tribes and rapidly spread into the interior. The successive waves of Old World diseases among southeastern Indians began a series of changes that destroyed the old Mississippian culture and produced the historic cultures.

Many tribal and national groupings of Indians had lived in the Southeast for centuries and their cultures were not by any means destroyed. The four main cultural subdivisions, organized by language family and way of life, were Algonkian, Muskogean, Iroquoian, and Siouan. The Algonkian speakers, probably the original settlers of the Southeast, were scattered from eastern Canada down the Atlantic Coast to North Carolina. The Muskogeans were spread over a huge area of the central South, from the Ohio Valley to the Gulf Coast and from Georgia to eastern Texas. These two groups were divided into a multiplicity of small tribes, but some of these tribes were organized into large confederacies, such as the Powhatans of Virginia and the Creeks of Georgia and Alabama.

The Iroquoians, centered in the southern Appalachians and the Carolinas, were more recent migrants into the Southeast, but how long they were in the area is debatable. Archeological and linguistic evidence suggests that the Cherokees, the largest group of Iroquoians, migrated from the Northeast before the time of Christ, while the Tuscaroras may have arrived at a later time. The Siouan

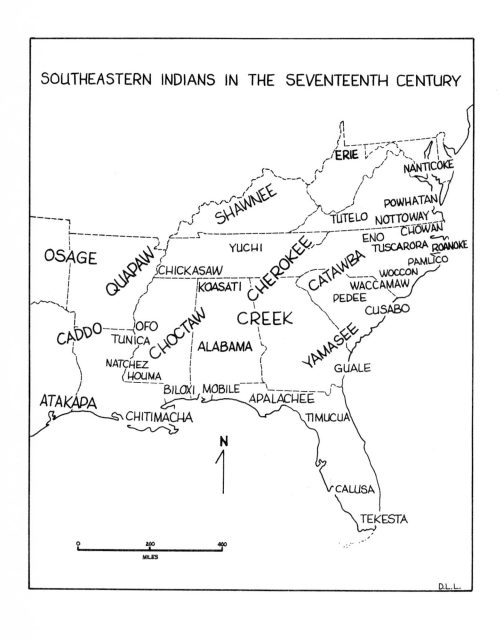

SOUTHEASTERN INDIANS IN THE SEVENTEENTH CENTURY

ERIE

NANTICOKE

POWHATAN

SHAWNEE

TUTELO   NOTTOWAY

CHOWAN

ENO

OSAGE   YUCHI   TUSCARORA   ROANOKE

QUAPAW   CHICKASAW   CHEROKEE   CATAWBA   PAMLICO

WOCCON

KOASATI   WACCAMAW

PEDEE

CADDO   CUSABO

OFO   CHOCTAW   CREEK

TUNICA

NATCHEZ   ALABAMA   YAMASEE

HOUMA   GUALE

ATAKAPA   BILOXI MOBILE

APALACHEE

CHITIMACHA   TIMUCUA

N

CALUSA

TEKESTA

0   200   400
MILES

D.L.L.

languages were spoken mostly in the western plains, but scattered languages in the South have been classified as related to them, including Biloxi, Ofo, Catawba, Yuchi, and languages of small groups in eastern Carolina. So little is known about other languages as to make them unclassifiable, because they became extinct so early. For example, the Timucuans of Florida were severely depopulated early in the colonial era by diseases brought by Spanish settlers, and the survivors amalgamated into Spanish society.

Because of depopulation, two trends occurred among small coastal tribes that changed their ethnic identity. First, if a large tribe lived nearby, individuals from the decimated tribes tended to merge into that larger group. The larger tribes, particularly the Tuscaroras, Catawbas, and Yamassees of the Carolinas, which also were experiencing depopulation, welcomed additions. They thus became receiving cultures of individuals from diverse backgrounds, but managed to retain their ethnic identity.

A second result occurred in areas where there was no predominant tribe, so that individuals of numerous groups tended to coalesce into small multitribal communities. These diverse communities, often of very small numbers of people, sometimes adopted English as their only mutually understandable language, and retreated into isolated, economically marginal lands that white settlers did not want. They gradually absorbed more European culture, sometimes through individual whites or escaping black slaves who joined them, but remained in isolation from the surrounding white society. This process accounted for the rise of numerous "tri-racial isolates" in various areas of the South. The North Carolina Lumbees are the best example of this amalgamation process, though there are other such groups in Virginia, the Carolinas, Kentucky, Tennessee, and Louisiana.

Among the large interior nations, their very size and greater distance from whites offered some protection from total decimation by disease. Nevertheless, each tribe experienced a large population decline due to Old World epidemics during the seventeenth and eighteenth centuries.

Although disease was the most destructive aspect of contact with Europeans, the Indian nations that survived this onslaught built up another economic system, based on this contact. Another revolutionary change in southeastern Indian cultures of the early historic period was trade. A trading relationship offered advantages to both Indians and Europeans, and a large part of the early colonial economy was tied up with the fur trade, especially in South Carolina and French Louisiana.

White traders made fortunes by selling skins of fur-bearing mammals (especially deer) to European markets. The Indians, on the other hand, were greatly attracted to European manufactured goods. Cooking utensils, needles, knives, and all kinds of metal tools quickly replaced most stone tools and pottery. Agriculture continued to be the major source of food, but hunting, for the fur trade, became much more important in the Indian economy. European firearms and ammunition, which made hunting easier, became major trade items. Other products of the trade included cloth, horses, and alcohol. The large interior nations, such as the Cherokees, Creeks, and Choctaws, with large territories of their own, occupied a middle-man position between the whites and other Indians farther west. They developed a prosperous trade that revolutionized their material culture. Because they were able to play off rival traders from English Atlantic coastal colonies, Spanish Florida, and French Louisiana, the interior southeastern Indians occupied an important economic position in the seventeenth and early eighteenth centuries.

It is ironic that while trading relationships were producing revolutionary changes in the economic situation of the interior Indian nations, another revolution was beginning in the English colonies. This revolution was more dangerous, because it involved something that the white colonists wanted even more than furs, and that was land. Most English colonists were farmers, not traders, and their population growth by the mid-eighteenth century was beginning to create pressure on the lands of the interior. Almost from the beginnings of settlement in Virginia and the Carolinas, there had been conflicts over land because of white expansion. As settlers won more influence over their colonial governments, the role of the British government in restricting settlement became less important. The final attempt by the royal government, to restrict white settlement east of the Appalachians, failed. The Proclamation of 1763 only succeeded in angering white expansionists.

Given this situation, it is surprising that whites did not expand over Indian lands and attempt to incorporate them into the economy and society of the Anglo-Americans. The usual explanation for English exclusiveness is their particularly strong sense of race. Whether racism was a cause or a reflection of their physical situation can be debated, but a number of other factors help explain why ideas of racial separation flourished among the British colonists.

First, the English colonies were strong enough to push the Indians back, or demand land cessions, but they were not yet strong enough to conquer them. Therefore, Native Americans generally remained beyond the frontier. Second, most colonists came to America as settlers, either in family or community groups. Such patterns, especially as there were enough white women to decrease the need for intermarriage with Indian women, meant minimal integration of the two peoples. Third, unlike the Spanish in Latin America and the French in Canada, the English in America had other labor sources besides Indians. What labor they could not attract from Europe, they made up for with African slaves. Thus Indians remained basically outside Anglo-American society.

The major attempt to integrate southern Indians into white culture was another threat to the native population: enslavement. A flourishing Indian slave trade centered in South Carolina by the early eighteenth century, but a series of Indian wars and revolts by African slaves made the whites fear that the two exploited groups might form a red-black alliance to overthrow the white minority. Therefore, the South Carolinians consciously began a policy of divide and rule to keep Africans and Indians separated. Indian tribes were offered bounties to capture escaped black slaves; Indians were paid to torture rebellious slaves; black militia were used to fight against Indians; and enslavement of Indians was ended.

There had been considerable intermarriage between Indian and black slaves, but by the mid-eighteenth century most Indian slaves had been sold to the West Indies. This trend not only further reduced Indian population in the Southeast, it decreased the whites' dependency upon Indian labor. With the exception of the fur trade, most of the economic basis for southern prosperity would rest upon agriculture and black, not Indian, labor.

The revolutions in southeastern Indian societies that were brought about by European contact, disease, trade, and land loss spawned another revolution: warfare. Evidence of Indian warfare exists for the prehistoric era, but warfare increased significantly during the colonial era. Some of this war between Indians and whites originated over enslavement of Indians and exploitative trade practices, but the major conflict was over land. White expansion left Indians little choice between armed resistance or forced migration.

Indian attacks almost destroyed the Virginia colony in 1622 and the South Carolina colony in 1715, but after those wars were lost the Indians could only fight defensively, to protect their lands from invasion by whites. To get away from encroaching whites, numerous groups migrated from the area. The North Carolina Tuscaroras moved north to join their Iroquois relatives in Pennsylvania, New York, and Canada. Savannahs, or Shawnees, moved northwest to Tennessee and the Ohio Valley. Yamassees, with tribal allies and escaping black slaves, moved south into Florida to form one part of a new, amalgamated group, the Seminoles. This heritage of opposition to whites, and incorporation of Africans into their society, helped form the defiant attitude which characterized Seminole resistance to whites in the nineteenth century.

Fighting against whites was only part of the expanded warfare that engulfed southeastern Indians during the colonial era. As different groups migrated in response to white expansion, they clashed with other tribes. In addition, competition over hunting territory for control of the fur trade exacerbated old rivalries. Whites encouraged intertribal warfare, in part to reduce the Native population still further. Europeans in North America pioneered the use of Native peoples to do their fighting for them, in their competition to expand (a technique that was later perfected in European imperial ventures in Asia and Africa).

The Indian nations had become so dependent on the European trade that they could not be uninvolved in these European national rivalries. Yet many Indian leaders skillfully used their position to play off one white nation against another, in a complicated type of balance-of-power politics. The convergence of English, Spanish, and French interests made the Southeast a major battleground in the so-called Second Hundred Years' War.

Thus by the mid-eighteenth century interior Indian nations of the South had adapted rather successfully to a new economic and political order based upon European trade and military alliances. But this adaptation was not to last, because of major changes after this period. The first change was ecological, caused by the overhunting of game in the South. As game was almost wiped out by the competitive European trade, the Indians had a diminishing product to trade for the manufactured goods on which they had grown dependent. With disease-afflicted populations, they were unable to keep up their game preserves, so there was also less food for the deer.

About the same time, political changes had a catastrophic effect on southern Indians. The British had gained a decisive victory over the French and their Spanish allies in the Seven Years' War. By the Treaty of 1763, the French gave up their entire North American empire and Spain gave Florida to the English. Besides failing to provide for the interests of French- and Spanish-allied Indians, this treaty meant that all southeastern Indians no longer had the opportunity to exploit European rivalries. A partial balance-of-power situation existed for the Indians during the conflicts between Britain and the Anglo-American colonists during the Revolution and the War of 1812, but in a war between a faraway trading ally and nearby land-hungry settlers, there was not much choice for the Indians; so most of them aided the British in a gamble to prevent further encroachment on their lands. British losses in both these wars left the Indian nations in a precarious position.

With the British gone, the French out of western Louisiana in 1803, and the Spanish out of Florida by 1819, southeastern Indians were faced with a united white power in the United States. Although the new national government was weak, its citizens were bent on expansion over Native lands. Also, there was virtually total agreement among white Americans that Indians were racially inferior and destined for extinction. The interior Indian nations had avoided the cultural disintegration of the coastal tribes, but their weakened economic and political power did not offer much hope for the future.

By the beginning of the nineteenth century, the Native peoples of the Southeast had gone through a number of revolutionary changes

in the preceding two centuries. The coastal tribes had been decimated by disease, enslavement, warfare, or migration, and the interior nations had experienced great changes in material culture,
economic base, and political status. Yet, despite these changes,
much of the day-to-day way of life of the surviving large Indian
nations continued to reflect their aboriginal cultures. Communal
agriculture was still the basis of their food supply, and most of the
farming continued to be done by women. Most southeastern Indians
continued to organize their societies around matrilineal kinship
groupings, with women exerting a more active role than was true for
European women. Political organization, language, and religious beliefs remained primarily indigenous.

This new era of economic and political decline marked another
period of revolutionary change. This time the change extended to
cultural aspects previously unaffected by the earlier trading and
military relationships. The primary pressure for change came from
two groups: missionaries and "mixed bloods."

During the colonial era, English missionaries were not especially
active in North America. But by the beginning of the nineteenth
century missionary sentiment was clearly rising among white
Americans, partly because of the influence of religious revivals
and partly because the new nationalism promoted enthusiasm to
expand this new, democratic experiment. Missionaries were therefore agents for cultural change as well as religious conversion.

When the missionaries arrived among the southern Indians, their
influence would probably not have received much attention were it
not for the sense of declining economic and political status among
the Indians. Land losses were continuing and demoralization, re-
flected by rising rates of alcoholism, was evident. Thus some Indians
were in a mood to listen to the revolutionary changes the missionaries proposed. To save themselves from further decline, which was,
according to the missionaries, evidence of God's displeasure for following pagan lifestyles, the Indians must become like the "chosen
people" (whites) in religion and culture.

One group of southern Indians who were particularly susceptible
to the missionary arguments were those who had already had significant exposure to white values in their own families, that is, the

"mixed bloods." Usually the product of marriages between white frontier male traders and Indian females, the children of these unions were given the derogatory title "mixed bloods" by whites. Yet among the matrilineal societies of the Indians, in which descent was traced completely through the female line, the children of an Indian mother would be accepted as a full member of the society, no matter what ethnic group the father belonged to. This total acceptance paved the way for the emergence of a new class of leaders, who could more effectively deal with outside whites because of their familiarity with the culture. Some of these "mixed bloods" had been sent by their white fathers to the East for an education; so they were thoroughly familiar with the "strange ways" of the whites.

It is significant that all of these southern Indian nations had experienced long periods of European contact before becoming interested in Christianity. As traditional mores and religious ideologies were not adequate to deal with the new problems brought about by economic decline, some Indians began to listen more seriously to the missionaries. Others wanted the schools that the missionaries would bring, so that they could become educated and able to deal more effectively with the white government. Still others took whites at their word, that Indians should be exterminated because they were "savages." If they could prove to whites that they were not savage but had become "respectable and civilized," perhaps the whites would accept them and not take more of their lands.

The acculturated Indians, led by "mixed bloods" and mission converts, realized that military opposition to white expansion only enflamed whites with stories of Indian savagery. Therefore these acculturated Indians, with the advice of the missionaries, set upon a new peace policy of accommodation designed to gain white respect by adopting white culture. By the 1820s the Cherokees, Chickasaws, Choctaws, and Creeks were becoming known as the Civilized Tribes. The Cherokees of north Georgia, whose lands were under the most pressure by whites, made particular progress in acculturation. Not only did they adopt Christianity, they set up schools, an English-Cherokee newspaper, and an elected government modeled after the United States Constitution. Prosperous "mixed bloods" even bought black slaves and practiced cash-crop agriculture based on private ownership of land. In their technology, economic system, social organization, political structures, and ideology, they were becoming more and more like the white Southerners who surrounded them.

Naturally, not all southern Indians wished to follow this new departure. Traditional leaders, non-Christians, and probably the majority of all the nations felt uncomfortable about acculturation to white social norms. Therefore each nation became progressively more factionalized between acculturationists and traditionalists, and developed into a heterogeneous society based on different attitudes toward Anglo-American culture.

Regardless of faction, almost all southern Indians were united in a determination to hold onto their remaining lands. They were finding it progressively more difficult to resist land losses. The new United States government, while too weak to conquer the Indians, managed to gain cessions of Indian lands by an ingenious system of trade and treaties. Government-sponsored trading posts were set up all along the frontier and credit was liberally extended to individual Indians. When Indian debts for the factory goods became large, so that the Indians could not pay these debts, government agents demanded payment of the tribal councils. Of course, the government had never expected the Indians to be able to pay in cash, so it demanded payment in land. By this process, repeated over and over again by the government in a conscious attempt to get more land from the remaining Indian nations, the Indian-occupied land base was gradually reduced.

The only problem with this "factory system" was that it required government officials to deal with Indian tribal councils as independent nations, by the use of treaties, and the treaties implied an independent status for Indians that made expansionist whites uncomfortable. By 1820 white settlement had completely surrounded the southern Indian nations, and sentiment to ignore the treaties and bring the Indians under the state governments grew significantly.

Indian affairs now merged into a larger power struggle that was developing between the state and federal governments. In an attempt to solidify the jurisdiction of the federal government over Indian matters, as opposed to the state governments, Chief Justice John Marshall made a ruling in *Cherokee Nation* v. *Georgia* (1831) that established the concept of "domestic dependent nations." While attempting to rescue the Cherokees from the Georgia state government's control, however, Marshall established a much more restricted view of Indian national sovereignty than the treaties implied.

Continued pressures for white expansion undercut the Marshall decisions, which at least recognized the Indians' right of continued occupancy of their lands. By the 1820s the call was for total removal of the remaining Indian states. Removal was now possible because the United States had acquired the huge Louisiana Purchase from France in 1803. Much of this land became known as the Great American Desert and was considered uninhabitable for whites; so it was felt that these lands could best be used as a place for unwanted Indians.

Removal sentiment gained a great victory with the election of Andrew Jackson as president in 1828. Jackson, a western expansionist from Tennessee, strongly favored Indian removal, even though a Cherokee had once saved his life. He pushed hard to get a Removal Act passed by Congress, and it was signed into law in 1830. Furthermore, Jackson essentially ignored Marshall's decisions and allowed the state of Georgia to establish its authority over the Cherokees.

It is ironic that President Jackson became famous for his tough stand in protecting national authority against the Nullification Movement in South Carolina, while he told southern Indians that the federal government had no power to protect them from intrusions by the states. Probably the main reason why the other southern states did not back up South Carolina was that they wanted the assistance of the United States government in removing Indians.

During the administrations of Andrew Jackson and Martin Van Buren, one group after another of the southern Indians was forced to sign removal treaties, exchanging their homelands for new land in the Indian Territory (present-day Oklahoma). Even though some removals were executed with relative efficiency, such wholesale displacement of peoples is difficult to justify. But for several groups

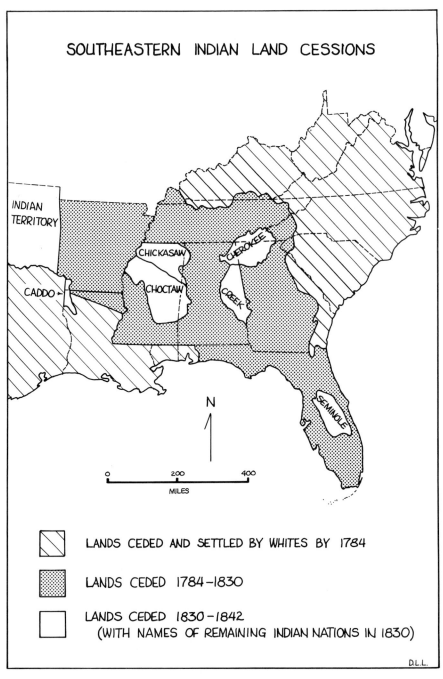

SOUTHEASTERN INDIAN LAND CESSIONS

INDIAN TERRITORY

CHICKASAW

CHEROKEE

CADDO

CHOCTAW

CREEK

SEMINOLE

N

0   200   400
MILES

LANDS CEDED AND SETTLED BY WHITES BY 1784

LANDS CEDED 1784–1830

LANDS CEDED 1830–1842
(WITH NAMES OF REMAINING INDIAN NATIONS IN 1830)

D.L.L.

ADAPTED FROM SAM HILLIARD, "INDIAN LAND CESSIONS," ANNALS OF THE
ASSOCIATION OF AMERICAN GEOGRAPHERS, LXII (JUNE, 1972), 374 AND MAP INSERT.

the removal process was especially tragic because of incredible mismanagement. Indians were herded into armed "concentration camps" and resistant individuals were captured. Sometimes the journey was made over the winter and government promises of food, clothing, and medicine were often unfulfilled. The most publicized removal was that of the Cherokees, the most acculturated of the Civilized Tribes. Of the 16,000 Cherokees who made the march to the Indian Territory, over 4,000 died on the infamous Trail of Tears.

In vain the acculturated Indians pleaded for the white government to enforce its own treaties and Supreme Court decisions, but the removal continued. Essentially, the removal of the Civilized Tribes proved that fears of "savages" were not as important as white desire for valuable lands.

The failure of the acculturation policy to forestall land losses was not lost on the Seminoles, the last major Indian group to be removed. The Seminoles were an exception to almost every trend of southern Indian history. They were not even an identifiable ethnic group until the late 1700s, when various bands of Creeks joined Yamassees and other tribal remnants to escape white contact by moving south into Spanish Florida. They welcomed escaped black slaves, to add them to their population. All of these groups had a heritage of hatred for Anglos, who had either fought or enslaved their forefathers. Even after the United States pressured Spain into giving up Florida in 1819, the Seminoles retreated farther into the swamplands to avoid contact with whites.

White Southerners were not especially interested in Seminole lands, but they felt threatened by the welcome Seminoles were giving to runaway slaves. Such a Maroon society, not far from the heart of the plantation belt, offered a threat to the continued existence of the South's "peculiar institution." Especially after the 1831 Nat Turner slave revolt in Virginia, whites were paranoid about slave uprisings. The old colonial fear of a red-black alliance was coming true among the Seminoles; so even if their lands were useless, they must be gotten rid of.

Seminole leaders, who had strongly resisted attempts at acculturation, had already fought a war against the United States. They still distrusted the Americans, but considered removal just to get away from the whites. Stupidly, slaveowners influenced the government agents to insist on the Seminoles' returning all escaped slaves before they could move away. When the Seminoles refused, war broke out again in 1835. This war was one of the most costly and frustrating the United States ever fought, and it did not end until 1842, after the United States commander had captured the Seminole leaders by violating a flag of truce. With the capture of the defeated Seminoles, the last removal to the Indian Territory took place. The United States had at last got rid of the major Indian nations in the South.

The removal era marked the great transition for southern Indian history, and the 1830s were as significant for them as the 1860s would be for black Southerners. Yet some Indian groups were never of concern to government removal agents, and some members of removed nations avoided migration. Why various remnant Indians were allowed to remain in the South, and what has happened to them since the 1830s, can tell us much about their diversity and about race relations in the South.

In this collection, "Indian" is defined as referring to groups of people who have consistently defined themselves as Indians. The remnant groups of Native Americans in the South were diverse peoples by the nineteenth century, and they have remained so in the twentieth century. Not only are they geographically diverse, they are culturally diverse as well.

Charles Hudson, in his excellent synthesis of the archeology, ethnography, and history of the southeastern Indians, distinguishes three categories of Indianness: genetic, cultural, and social. Based upon these categories, he divides southern Indians of recent times into three groups: (1) those who have retained parts of their aboriginal culture (Cherokees, Seminoles, Choctaws, and Alabama-Coushattas); (2) those who have lost their aboriginal culture but retain strong genetic and social identities as Indians (Lumbees, Catawbas, Houmas, Creeks, and other small groups); and (3) racially mixed peoples who have only a tenuous cultural and genetic Indian background but are establishing social identity as Indians (Haliwas of North Carolina and other *mestizo* "little races"). Beyond these groups, Hudson points out that many white and black Southerners have Indian ancestry but otherwise no claim to an Indian identity beyond the general Native American influences upon southern folk culture.[2]

The historical situation of Native peoples in the post-removal South is in several aspects very different from the problems that have faced most Indians in the United States since the 1840s. The end of the removals marked a transition for United States Indian policy, because after that decade the primary attention of the government was directed toward Native Americans of the West. By the mid-nineteenth century, American settlement was pushing over the Great Plains to get to the Pacific coastal regions, and gradually the interior was being settled. This invasion of their lands caused western Indians to react in much the same way as eastern Natives of the previous century: by armed defense of their homeland.

Such clashes were usually settled not by total military defeat of a Native group but by a negotiated settlement, certified by a treaty. The revival of the treaty system gradually restricted Indian lands to areas called reservations, but the treaties specified that most rights of self-rule within the reservation were retained by the group itself.

By the 1870s, however, after most western tribes had been settled on reservations, the government began to negate those treaties. Congress ended the practice of giving agreements with Indians international status as treaties, and the Supreme Court declared that Congress had the right to pass laws contradicting treaties, without the consent of Indians. Progressively, tribal governments were allowed less and less power, while local agents of the U.S. Bureau of Indian Affairs took more control over affairs on the reservations. This trend culminated in 1887 with the passage of the Dawes Indian Allotment Act, by which Congress hoped to do away with reservations by dividing the remaining lands into individually allotted plots. Since most Indians were not citizens, this meant they would be almost totally powerless without the protection of their treaty guarantees and their tribal governments.

The Dawes Act became the basis for United States Indian policy from 1887 to 1934, and its main effect was not to assimilate the Indians, as some of its "humanitarian" sponsors had hoped, but drastically to decrease the Natives' land base. During the years of its operation, the Dawes Act was responsible for the loss of 86 million acres of land and further decline in Native self-government. Much of

the remaining land was economically barren, and as Indian populations grew in the twentieth century, this restricted land base was
overtaxed even more.

The resulting poverty and despair within the reservation context
became justification for treating Indians as helpless and dependent
wards of the government. Consequently, the power of the federal
Bureau of Indian Affairs over the daily life of Native peoples became
virtually unchallenged. Native religions were outlawed, white social and economic mores were enforced, and children were forcibly
separated from their families to attend distant boarding schools.
Such policies were rationalized on the grounds that the only solu-
tion for the "Indian Problem" was for Native peoples to be absorbed
into the American melting pot and "become citizens just like everyone else." This policy of forced assimilation ignored the fact that
Native Americans had never asked to be assimilated. They had to
struggle to retain what elements of their traditional way of life they
could preserve in a society which did not value cultural diversity
and pluralism.

Allotment and forced assimilation continued to be the hallmarks
of United States Indian policy until 1934, when Franklin Roosevelt's
new commissioner of Indian Affairs, John Collier, began a comparatively enlightened "Indian New Deal." Under the Indian Reorganization Act, Collier ended allotment, began land reclamation
projects, sponsored tribal government reorganization, and encouraged Native cultural revival. However, before Collier's ideas could
be enacted, many of his emphases were negated.

In the early 1950s a more conservative sentiment arose; the government favored ending the federal treaty obligations to Indians.
This idea, "termination," marked a revival of the old melting pot
theory that Indians should be "freed" from their reservations. Most
Native Americans, however, saw it as just one more attempt to separate them from their land base. The government coerced several
tribes into accepting termination—most notably the Menominees
of Wisconsin. Economic disaster followed, and it was only in 1974
that the Menominees succeeded in having their federal reservation
status restored. Though the government has backed away from the
policy, termination is still a scare word on Indian reservations.

Another threat, especially for western reservations with mineral resources or water supplies in arid areas, concerns large-scale leasing of reservation lands by corporations. Tribal governments are often forced to cooperate with BIA-negotiated leases because there are few alternative financial sources for supporting the reservation economy. Even though it takes a different form, large areas of land leased to outside interests means de facto land dispossession. This issue of land loss, after 200 years, is still the central theme of Indian–white relations in the United States.

The preceding discussion is not and is not meant to be a complete summary of general Native American history, but only a basis for comprehending how such trends do *not* apply to remnant Native peoples in the South. Only gradually in the late nineteenth and early twentieth centuries did the federal government begin to recognize the southeastern Cherokees, Choctaws, and Seminoles. Most other groups felt little effect from heavy-handed allotment and forced acculturation policies and the reforms of the Indian New Deal. Moreover, the small size and isolated conditions of most southern Indian groups meant that their history was determined much more by local situations than by federal Indian policy. Federally unrecognized groups have often had to turn to the national government in hope of protection against local interests which were taking their lands.

Besides their isolation from other Indians, the various groups of Native people remaining in the South have been in a unique situation (for Indians) by virtue of being in a society that also contains large numbers of Afro-Americans. The dichotomy between white and black has had a tragic effect on southern Indians, as they struggled to establish themselves as a third race in a society that defined itself biracially.

The following chapters have been arranged according to each group's acceptance by white Southerners, beginning with groups who have had the most difficulty gaining recognition of their Indian status. To understand these peoples, and the reasons for their cultural and social diversity, we must examine each group separately before we attempt to analyze general historical patterns for all southern Indians. Their story of ethnic survival is the subject of the following essays.[3]

Notes

1. U.S. Bureau of the Census, *1970 Census of Population* (Washington: Government Printing Office, 1971), Subject Report PC(2)-IF, "American Indians," Table I, "Indian Population by Sex and Urban and Rural Residence, 1970," p. 1. Texas was not included in these calculations because its large population of western Indians would tend to distort the figures for the Southeast.

2. Charles Hudson, *The Southeastern Indians* (Knoxville: University of Tennessee Press, 1976), pp. 478–501.

3. The sources for this chapter are discussed in the bibliographic essay at the end of the volume.

I

Native Groups
that Avoided Removal

2

The Indians of Virginia
A Third Race in a Biracial State

HELEN C. ROUNTREE

W hen the English began migrating to what is now eastern Virginia, they found three families of Indian peoples.[1] First there were the Algonquian-speaking Powhatan tribes, who occupied all of present-day eastern Virginia below the falls of the rivers and whose population was estimated at 14,000.[2] Then there were the Iroquoian-speaking Nottoway and Meherrin, who lived south of the upper James River and probably did not exceed a few thousand. And finally there were various little-known tribes of Siouan speakers, such as the Monacan, in the piedmont of the state. Beyond that, English knowledge did not go.

The English inundation struck the Powhatans first. For them, the seventeenth century was a time of war, population loss, and erosion of the land base. By the end of the century, only about a thousand Powhatans were left, on and off reservations—a figure that has been preserved ever since by the joining and "spinoff" of individuals. Oddly enough, however, serious culture change did not occur until well into the eighteenth century.[3] The Nottoway and Meherrin were not much affected by English settlers until the early 1700s, at which time treaties were made with them and land was set aside for reservations. Much of their vigor derived from ties with their relatives, the Tuscarora, and when the Tuscarora moved north after 1715, the Meherrin melted away and the Nottoway began to decline. The Siouan-speaking tribes had always remained on the fringes of the English settlements; after the early eighteenth century they, too, melted away. In all probability, they, together with a few migrants from other Virginia tribes and from non-Indian society, settled in the Blue Ridge Mountains of Virginia and adjacent colonies.

By 1800 only four small reservations were left in Virginia. The Algonquian Pamunkey and Mattaponi of King William County, administered as one unit, contained about 800 and 100 acres respectively, with populations of about 100 and 50 respectively (no census survives). The Gingaskin reservation in Northampton County had 690 acres; in 1813 there were 29 adults there who qualified as Indians, together with a larger number of children and "non-Indian" relatives and friends.[4] Its Indian element was a distillation of the several Algonquian tribes of Virginia's Eastern Shore. The Nottoway reservation had about 3,900 acres left. In 1808 there were seventeen Indians living there; some were adults with non-Indian spouses.[5] All of these reservations had been formed through treaties with the colony of Virginia before the Revolution.[6] Therefore they have always been considered state reservations, and until very recently the federal government has not recognized their inhabitants as Indians or assumed any special responsibility toward them.

Each reservation unit had four or more trustees, who were prominent white men in the community, appointed first by the state legislature and later by other, surviving trustees. Their job originally was to run the tribal finances for the Indians, who were mostly illiterate, and to represent the tribes during the years when nonwhites were not allowed to appear in court cases. They were knowledgeable local men who could be consulted either by the Indians or by the state legislators; this is the remaining function they have today.

In addition to the reservation Indians in 1800, there were several groups, such as the Chickahominy and Portobacco (now called Rappahannock), who lived in seclusion without reservations but kept up a tribal identity among themselves. There were still others, living along the Blue Ridge, who knew that they were partly of Indian descent but had no particular group identity. All of these kinds of Indians followed a lifestyle that by 1800 had come to be much like that of their small-farmer neighbors. And this got them into new trouble with those neighbors: the Indians no longer seemed like "real Indians" to many Virginians.

"Real Indians," of course, were fossils: they were full-blooded aborigines who wore buckskin clothing, lived in wigwams, hunted for a living with bow and arrow, and mouthed pidgin English. Non-Indian Virginians—and Americans in general—have always kept their own identity up to date in the face of changing times, but Indians were expected to be different, and in reality, of course, they were not different. Most of them farmed the land in order to eat and tried to get an education in order to defend their remaining civil and treaty rights. Many of them found strength and solace in Southern Baptist Christianity. And because of their small, inbred populations they sometimes married congenial non-Indians, at the risk of expulsion from the tribe, rather than inbreed any further. In some defunct tribes, the non-Indian spouses included Free Negroes; thus many Virginians believe that the surviving tribes have African ancestry also, though reliable scientific documentation is lacking. The belief was enough, however, and this, together with obvious changes in the Indians' lifestyle, has always damaged their credibility as "real Indians."

There were never any removals in Virginia. The situation had gone beyond that by 1800. It was not likely that anyone would try to find new reservations for a people believed by many to be no longer Indian. Instead, efforts were made to make them disappear *in situ* through assimilation into the neighboring population. The efforts were successful to the extent that two of the four reservations were broken up, and all the tribes, with or without reservations, suffered a constant loss of people to the non-Indian population. But in most tribes a stubborn, beleaguered core has always remained to carry on Indian identity, in spite of all the pressures. The history of these pressures and the core peoples' reactions to them will be documented in the following pages.

Allotment and Termination in Virginia

The early nineteenth century witnessed a rising intolerance toward all non-whites in Virginia, which was expressed in a series of discriminatory laws for Free Negroes and a concerted effort to make

Indians assimilate into that persecuted group. The effort against reservation Indians took the form of allotment and termination.

I use the terms allotment and termination advisedly. They are usually applied to specific federal policies of the 1880s and 1950s respectively, but closer inspection shows they were used in certain eastern states well before that. "Allotment" means dividing a reservation and assigning plots to individual Indians; the Gingaskin reservation was allotted in 1813, while allotment as a policy was not even considered in Washington until 1816. "Termination" means dividing the whole tribal estate among the Indians and ceasing all government services to the tribe; termination of state reservations occurred in Virginia (Gingaskin, 1813; Nottoway, 1824), Massachusetts (Wampanoag, 1828), South Carolina (Catawba, 1840, but later rescinded), and Rhode Island (Narragansett, 1880). In cases where the state rendered the Indians no services other than protection of the land, as with the Gingaskin, allotment and termination were the same thing. Termination was not removal in any of these cases: no other reservations were provided, and the Indian inhabitants remained in the area as "ordinary citizens."

Pressure on the Gingaskin began in the 1780s, when two petitions were sent to the state legislature by white citizens of Northampton County.[7] The first petition asked that part of the reservation lands be leased to non-Indian farmers, while the second asked for outright sale of the land and division of the money among the Indians (i.e., termination). The reasons for sending the petitions were to become standard in the minds of nineteenth-century whites in Virginia, and in the rest of the country as well. The Gingaskin were considered a nuisance to the community, due to their "fondness for fishing, fowling & hunting, the natural insolence of their disposition, & their disinclination to Agriculture," which was also viewed as a waste of good land. There were "not more than three or four of the genuine Indians at most," for the reservation had become a haven for "an idle set of free negroes who had of late years connected themselves with the Indians" (i.e., married them).

Not only did these Free Negroes cut down reservation timber to build houses for themselves, but "the adjacent neighborhood" had also cut trees illegally, until hardly any were left. Instead of suggesting a way of helping the Indians defend themselves against such illegal depredations, the people who petitioned the legislature felt that the land should be sold to someone who was able to defend it (i.e., a white person). Finally the petitioners, in common with whites to the present day, resented the fact that the Gingaskin paid no taxes on reservation land, thereby contributing nothing to the public treasury. They overlooked the fact that the Indians had paid long ago by signing away their lands in a treaty.

The state legislature declined to act until it heard from the Indians themselves. No message from the Gingaskin arrived until 1812, when eleven members of the tribe petitioned through their trustees that the tribe's land be divided and held by individuals (i.e., allotment).[8] The reason they gave was that they were living by agriculture while much of the reservation was leased out, and larger plots would be an advantage. No mention was made of racial matters or association with Free Negroes. In fact, the Gingaskin never responded in any way to the racial charges made by their neighbors, unlike Virginia Indians of a later time. The Indians' bland petition was accompanied by a strong letter from one of their trustees, George Parker, that reiterated many of the complaints of the petitioners of the 1780s concerning association with undesirable Free Negroes and the destruction of the reservation's timber resources. Parker's letter shows that the tribe's trustees, far from being able or willing to help, regarded the tribe as an increasingly dangerous nuisance and looked forward to its dismemberment. Now that the Gingaskin had somehow been brought to give their consent, that dismemberment could take place.

In February 1813 a law was passed allotting the reservation to individuals considered by the trustees to be descendants of the Gingaskin.[9] The land was surveyed and allotted to twenty-nine people; no restriction was placed upon its immediate sale.

The tacit assumption behind the Gingaskin allotment law (which was not tacit in many other cases in the United States) was that the allottees, being illiterate, naive, and irresponsible, or all three, would sell out quickly and disappear. And as in other cases in the United States, that assumption seemed at first to be justified—but only at first. There was an initial burst of sales, and then things slowed down. The decade of the 1820s saw only four plots sold, and four others were used as collateral for debts. By 1830, only half the reservation had been sold.

Eighteen hundred thirty-one was the year of the Nat Turner slave insurrection in Southampton County. Little effect was felt by the Nottoway, right next door, but on the Eastern Shore the white population panicked. Tremendous pressure was put on non-whites there to leave. The Gingaskin were made to feel that pressure, for in November 1831 seventeen sales were made to seven white buyers and two more plots were put into litigation to determine ownership. After one month, nearly all the reservation land was in white hands, and the remaining pieces were sold over the next twenty-eight years, often by multiple heirs who lived outside Virginia.[10] The Gingaskin who remained in the area gradually merged with the black population, and some of their descendants still live in Northampton County.

The Nottoway reservation in Southampton County was the next to go, but this case differed from that of the Gingaskin in some ways.[11] Though the Nottoway seem to have intermarried with whites and Free Negroes, there is no record of their spouses' having a bad reputation. Instead, the Indians themselves had a bad reputation; they had refused to adjust to the Anglo world around them, and many of them were known as vagrants and alcoholics, according to their own trustees.[12] They lived primarily on the proceeds of sales of reservation land, of which they had a sizable quantity. The petitions which went to the state legislature came not from disgruntled white neighbors but from the Nottoway themselves, asking to sell ever more land. Their trustees acquiesced, not knowing what else to do in the face of Nottoway refusal to take up farming on their reduced land base or let their children be apprenticed to tradesmen.

In 1821 the Nottoway petitioned for allotment (and therefore for termination) and were prevented from getting it only because the legislature wrote to consult the trustees about it. One of the trustees, Jeremiah Cobb, wrote back, saying among other things, "I have no hesitation in saying that they are destitute of both economy, prudence, or industry, and were their lands to be divided among them at discretion, they would scarcely have a hut to shelter themselves in five years." Cobb did not see this as a way to make the Not-

"Dressing up" as Indian and growing long hair have been a means of emphasizing Native identity. This Pamunkey man, William T. Bradby, posed for
the Bureau of American Ethnology in 1899. *Courtesy of Smithsonian Institution National Anthropological Archives, photo no. 893.*

toway disappear. Instead he was sure that "we will be faced with them on the parish" (i.e., on welfare). The legislature sensibly believed him and rejected the Indians' petition.

In 1823 the one and only literate Nottoway petitioned the legislature for his share of the tribal estate so that he could get a start in life. Since the trustees backed him, the legislature passed a law which later opened the door to termination.[13] The young man could get his share in money and/or land, and so could anyone else of sufficiently good character who was descended "from a female of the Nottoway Indians." No one, however, claimed a share immediately. In 1830 the young man and the aged "female chief" of the tribe claimed their shares and sold them soon afterward. Not until 1835 was there a rash of sales, and most of the Nottoway who came of age and claimed their shares after 1840 hung onto them as long as they could. The last chunk of reservation land was divided in 1878, and heirs of those people continued to hold their plots well into the twentieth century. The last plot was lost to Indian-descended ownership only in 1953. Nottoway descendants are now scattered over southeastern Virginia.

The next tribe to face termination was the Pamunkey/Mattaponi of King William County. The pressure came from some of their white neighbors, led by T. W. S. Gregory, who petitioned the state legislature and used the same arguments that had been used against the Gingaskin as to marriage, associations, and vagrancy. In addition, Gregory added a more current grievance: not only were these free non-whites a bad example to the slaves, but the reservation, being on the waterfront, "could be readily converted into an instrument of deadly annoyance to the white inhabitants by northern fanaticism." The petition asked the legislature either to sell the reservation and divide the proceeds among people of Indian descent (i.e., termination) or to allot the land to Indian-descended people, with full power to sell. This latter course "would in progress of time, lessen or remove the present grievance," for the allottees were expected to sell out. The petition was signed by 144 men, plus four "Acting Trustees."

The Pamunkey got wind of the petition, and before it was sent they sent two counterpetitions of their own to Richmond.[14] These petitions were endorsed by five trustees—whose names do not correspond to the four "Acting Trustees" mentioned above. It would seem that the white petitioners had indulged in some dishonesty of their own. The Indian petitions were written by one of their number, Tazewell Langston, who had some education. Langston made it plain that the Pamunkey were industrious farmers, not vagrants, and that no one in the tribe had been in trouble "for stealing, or hostility with our white neighbors, or one another, since our tribe has become civilized." None of the tribe's near neighbors had signed Gregory's petition; some signers found out Gregory's intentions later and had their names removed. As for not being "real Indians," Langston stated that "if anything can be proved, there are many here that are more than one half blooded Indian, tho we regret to say that there are some here that are not of our tribe." This statement, the only one about race in either Indian petition, is ambiguous, but it represents a clear recognition of the dire consequences if Indians married blacks.

Some of the non-Pamunkey who lived on the reservation may have been Catawbas from South Carolina, who had been visiting and intermarrying with the Pamunkey since the American Revolution. Around the time of the Gregory petition, the Pamunkey had invited Catawbas to migrate to Virginia, specifically for keeping up the Indian-blood quantum on the reservation.[15] Langston emphasized that breaking up the reservation would be a disaster for the tribe, who were "like as one family," and he asked the legislature to consider all this. The legislature seems to have been impressed by this message directly from the Indians, as well as by the trustees' unequivocal statement, "We are opposed to the sale of their land." When the Gregory petition arrived in Richmond, it was rejected and filed away.

This, unfortunately, was not the end of the matter. The Pamunkey had beaten off termination, but at a terrible cost. Their whole existence as Indians, descendants of King Powhatan's people, had been threatened by whites who scarcely knew them. This left a tremendous psychological wound that has persisted to the present day among the reservation people. The wound has been kept open by the fact that in the 1920s the Gregory petition was disinterred, mimeographed, and circulated in an attempt to prove that no "real Indians" were left in Virginia. As we shall see, in its second lifetime the petition involved another misrepresentation. The struggle of words continued.

The Racist Years

As the Civil War drew closer, the tension between whites and free non-whites grew. Ironically, these were the years in which the non-reservation groups began to establish themselves as real enclaves. The Chickahominy, for instance, had lost their reservation back in 1718, in a mysterious and possibly shady land deal.[16] The reservation had been in upper King William County, and after its loss the tribe simply disappeared from the records. However, by about 1820 a few non-white people with modern Chickahominy surnames had settled in Charles City County, the ancient Chickahominy tribal area, and had surfaced in the census records. By the mid-1850s, more Chickahominy were appearing in the records of Charles City County, several as landowners. An Indian enclave had been established, although it did not gain recognition as a tribe until 1908.

The Portobacco/Rappahannock had lost their reservation in Caroline County shortly after 1700 and had quietly settled nearby and been lost to sight. They resurfaced in the records at about the same time as the Chickahominy, as did the Upper Mattaponi or Adamstown people, who live near the old Chickahominy reservation in upper King William County and may be related to either the Chickahominy or the Pamunkey/Mattaponi. Some Nansemond also surfaced in what is now the city of Chesapeake. They registered at the courthouse as persons of Indian descent, "not negroes or mulattoes," as had some of the Nottoway; they were regarded as Indians in the community.

The Indians of Virginia were not in sympathy with the South in the Civil War era, and their white neighbors recognized and resented this. As early as 1857, the Pamunkey had their firearms taken away, on the excuse that non-whites were not allowed to carry them. The Pamunkey, who still hunted for part of their living, complained to the governor of Virginia that their treaty rights had been violated, and their arms were returned to them.[17] During the war, no Indians fought with the Confederacy, and only a few Chickahominy fought with the Union. Some Chickahominy families fled north, going as far as Ontario and settling with an Ojibwa band until the war was over.[18] Everyone else in the tribes apparently waited out the war and tried to survive the destruction that was going on around them.

The post–Civil War years were a time of upheaval and then re-settlement into old patterns. Initially, black people tried to take a higher place in society, which was resented by whites and Indians who considered themselves superior. When the local whites re-turned to power, they erected higher barriers against all non-whites, and the Indians—caught in the middle as usual—had to erect even higher barriers between themselves and the blacks. The result was rigid three-way segregation in schools and churches and, where the Indians could manage it, racial listings in official records.

Tribal rules crystallized into laws prohibiting marriage with blacks. Appearance of Indian ancestry became even more important and desirable: "typical Indian" traits of copper skin, dark eyes, hawk nose, and straight black hair. Men wore their hair long to show it was straight, not kinky. James Mooney, the Smithsonian anthro-pologist, visited the Pamunkey in 1899 and recorded in his field notes that "all [the men] agree th[at] none cut the hair above [the] shoulders before t[he] [Civil] war." He was told that two chiefs of the tribe, who died around 1880, always wore their hair long.[19] Mooney, who had just returned from long, intensive field work among the Kiowa Indians in Oklahoma, wrote to one of his col-leagues: "I was surprised to find them so *Indian*, the Indian blood being probably nearly ¾. . . . Some would pass unquestioned in any western tribe."[20]

Visits by Mooney and by Albert S. Gatschet gave a great boost to Indian morale in Virginia. The experts believed they were Indians; now maybe the public would, too. The Chickahominy came further into the open; they informally elected a chief and tribal officers.[21] In 1901 they reorganized Samaria Baptist Church into Samaria In-dian Baptist Church, and they secured the Pamunkey church pastor as their part-time minister. Beginning in 1904, they issued tribal membership cards. They held gatherings as a tribe, to which they invited white and Indian friends. Finally, in 1908, with the help of

There has been some intermarriage between Virginia and Native Americans of other areas. On the left is Western Chickahominy Chief O. Oliver Adkins, standing with a Cuna (San Blas) man from Panama who married into the group. Note that both are wearing Plains-style clothing as a symbol of their Pan-Indian identity. *Courtesy of Helen Rountree, 1970.*

Pamunkey Chief Terrill Bradby (Mooney's main informant), they formally organized themselves as a tribe.

The Chickahominy had need of a tighter organization, for they and other Indian people in Virginia were to be affected by authorities other than Mooney and Gatschet. In 1894 John Garland Pollard published a brief monograph on the Pamunkey[22] in which he emphasized the "race pride" of the tribe, but alleged that they had "not a little" black ancestry. Pollard gave no source for this statement, but it was used in the article on American Indians in the eleventh edition of the *Encyclopaedia Britannica*. In 1913 a scholarly study on the Free Negro of Virginia came out,[23] in which the Pamunkey tribe was mentioned as an example of Indian-Negro intermarriage, the sources being the abortive Gregory petition of 1843 and "a prominent citizen of Richmond who has observed them." That citizen may have been Pollard, who by then was a high official in the Byrd machine, or a very biased man of whom we shall hear later: Walter Ashby Plecker. Whatever the scientific value of the sources, the book affected the reputation of the Pamunkey in scholarly circles, for it was cited in various books on the Free Negro.

There were greater troubles for the Virginia Indians in the early twentieth century. In 1900 a Jim Crow law was passed requiring separate railway coaches for whites and "colored" people. The Pamunkey and the Chickahominy were immediately affected by this, for railroads to the city of Richmond ran through their territories. The Pamunkey complained, first to the county judge and then to the Richmond commissioner, and they won a ruling that Indians could ride in the "white" coach. After that, Indian people carried membership cards to avoid embarrassing incidents. There were also problems about treaty rights on the reservations. When the United States entered World War I, Pamunkey and Mattaponi men were drafted. The chiefs of both tribes protested—probably not from lack of patriotism but from a fear that tribal rights were being encroached upon, for reservation Indians at that time were not "citizens." The state attorney general's office ruled that since they were not citizens, they could not be drafted.[24] Their status upheld, Indian men went to war as volunteers. Soon after that, a dispute arose over county taxes that were levied on a general store on the Mattaponi reservation that was run by a tribesman. The case was taken to the county circuit court, which decided that the store was technically not in the county and so was not subject to county taxes.[25]

From 1919 through the 1940s the Powhatan tribes were visited by another anthropologist, Frank G. Speck of the University of Pennsylvania. Speck was intrigued with the canoes, baskets, wooden bowls, corn-husking pegs, turkey-feather mantles, etc., that some individuals still knew how to make. He collected recipes for herbal remedies. He saw as "Indian" the men's expertise in hunting and fishing, and he felt that the division of the Pamunkey reservation's woodland into hunting territories for individuals was traceable to a general Algonquian heritage of hunting territories (which has since been disproved for the northern Algonquians).[26]

Speck's visits and writings had tremendous impact upon the Virginia Indians, and under his influence three things happened. First, some of the tribes began holding powwows for all Powhatan groups and going to other gatherings in Maryland and Delaware. Second, some of the nonreservation enclaves organized into tribes. In 1921, the Rappahannock took out a charter as a tribal corporation under the State Corporation Commission, but otherwise they remained ordinary citizens. The Upper Mattaponi and the Nansemond organized informally in 1923. For these people, as for the Chickahominy in 1908, organizing meant coming further into the open and being more vulnerable to attack. It was a very hard step for some of them to take. The Rappahannock, more than the others, lived scattered in an area that was unusually hostile to non-whites. Speck met the people several times in 1920, and after one meeting he wrote, "Very timid about the move toward organization. Some even asked if they were in danger of being killed by white people."[27] The third result of Speck's activities was that the Chickahominy, who were already organized, began to press for formal recognition as Indians by the state. To this end, they began in 1920 to gather affidavits and petitions from their white friends, stating that the Chickahominy were Indians and had always been considered such in the community. The attempt came to an end in the mid-1920s, when other troubles engulfed the tribe.

The organization of Indian-descended people into tribes was, in a sense, asking for trouble, and trouble was not long in coming. A powerful white backlash materialized. Its leader was Walter Ashby

Plecker, M.D., registrar of the state's Bureau of Vital Statistics. Plecker was an extremely strong-willed man and his correspondence with everyone, even federal officials, was apt to have a domineering tone. Opposition only made him angry and more determined. He had a passion for neat classifications, which extended to racial matters. He also believed that "contamination" of the white race would surely lead to the country's ruin, as it had supposedly done in civilizations of the past. This idea was very common among Plecker's contemporaries. But Plecker was armed with "scientific" credentials and a position as head of the bureau which handled the state's records of births, marriages, and deaths. He quickly became an "authority" on race in Virginia, and he was only too willing to use his power to try to keep the white race "pure."

For Plecker, there were only two races in Virginia: white and "colored," which to him and to most people meant black. Unfortunately for Plecker, some of the most aristocratic families in the state could trace their ancestry back to Pocahontas, who was obviously not white. These people *had* to be admitted to the white category, and so a white person was legally defined as one-sixteenth or less Indian and the rest white. "Indians" had to be at least one-quarter Indian and less than one-quarter black. This, of course, opened a chink in the wall. People of dark complexion claimed that their "suspicious" ancestor had been an Indian, sufficiently far back, and they were then classed as whites. Plecker and his associates were outraged at this; it did not seem to occur to them that the menial jobs and second-rate schools and hospitals set aside for "colored" people were enough to make anybody pass for white who could. Some non-whites went through a stage of first claiming to be Indian in order to establish credibility for the "suspicious" ancestor. And this, needless to say, outraged the descendants of the Powhatan tribes, whose credibility was already poor.

Plecker was methodical. If the Indian category was a way station to whiteness, it had to be eliminated, or at least discredited. This meant proving that all people in Virginia who claimed to be Indian were actually of African ancestry and were therefore colored. He set about collecting old federal censuses; county birth, marriage, and death records (which were fragmentary or nonexistent before the Civil War); and information from "reliable" people in the counties. The last category of information was hearsay; the former category consisted of racial classifications on records made by untrained local people who usually wrote down their opinions on race in front of people who were illiterate. Or if the people could read, the "Race" box was filled in after the interview was over (which the Indians claimed was done by the takers of the federal censuses of 1930 and 1940). It is not surprising, then, that many old records of Indian ancestors say "colored."

Armed with this "scientific" evidence of African ancestry, Plecker set about discrediting all Indians in Virginia. When anyone wrote to him for an opinion, he did not hesitate to put his views in writing, sometimes using such terms as "mongrels." In 1925 he began a campaign aimed at the U.S. Census Bureau, in the hope that in the 1930 census no Indians would be listed in Virginia. In one letter, he wrote to the director that he had "absolute proof" that the Indians were actually blacks, because "we have their pedigree back."[28] His campaign was successful to the extent that in that census there is a footnote qualifying the classification of people as Indian.

Plecker circulated a pamphlet on eugenics, published by the Vital Statistics Bureau, which included a warning to the public about the racial machinations of ambitious non-whites. In 1928 he secured legal backing for attaching a "warning" to Indian birth and death certificates. Citing various sources, such as the Gregory petition of 1843, the warning concluded that though a certificate read "Indian," the person should be classed as "colored" and treated accordingly. In later years Plecker wrote directly on the back of the certificates instead of attaching the wordy warning. Not until 1972 did it become illegal for the bureau to send a photostat of these writings or the warning with each copy of the certificates.

The Gregory petition was mimeographed and circulated, and Tazewell Langston's counterpetitions were summarized in an outright lie: "They beg for pity and admit the truth of the claims made by the white petitioners." The petition found its way in 1939 into the work of E. Franklin Frazier, who described the Pamunkey tribe as "typical of those communities of mixed-bloods which, having originated in the association between Indians and Negroes, gradually lost their Indian character."[29] Frazier's only source for this statement was the Gregory petition. It was at this very time that Frank Speck was having his graduate anthropology students do field work with those same Pamunkey *because* they were still Indian.

In January 1943, Plecker issued a circular which listed, county by county, the surnames of people who claimed to be Indian or white but were suspected of having black ancestry. The circular was sent to local registrars, doctors, nurses, clerks of court, school superintendents, and public health workers with the intention that these personnel would prevent "suspicious" people from using white facilities. As with the mimeographed Gregory petition, the Indians knew nothing about this circular until a sympathetic white showed them what Plecker was doing. The witch-hunting quality of the circular prompted a good friend of the tribes, James Coates, to start a campaign of his own against Plecker. Coates collected tribal rolls and affidavits of influential, friendly whites. He induced the president of the Medical College of Virginia to state publicly that the Virginia Indians had always been admitted to the hospital as whites, and they would be in the future, no matter what Plecker said. Coates also attacked Plecker in the press, and altogether won much sympathy for the tribes.

The Indians had their friends in academic, government, and other circles, but never quite enough to counteract the pressure that Plecker put on them. Whenever Indian people wanted to transact legal business, there were forms with the box for race and the Plecker-influenced Racial Integrity Law of 1923, stating that the box had to be filled in accurately (i.e., in conformity with the records of the Vital Statistics Bureau). The reservation tribes survived it pretty well, but the nonreservation tribes were less secure, and one of them, the Chickahominy, cracked under the strain. The tribe became badly factionalized over the issue of trying to get a reservation, and the matter was complicated by religious dissension within the tribal church.[30] By 1925 the tribe had split into two sections, and in 1940 the reservation-oriented Eastern Division Chickahominy incorporated as a separate tribe.

World War II presented another set of problems to the Indians of Virginia. All of them were draftable, since a federal law of 1924 made reservation Indians citizens without jeopardizing their treaty rights. When a question arose whether Indian men should serve in white or "colored" regiments, the Selective Service Board took opinions from Plecker, the Indians, and others such as Frank Speck, and then turned the problem back to the local draft boards. The reservation men were classed as Indians and served with whites; so did the Upper Mattaponi men, after some difficulties. The Western Chickahominy found themselves inducted with blacks and refused to leave the barracks until their chief and an influential army friend got them reclassified. An Eastern Chickahominy man, living in Hampton, fought his draft board until in desperation it classified him "nationality unknown"; he served with whites. The Rappahannock had the worst time, for some men who lived in Caroline County and were classified "colored" refused to go and were taken to Selective Service court, where they were convicted on the basis of racial classification in old county records and one of the men's having attended "colored schools and churches." They were sent first to prison and then to hospitals in a program for conscientious objectors.[31]

In those same years the Indians of Virginia were trying to get better education for their children without jeopardizing the children's status as Indians. The separate Indian schools did not go beyond the eighth grade, and the state and counties were reluctant to provide separate high school education for children whose racial status was not secure. Pressure could not be brought on Richmond because the tribes would not unite even for such a basic common good. As one reservation chief wrote to Frank Speck, "Some of these [nonreservation] people . . . are not even recognized as Indians by the State of Virginia. Therefore . . . we feel that it is best to fight for [ourselves] exclusively." In view of what the reservations had been through with Gregory and Plecker, this attitude is understandable, but since the nonreservation people needed the support and greater prestige of the reservation tribes to *get* that recognition, this aloofness was (and is) bitterly resented. To remedy the school situation, various white friends of the Indians applied to the federal government for permission to enroll Virginia Indian children in the federal school at Cherokee, North Carolina. The initial response was that since none of the Virginia tribes had a treaty with the United States, they were not eligible for services provided by the Bureau of Indian Affairs.[32] A couple of years later this opinion was altered, and the school at Cherokee admitted reservation (but not nonreservation) children.

A Gradual Improvement

Walter Ashby Plecker retired from the Vital Statistics Bureau in 1946 at the age of 85 and died in a traffic accident soon thereafter. His successor at the bureau continued his policies, though with less success, and the opposition to Indians in Virginia slowly diminished as people became willing to listen to Frank Speck, James Coates, and the Indians. In 1959 a new registrar came to the bureau, who thoroughly disapproved of Plecker's extracurricular activities and destroyed his Racial Integrity File.

High school courses came to the Indian schools in the late 1950s. The Chickahominy school, which as a nonreservation school was supported by Charles City County, came to be staffed largely by people from the tribe who had gone to Bacone College in Oklahoma. Today, most young people in the tribes finish high school, and many go to college. The separate Indian schools were lost with integration in 1966–68, but Indian youth is keeping its image by wearing Indian jewelry and their elders are getting grants for Indian education from the federal government. Job skills have improved as a result of better education, and so has the hiring situation in Virginia, thanks to the Civil Rights Movement. Many young Indians have migrated to the cities for jobs, while others live in their communities and commute to the cities. With the liberalizing of ideas about the federal government's responsibility toward Indian people who are not enrolled on federal reservations, money has become available to the Virginia tribes for education, community improvement, and tribal centers, and they are taking full advantage of it.

A certain amount of "word struggling" is still being waged in Virginia as Indian people live with a public that cannot believe they are Indians unless they dress in buckskin and feathers. As we have seen, that stereotype has been badly out of date in Virginia for nearly two centuries. Indians in Virginia resemble their non-Indian neighbors in many ways, but there are still internal differences: nuances of

worldview, attitudes toward government policies, the feeling of belonging to a certain group (as opposed to other groups), and resentment of the type of American history that paints the country's aborigines as bad. If nothing else, people who are reared to emphasize their Indian descent have a special, not to say cynical, sensitivity to what the United States is all about. For them, it is a country of migrants who pushed the aborigines aside and tried to make them disappear, rather than give them a working chance to hold their groups together while adjusting to the loss of their homeland.

The successes of the Civil Rights Movement have not altered the fact that to the Virginia Indians, their image as Indians is very important. Sometimes they themselves idealize the Indian as the Noble Savage, and yet this concept has kept them going in the past. Some of them occasionally dress up in buckskin and feathers, for important tribal occasions or for the Chickahominy Fall Festival each September, but the latter is mainly for an ignorant public who would otherwise not be aware of their existence. Understandably, they remain supersensitive to real and imagined racial slights.

Relations with non-Indians are more promising than ever before. At the same time, the Indians of Virginia are reaching out to other Indian people in the country, and are finding that they have not been alone in what they have endured and they are not alone in what they are.

Notes

1. I am greatly indebted to the following people for reading earlier drafts of this paper: Chief O. Oliver Adkins (Western Chickahominy), Chief Marvin Bradby (Eastern Chickahominy) and his tribal council, Linwood Custalow, M.D. (Mattaponi), Chief Andrew Adams (Upper Mattaponi), Chief Captain Nelson and Councilman Oliver Fortune (Rappahannock), James R. Coates, Dr. Nancy Oestreich Lurie, and Calvin L. Beale. In addition, Mr. Beale kindly allowed the use of his private papers. Quotes from the Frank Speck Papers are used with the permission of the Library of the American Philosophical Society, Philadelphia.

2. Christian F. Feest, "Seventeenth Century Virginia Population Estimates," *Quarterly Bulletin of the Archeological Society of Virginia* 28 (1974):66–79.

3. Helen C. Rountree, "Change Came Slowly: The Case of the Powhatan Indians of Virginia," *Journal of Ethnic Studies* 3 (1975):1–20.

4. Northampton County, Virginia, unnumbered plat book (early 1800s), Plat 37; Order Book 37, pp. 416–17.

5. Virginia State Library, Executive Papers, Box 154a, letter of July 18, 1808.

6. The latest treaties were as follows. For the Algonquian-speaking Pamunkey, Mattaponi, and Gingaskin: "A Treaty between Virginia and the Indians, 1677," *Virginia Magazine of History and Biography* 14 (1906–7): 289–96. The Nottoway signed that treaty and also a later one, transcribed in Sadler Phillips, *The Early English Colonies: A Summary of the Lecture by the Rt. Hon. and Rt. Rev. Arthur Foley, Lord Bishop of London . . .* (London, 1908), pp. 201–5.

7. Virginia State Library, Legislative Petitions, Northampton County, January 26, 1784, and October 10, 1787.

8. Ibid., December 2, 1812.

9. State of Virginia, Acts of Assembly, 1812–13, pp. 117–18.

10. All sale records: Northampton County, deed books 26–30.

11. For a detailed discussion of the Nottoway case, see Helen C. Rountree, "The Termination and Dispersal of the Nottoway Indians of Virginia" (in press).

12. See especially the following: trustees' letter of July 18, 1808, in Virginia State Library, Executive Papers, Box 154a, and Jeremiah Cobb's letter accompanying the 1821 petition, in Virginia State Library, Legislative Petitions, Southampton County, December 11, 1821.

13. State of Virginia, Acts of Assembly, 1823–24, pp. 101–2.

14. White petition of January 20, 1843, and Indian petitions of November 26, 1842, and January 12, 1843, are filed together in Virginia State Library, Legislative Petitions, King William County.

15. Douglas S. Brown, *The Catawbas: People of the River* (Columbia: University of South Carolina Press, 1966), pp. 271–72, and Frank G. Speck, "The Catawba Nation and Its Neighbors," *North Carolina Historical Review* 16 (1939):416.

16. Helen C. Rountree, "Indian Land Loss in Virginia: A Prototype of Federal Indian Policy" (Ph.D. dissertation, University of Wisconsin–Milwaukee, 1973), pp. 100–103.

17. Virginia State Library, Executive Letter Book, 1856–60, pp. 47, 49.

18. Theodore Stern, "Chickahominy," *Proceedings of the American Philosophical Society* 96 (1952):206.

19. Smithsonian Institution, National Anthropological Archives, MS 2218. [This visit resulted in his article "The Powhatan Confederacy, Past and Present," *American Anthropologist* 9 (1907):128–52.]

20. Ibid., correspondence with the Bureau of American Ethnology.

21. The *Times* (Richmond), July 15, 1900, p. 2.

22. John Garland Pollard, *The Pamunkey Indians of Virginia* (Washington: Smithsonian Institution, Bureau of American Ethnology), Bulletin 17.

23. John H. Russell, *The Free Negro in Virginia—1619–1865* (Baltimore, Johns Hopkins Studies in Historical and Political Science, series 31, no. 3, 1913).

24. Copy of ruling in Mattaponi Museum, Mattaponi Reservation, Virginia.

25. Mentioned in attorney general's ruling of June 26, 1957; copy is on file in King William County Courthouse.

26. Frank G. Speck, *Chapters on the Ethnology of the Powhatan Tribes of Virginia*, Indian Notes and Monographs, no. 5 (New York: Heye Foundation, 1928), vol. 1; *The Rappahannock Indians of Virginia*, Indian Notes and Monographs, no. 3 (New York: Heye Foundation, 1925), vol. 5. For a discussion of northern Algonquian hunting territories, see Eleanor Leacock, *The Montagnais "Hunting Territory" and the Fur Trade* (n.p.: American Anthropological Association, 1954), Memoir No. 78.

27. Frank G. Speck, Field Notes: Field Notebook No. 1, American Philosophical Society Library, Philadelphia.

28. Personal papers of Calvin L. Beale, letter of January 15, 1926, to U.S. Census Bureau.

29. E. Franklin Frazier, *The Negro Family in the United States* (Chicago: University of Chicago Press, 1939), p. 215.

30. Helen C. Rountree, 1975 field notes.

31. Sources are oral recollections in 1975 and 1976 by Chief Curtis Custalow, Mattaponi; for Upper Mattaponi, Chief Andrew Adams; for Western Chickahominy, Chief O. Oliver Adkins; for Eastern Chickahominy, Councilman William Stewart, the man involved (and also a story from my family, for my grandfather was on that draft board); for Rappahannock, Chief Captain Nelson and Councilman Oliver Fortune, one of the men involved. Also for Rappahannock, Frank G. Speck's field notes.

32. Frank G. Speck, Field Notes: letter of assistant commissioner of Indian Affairs to Hon. Dave E. Satterfield, U.S. House of Representatives, November 25, 1944.

3

The North Carolina Lumbees
From Assimilation to Revitalization

W. McKee Evans

The term "Lumbee" has come into general usage only since 1953. It designates 30,000 or more brown-skinned people who live along the Lumbee River in Robeson County, North Carolina, and in neighboring counties in North and South Carolina. At various times in their history these people have been known by other names, including Scuffletonians, Croatans, Cherokees, and Indians of Robeson County.

The profusion of names reflects some unsolved problems concerning the origin of the Lumbees. They are probably descended from the remnants of a number of tribal groups that largely disappeared from the Carolinas during the eighteenth century. Many also show varying degrees of European and/or African ancestry. They were speaking English when they were "discovered" by the white settlers and they have retained virtually no features of distinctively Indian culture.[1]

In the 1830s, during the Age of Jackson and the period of Indian removal, the Lumbees suffered a catastrophic loss of legal and economic status. The explanation for this development is not obvious. Nothing so dramatic or sudden took place as removal. Indeed, the Lumbees were not tribal Indians who were subject to removal. They held their lands as individual farms exactly as the whites, whose culture and lifestyle they had shared from the time of the earliest white settlement a century before. Until 1835 the Lumbees had enjoyed the same legal rights as the whites.

Like tribalized Indians, they suffered ruin during the Age of Jackson, but as a result of more general causes, especially the rise of North–South tensions and the hardening of racial attitudes. The

North Carolina constitution of 1835 stripped "free persons of color" of most of their civil rights, including the rights to vote, to serve on a jury, to testify in a case involving a white person, to bear arms, to learn to read and write.

Soon afterward, castelike restrictions were also imposed to prevent any blurring of racial distinctions. Whites were forbidden to marry blacks, Indians, "Mustees," and mulattos, as well as other non-white groups. By outlawing any interracial kinship ties that whites might have or might develop, the law seems to have promoted white racial solidarity and enabled the dominant race to act with less restraint in its efforts to control and exploit non-whites. There is no reference in any of these measures to Scuffletonians, the name by which the Lumbees were then known, but subsequent court decisions applied all the legal disabilities to them.[2]

Contrary to a widely held opinion, Indians and other non-whites were not legally prohibited from owning land in ante-bellum North Carolina. The belief that they were not allowed to own land arose, perhaps, from an Indian custom of transferring the title of their land to the name of a white friend. Faced with a rising tide of racial prejudice, Indians were afraid that their legal rights might not be respected.[3]

Yet they in fact held little land and seem, with the passage of time, to have held less and less. From the fragmentary documents that have come down to us from the eighteenth and early nineteenth centuries[4] it would appear that the people of Robeson County during these years, both Indian and white, can best be described as "rustic" or "old-fashioned" rather than poor. They seem to have enjoyed a certain backwoods prosperity. But along with and following the loss of their civil rights, people with Lumbee surnames seem to have suffered genuine impoverishment. By the time of the census of 1860, almost all were land poor. Most were completely landless.[5]

Even though no one has yet documented the precise process whereby the Lumbees were impoverished, the memories that they themselves hold from the ante-bellum period are certainly highly suggestive as to what happened. Scholars who study present-day Lumbee traditions report that the

Lumbee still refer with bitterness to what are called "tied mule" incidents. Such an incident occurred when a white farmer tied his mule on an Indian's land, freed several cows in the Indian's pasture, and put a hog or two in his pen. Then, the white farmer would arrive with the authorities and claim that the Indian had stolen his animals. Knowing he had little chance for justice in the courts, the Indian would agree to provide free labor for a period of time, so that charges would not be pressed, or to give up a portion of his land as a settlement. This was, of course, only one way in which the Indians were deprived of their labor and property; other, more "sophisticated" quasi-legal means were also used.[6]

The Civil War years are the low point in the history of the Lumbees and, paradoxically, the beginning of their self-consciousness and revitalization. They had the misfortune to live near the lower Cape Fear River, where, at the outbreak of the war, the Confederate government undertook what would be its greatest enterprise of military engineering: a system of forts designed to defend Wilmington, the most important Confederate port, the Confederate navy headquarters, and the home port of most commerce destroyers and blockade-runners. In 1862, however, a yellow fever epidemic struck lower Cape Fear, killing perhaps 10 percent of the people and causing a flight of free labor from the area. Convinced that the Union fleet would attack Wilmington as soon as the epidemic subsided, the Confederate government pushed grimly ahead with the defense project, first by impressing black slaves. After a group of planters protested to the North Carolina House of Commons the harsh treatment their slaves were receiving, the government began conscripting Lumbee Indians.[7]

These events triggered a guerrilla war that lasted almost a decade. The chief guerrilla leader, Henry Berry Lowry, and most of his followers were Lumbees, but at various times they were joined by Union soldiers who had escaped from Confederate prisoner-of-war camps, by escaped slaves, and perhaps by Confederate deserters. The Lowry band opposed the Confederacy and after the war, when the new authorities sided with the former Confederates against them, they opposed the state and Federal troops.

Under the faminelike conditions that prevailed in the area from the late war years through 1867, the Lowry band seized corn and other food from planters and distributed part of it among the destitute of all three races. Such Robin Hood tactics tended to polarize the population of Robeson County along class lines and into friends and enemies of the Lowrys. Friends of the Lowrys were sufficiently numerous to make possible a one-way flow of information: the Lowry band usually knew exactly where its enemies were, but the soldiers who were hunting for them rarely knew where to look.

Lowry sympathizers—black, white and brown—also became a force within the local Robeson County organization of the Republican party, which resulted in splitting the organization into a pro-Lowry faction and those who were loyal to the state leaders. This split contributed to the subsequent victory of the conservative Democrats at the polls. Most North Carolina Republicans, including a few regular Republicans in Robeson County, took the position that the Lowrys were bandits. Thus they supported the efforts of the conservative Democratic legislature to suppress them. By 1874 the band had been defeated and its principal leaders killed or driven from the area.[8]

During the two decades after the defeat of the Lowry band and the defeat of the Radical experiment in Reconstruction there was an important redefinition of the status of the Lumbees by the reestablished conservative Democrats. For fifty years the dominant white group had insisted that they were black or blackish. Abandonment of this view in the 1880s can probably be explained by the fact that these whites were finding that such an interpretation had become a political liability.

The stability of the newly reestablished post-Reconstruction state governments depended largely upon the expectation that the blacks would acquiesce to the status of half-freedom that they were accorded. There was much in southern history, furthermore, to make the leaders of the New South optimistic about their ability to contain black unrest: the slaves had not answered John Brown's call for revolt, and the Nat Turner insurrection had been put down in less than two weeks. But the Lowry revolt had lasted ten years! If the Lowrys were indeed black, they had set a dangerous example for people who were supposed to serve as the mudsills of the New South. Beginning in the 1880s, it became the new style in writing North Carolina history to ascribe these years of violence to the passing era of Indian wars, to make them part of a diminishing threat rather than part of a threat that seemed likely to continue.

The editor of a conservative Democratic newspaper wrote a book in which he concluded that the Lumbees, far from being black, were actually Indians with a strong admixture of white blood. They were, he thought, descended from the Croatans, an Indian group in eastern North Carolina which in the sixteenth century is supposed to have assimilated the survivors of Sir Walter Raleigh's lost colony.[9] Angus Wilton McLean, later a governor of North Carolina, in "Historical Sketches of the Indians of Robeson County" found them to be Cherokees.[10] Still later investigations found them to be Sioux.[11] The fact that some Lumbees trace their descent in part from the Tuscarora was also noted.[12]

It is not at all clear how much these efforts have contributed to the question of Lumbee origins. What is more evident is how much the Spencer rifles of the Lowry band contributed to the perceptions of the dominant white group: white historians expended considerably more energy in the late nineteenth and early twentieth century demonstrating that the Lumbees were Indians than they had expended in the previous half-century demonstrating that they were not.

The rediscovery by the whites that the Lumbees were Indians scarcely revealed anything to the Lumbees that they did not already believe. Yet the changing perception of them by the dominant whites was of great importance to them. It provided them with a way of escaping some of the disabilities that were being visited on the blacks following the fall of the Reconstruction governments and the disintegration of the Republican party in the South. By recognizing them as Indians,[13] the conservative Democrats were offering them a middle legal status: they would have more rights than the blacks but not so many as the whites. Now that the Reconstruction dream of the equality of all men before the law had been shattered, the Lumbees responded to the conciliatory gestures of their former foes.

The defeat of the Lowry band and the emergence of various Lumbee origin theories are thus twin developments that mark the beginning of a period of accommodation between the Lumbee people and

the conservative Democratic authorities. As a result, with the establishment of one-party government in eastern North Carolina the
Lumbees, unlike the blacks, were allowed to continue voting, albeit
for their former opponents. The Lumbees would not be able to exercise as much influence in the Democratic party as they had once
exercised in the smaller and poorer Republican party. Nor were they
able to win for themselves as many positions of local importance,
especially that of justice of the peace.

Yet even in the twentieth-century one-party system, Lumbees
have continued to exercise a measure of influence. A recent scholar
has noted that in each Lumbee community there is a "locality
leader" who

> is contacted by the Whites at election time, and paid to "deliver" a vote in
> a particular way. He uses some of the money paid to him to give a dollar
> apiece to people in his area to vote for the candidate. In return for delivering
> the vote, the locality leader is in a position to do small favors for the people
> in his area through his political contacts, which strengthens the locality
> leader's position for the at least partial benefit of all concerned—the candi-
> dates, the leader, and to a less extent, the people of a locality.[14]

The disfranchisement of the blacks and the establishment of the
one-party system was followed at the turn of the century by the passage of the segregation laws. In Robeson County this resulted in
imposing a curious three-tier status system: three separate but equal
racial drinking fountains in public places; three separate and un-
equal seating areas in theaters, each with its own entrance; and six
bathrooms for two sexes and three races in public buildings. However, the most remarkable achievement of the founding fathers of
segregation (with three official races) may be the construction of
four racial school systems in Robeson County: one for each of the
official races plus a fourth for a group whose racial identity was
considered debatable. This fantastic caste system, with all its com-
plications, inconsistencies, and ironies, continued to be legally en-
forceable until the Second Reconstruction of the 1960s.

Yet the introduction of triple segregation does not appear to have
stirred great resentment among the Lumbees. Indeed, compared to
the Reconstruction years of near famine and guerrilla war, the early
segregation period seems peaceful. Perhaps an explanation for this
is the fact that segregation was introduced during a time when the

Oscar R. Sampson, Lumbee leader who helped pioneer Indian education in North Carolina. He served on the Pembroke State University board of trustees for thirty years. *Courtesy of Lucy Sampson and Adolph Dial.*

Lumbees were rapidly developing a strong ethnic consciousness. Not only were white historians rediscovering that the Lumbees were Indians, the Lumbees themselves were attaching much more importance to their Indian identity.

Until after Reconstruction the strongest locus of loyalty for Indians appears to have been kinship and family rather than ethnicity. Even though the Lowry movement had been overwhelmingly made up of Lumbees, the leaders had shown little racial exclusiveness and had worked easily with friendly blacks and whites. Indeed, among the closest lieutenants of Henry Berry Lowry had been a former slave, George Applewhite, and a white youth, Zachariah McLauchlin.[15]

But with the defeat of the Lowry band and the disintegration of the Republican party, the Lumbees no longer had political ties with blacks and with white Radicals. Such political connections as they were able to maintain were "vertical," extending upward through the locality leaders to the conservative white "courthouse ring." In the wake of defeat and in their ethnic isolation, the Lumbees were

turning increasingly inward—were taking intense interest in their
own kind, in the various theories about their origins, and above all
in the legend of Henry Berry Lowry, whose bold deeds seemed to
add inches to the stature of every Lumbee sharecropper who had to
work for a white landlord.

Their growing ethnic consciousness may be seen in their religious
history. As early as 1880, some two decades before triple segregation
was introduced, a group of Lumbee Baptists withdrew from the
Southern Baptist Conference to form the Burnt Swamp Association.
By 1973 this exclusively Lumbee body reported 6,000 members
organized into forty-two congregations. In 1900, Indian Methodists
formed what came to be called the Lumbee Methodist Conference,
which in 1974 reported 1,600 members in seven churches. Many
other Indians would remain affiliated to "white" church organizations, but as members of local congregations that were almost
exclusively Lumbee.[16]

The introduction of racially segregated schools does not appear to
have evoked the hostility of the Lumbees. It occurred at a time when
they were showing a preference for their own institutions. Also,
Indian schools were set up most often in communities where previously there had been no educational opportunities at all. Then too,
individual Lumbees, if not allowed real control over the Indian
school system, were allowed to manage it. Teachers were hired and
fired by the local school committeeman, an Indian who was appointed by the county school board, which until after World War II
was entirely white. Typically, the local committeeman was also the
locality leader, the Indian power broker who conducted negotiations
between his community and the white political machine.[17]

Traditionally, Lumbees had suffered such deprivation in educational opportunity that when their school system was set up in the
1880s, it was difficult to find Indians who could fulfill minimum
qualifications as teachers. For this reason a "normal" school for
training teachers was key to the development of the system. In
1887 the legislature appropriated $500 to cover two years' operating
cost for Croatan Normal School and appointed an Indian board of
trustees. But the legislators left the trustees and the Indian community the problem of procuring a building for the school.[18]

The response of the Lumbee community is striking. The legislative act was ratified in March. By fall, a two-story building had been completed by means of donated materials, cash contributions, and voluntary labor and fifteen young people began their training as teachers. This institution, with several changes in name and one change of location, had grown by 1941 into Pembroke State College for Indians. It was for a number of years the only state-supported four-year college for Indians in the nation. In 1971 it became Pembroke State University.[19]

The creation of a special school system for Indians was an important step in their definition as a middle-status group between the blacks and the whites. To evaluate their relative status in such practical terms as living standards and opportunity for advancement, we must compare the Lumbees with the whites and the blacks. But we must first consider the basis for this comparison— Robeson County, the largest community with which most Lumbees interact.

Because much of the land has poor natural drainage and is criss-crossed by swamps, Robeson County remained until the twentieth century an underdeveloped, backwoods society. The building of modern drainage systems and good roads, however, transformed the county into the most productive agricultural county in North Carolina and one of the most productive in the South. It has the largest cotton crop of any county in North Carolina, the largest soybean crop, the second largest corn crop, and the third largest tobacco crop—which brings in the greatest cash return. The county is also an important producer of beef, pork, poultry, peanuts, and sweet potatoes.[20]

Despite the productivity of its fields, Robeson is often called a poor county, and indeed many indexes of poverty bear out this characterization. A study based upon data for the 1960s shows that the county had a median family income well below $3,000 a year— scarcely one-third that for the United States as a whole. Fifty-two percent of all houses had no flush toilets and two-thirds of the houses were characterized by the Department of Health as "substandard."

Two-thirds of the children did not complete high school and the "functional illiteracy" rate was 25.3 percent. Its number of white males sentenced to the state prison was second highest in the state.

It ranked seventh of the 100 North Carolina counties in the instance of tuberculosis, and 72 percent of those examined for the armed services were rejected for poor health or mental deficiency. The mental retardation rate in the county varied between 20.0 and 29.9 per 100,000, as opposed to a statewide rate of 14.5. The county showed a "third world" birth rate of 28.7 births per 1,000 people, higher than any state in the Union or any country in Europe except Albania; and 15 percent of these births were illegitimate. Yet Robeson County, one of the nation's 100 poorest counties in terms of median family income, could nevertheless boast between thirty and forty millionaires.[21] The salient characteristic of the larger environment in which Lumbees live, therefore, is not the absence of wealth but the polarization of society into those who have a comfortable income and property and those who have little of either.

How successful have Indians been in achieving "middle status" in a society where there is scarcely any middle? It is hard to answer this question precisely because many statistics merge Indians and blacks into "non-whites." It is apparent, however, that Indians are the group most closely connected with farm labor. The population of Robeson County is about 40 percent white, while Negroes and Indians constitute about 30 percent each. Yet since blacks and whites live mostly in and around the towns, Indians make up about two-thirds of the rural population and supply about 80 percent of all types of farm labor. So when we cite figures that show, for example, that blacks are more likely than Indians to have running water and flush toilets in their homes, we are essentially comparing town blacks to rural Indians.[22]

But not all Lumbees are farmers. In and around the town of Pembroke the population is more than 90 percent Indian. Yet we find here an ethnic community in the fullest sense of the word. There is a wide range of social classes, including businessmen, professional people, and university students. There is an Indian newspaper, a variety of religious and civic organizations, and a dramatics group.

Elsewhere in Robeson County, however, the Lumbees appear most often not as a complete ethnic community but as a depressed social stratum in a rural economy that is dominated by whites. Lumbees sometimes admit to being without money, but they rarely characterize themselves as "poor," a word that does not seem to fit people who move in a rich web of kinship relations and have a positive conception of themselves.[23] Yet a great many are sharecroppers or farm laborers who are desperately poor by ordinary statistical measures. According to information collected by the North Carolina Fund, Robeson County in 1964 had the following racial distribution of income[24]:

Total Family Earned Income	White	Indian	Negro
$5,000 and over	46%	11%	2%
$2,000 to $4,999	33%	26%	39%
Less than $1,999	21%	63%	59%

A closer look at the poorest families, furthermore, reveals how little economic benefit Lumbees have gotten from the middle-status position they have enjoyed since the end of the Lowry period. In 1964, 44 percent of the Lumbee families in Robeson County earned less than $1,000, compared to 35 percent of black and 15 percent of white families.

There is a connection between the poverty of rural Indians and the prosperity of investors in agribusiness. The growth of agribusiness has been subsidized by the federal Agricultural and Conservation Program: Soil-bank payments are made to landholders for withdrawing acreage from production. In 1967, ten corporations or individual landholders in Robeson County received soil-bank payments in excess of $30,000, and one of them received more than a quarter million dollars. But as of 1971, only about 30 percent of Lumbee farmers owned enough land even to be considered independent. And for those who are sharecroppers or farm laborers, fallow land or land replanted to forest means fewer jobs. Landlords are supposed to share these payments with their tenants. Though this obligation does not seem to be widely observed, it prompts owners to reduce their tenants to day laborers in order to become legally entitled to the entire payment.[25] In addition, government payments to landholders create some of the capital for the modernization of agriculture, which eliminates still more jobs. By 1960, 45 percent of the work force in Robeson County was working fewer than forty weeks a year.[26]

Many local civic leaders have expressed hope that although the modernization process eliminates traditional jobs and intensifies rural poverty, in the long run the process will create new and better-paid jobs in up-to-date industries. They therefore have been optimistic about the potential benefits of industrialization, which expanded rapidly in Robeson during the 1960s. Of the eighteen plants in the county, which in 1971 were employing fifty or more workers, all but five had been built since 1960.[27]

But it remains to be seen whether the civic leaders are right about the long-term results of industrialization. In the short run, however, the process has not had a dramatic impact on the Lumbee poor. Indians often have had a hard time meeting the educational qualifications for industrial jobs.[28] The rural schools that most of them attended have not been as good as town schools.[29] Furthermore, in farming areas there has been a firmly established custom for children to join their families in the fields at key points in the agricultural cycle. Also, the wages offered by local plants have been less attractive than the wages paid in most American communities. In 1972, Robeson County wages were in the bottom 7 percent of North Carolina counties, and North Carolina was credited with having the lowest per hour wage rate in manufacturing of any state in the Union.[30] And finally, the adaptation of the Lumbees to industrialism has not been easy. Traditional family-organized agriculture and factory work do not offer the same rewards, nor do they pose the same psychological demands. The Lumbees are accustomed to hard work, but in response to the agricultural cycle and kinship and community obligations. They are used to long hours but also to a flexible work routine that lacks the sharp delineation between "work" and "life" that is characteristic of industrial society.[31]

The best example of the traditional work pattern of the Lumbees probably can be seen in their production of flue-cured tobacco. In Robeson County, tobacco may absorb more man-hours than all other crops combined. It is a crop which Indians have been cultivating by various techniques since long before the coming of the whites. Tobacco is the chief money crop, and the social standing of a family is influenced by how well they grow it. There is a local saying that one can tell what kind of man a person is by looking at his stand of tobacco.

The peak labor demand of the crop comes in July and August, the

Lumbee powwow for Indians of eastern North Carolina, Pembroke, 1972. *Courtesy of Walter L. Williams.*

harvest and curing season, when there is a specialized task for every member of the family, from boys and girls of five years to the very aged. The operation is carried out most efficiently when done by a barn and a field crew, which totals fifteen to thirty people. Since, despite the fertility of the Lumbee family, a sharecropper or farmer cannot ordinarily form these crews wholly from his own household, he must borrow "hands" from his kinsmen and neighbors, and in turn he must lend "hands" to help them secure *their* barns. The hours are extremely long; sometimes workers even sleep around the barns. The work is hard but not unrelieved. "Some jobs may be harder than others, some jobs may require more skill than others, but no job is more important than another. Out of this comes a sense of belonging, of belonging to a family and community group extending over three generations, and of being useful."[32]

In the final stage of the curing, when the tobacco must be frequently checked both night and day, the work becomes merged with a celebration of the harvest. Often people bring musical instruments to the barns. There is singing and drinking, and rumors of amorous adventures. Above all, the entire effort is enlivened by a ripple of anticipation that animates an agricultural society during the harvest season: golden and fragrant clusters of cured tobacco will soon bring a fleeting moment of prosperity to the harsh life of Indian farmers. When the smell of curing tobacco is in the air, even Lumbee professional people sometimes forsake their occupations to help their kinsmen with the harvest.

But Robeson County Indians have shown a different attitude toward industrial work. In the 1960s the B. F. Goodrich Company opened a plant in the area for making tennis shoes, which employed 1,400 workers, many of them Indians. The working hours were shorter and the pay higher than those to which the rural population was accustomed. Yet within a short time the company was faced with a monthly turnover rate of more than 10 percent.[33] The requirements of the assembly line are inflexible and divorced from the activities of one's family and his neighbors, and a foreman can be as exacting as a Lumbee patriarch but he does not have the same moral authority.

So far, industrialization has not solved the problem of rural underemployment and poverty. But as Lumbees are crowded off their ancestral lands by the federal soil conservation program and agri-business technology, they have found certain alternative employments. A few, who manage to go all the way through the school system, have found white-collar employment, especially as teachers. Many more seek work in less confining types of manual labor, such as the building trades. Since there are limited opportunities for these kinds of jobs in Robeson County, there has been a considerable migration of Lumbees to urban centers.

Lumbee colonies have emerged in Greensboro, North Carolina, in Baltimore, Philadelphia, and Detroit. There is also a Lumbee diaspora in many cities where the immigrants have not arrived in sufficient numbers to form ethnically distinct neighborhoods.

The largest and oldest exile community is the one in Baltimore, the so-called Reservation or "Lost Colony of East Baltimore Street," where, since the outbreak of World War II, Lumbees have been attracted by the almost continuous boom in the building trades in the Baltimore-Washington area. Yet, though this colony has already produced a second generation of city-bred Indians, it can hardly be called a stable community. A scholar who studied this settlement calculates that in a 23-block area of the city, one would find an Indian population no greater than 3,000 at any one time. But in any given year as many as 7,000 Lumbees would have resided for varying periods in that settlement. He estimates that six of every ten Lumbees who arrive in Baltimore return to Robeson County within one year.[34]

Yet too often the dream of the Lumbee exile to return to "my own home," with "my own land," "to be with my own kind," is not realized. He is likely to return only to confront the same economic pressures that still drive Indians out of the rural countryside. He may therefore reappear in Baltimore in a short while, or he may try another Lumbee ghetto.

Not all the Lumbees who leave the urban colonies return to Robeson County, however. Those who acquire skills, who achieve rank in the armed services, who obtain a higher education, generally do not return. For them the ghetto serves as their place of apprenticeship, where they learn to function in the larger American society. Those who move up generally move out, to become assimilated.

Compared to other Indian groups, the upward mobility of Lumbees appears little short of phenomenal. In a 1970 survey of thirty-six American Indian groups, the Lumbees, though one of the most numerous Indian groups in the nation (but only 7.5 percent of the number of individuals surveyed), accounted for one-third of the Indian college students and one-half of the Indian teachers in the sample.[35] An observer found that, in the quest for jobs, skills, and education, Lumbees had an advantage over the residents of other ethnic ghettos because they hold a positive image of themselves.[36] Unlike many other Indian groups, they are a people who know that in the years since the Civil War they have not lost every round.

Thus a number of developments would seem to suggest that, in the years following World War II, the Lumbee people, like many another Indian group, would disappear. Federal soil conservation policy and the technological advance of agribusiness, like two giant bulldozers, were clearing the countryside of small farmers, were "ghettoizing" the Indian poor. To be sure, many Lumbees brought with them to the ghetto the cultural resources necessary for climbing the American success ladder, but the American system has exacted a price for their success. They have succeeded as individuals rather than as a people. In order to ply their skills, to utilize their education, they have had to disperse, to remove themselves from the pattern of discrimination and limitations of opportunity that restrict the development of Lumbees in their ethnic communities.[37] The price is assimilation. They must trade a specific cultural heritage, which may be the source of their spiritual energy, for a nondescript, general American identity.

By the 1950s the survival of the Lumbees as a people seemed to depend upon their ability to find new opportunities in their home territory in Robeson County. Only this could stanch the outward flow of skill and talent and could call home the exiles. In the settlement at the end of the First Reconstruction period, Indians had been accorded a subordinate place in the rural economy. Now, with the modernization of agriculture, that place was rapidly phased out. To survive as a people, the Lumbees would have to negotiate a new place for themselves. For this reason, the modern movement against racial discrimination, often called the Second Reconstruction, has great significance for the Indians. It improves their prospects for survival.

Reconstruction II began in the early 1950s as a series of legal maneuvers by civil rights lawyers and counter maneuvers by their opponents. The tremendous publicity about token reforms inevitably led blacks and Indians to expect more substantive changes in southern society. This festering unrest of both peoples came to the surface in January 1958, as the result of activities of the Ku Klux Klan in Robeson County.

When the Klan conducted a series of intimidating demonstrations aimed at the blacks in the town of St. Pauls, the blacks organized a boycott of the local merchants. The merchants quickly got the message, took measures to guarantee the blacks police protection, and the Klan activities disappeared from that community.

But almost simultaneously, Klan activities in the nearby towns of Lumberton and Maxton were aimed at Indians. In 1870 Henry Berry Lowry had assassinated John Taylor, the presumed head of the Klan in Robeson County; few Lumbees had forgotten this bit of history. When the Klan scheduled an outdoor rally near Maxton, not only was it attended by armed Klansmen, it was also attended by armed Indians. They came from all over the county and even from the Lumbee settlements in Baltimore and Cleveland.

The Indians opened a noisy barrage of gunfire, but they clearly intended to intimidate rather than injure. No one was killed, though one Lumbee and a white reporter suffered gunshot wounds. The Indians pursued the Klansmen across the nearby border into South Carolina, ending the public activities of the organization in Robeson County. A few days later some Indians sent a jubilant wire to the head of the Klan at his home in South Carolina. They expressed "deepest sympathy" and signed it "General Custer." [38]

The 1958 routing of the Klan marks a turning point in Lumbee history—the beginning of a period in which the seething woes of many individuals were translated into public issues. To be sure, many (perhaps most) Indians continued to think of politics as a vertical process: if you have a problem, you go to your locality leader, who hopefully will intercede before the white authorities. But from unspectacular beginnings in four townships around Maxton in the early '50s there emerged what was called "the Movement," a different kind of politics that Lumbees had not practiced since the Civil War and Reconstruction I. Instead of looking upward in supplication, an Indian with a grievance was now more likely to look outward for allies. Movement people, though basing themselves primarily upon the Indian poor, worked also with blacks and whites who were seeking changes in the local power structure.[39]

Yet the Movement people did not simply revive Lumbee Radicalism as it had existed in the days of Henry Berry Lowry. They added something new: pan-Indianism. They cultivated interest in other Indian cultures and made common cause with Indians everywhere.[40]

Some Movement adherents developed their own origins theory. They reject the name Lumbee, which they associate with the accommodation policies of the locality leaders, who, at their worst, are capable of servility toward the white authorities and tyranny over Indians. Instead, they identify with the fighting Tuscarora of the eighteenth century. This theory appeals to the poor because, if they could establish their identity with such a well-recognized tribal group, they could qualify for badly needed federal benefits.[41] Indians who live under less desperate circumstances, however, tend to reject both the Tuscarora theory and the idea of federal aid. They feel that the success that Lumbees have enjoyed, relative to other Indians, is due to their stubborn independence and freedom from federal paternalism.

It seems possible that Reconstruction II and the Movement have not yet run their course in Robeson County, but certain results are already apparent. For one thing, Lumbees are much more active in politics. They hold more local offices, and are no longer content just to vote for a list of candidates drawn up by white county authorities. Furthermore, with the ending of legal disabilities more Lumbees hold jobs that once were exclusively held by whites. It is doubtful, however, that the new opportunities are sufficient to compensate for the loss of employment by Indian farm laborers and tenants. It would seem that migration is still the open wound of the Lumbee community. The flow has been slowed but not stanched.

Lumbees have mixed feelings about the changes that have come to the educational system. Segregated Indian schools were always starved for funds but they gave Lumbee children a sense of identity, which may be weakened in communities where the population is mixed and the schools are racially integrated. In the same way,

Indians are not entirely happy about the changes that have occurred in the institution that they often continue to refer to as "the college." After being racially desegregated in 1953, the college became, in 1971, Pembroke State University, a campus of the Consolidated University of North Carolina. To attract white students and achieve university status, the institution greatly improved its curriculum and increased its admission standards, which could be more successfully met by white students from good town and city schools than by Indians from poor rural schools. For a time, the university became almost 90 percent white. To many Lumbees it must have appeared that the tenfold expansion of the university consisted in a tenfold expansion of educational opportunities for whites.

On the other hand, it should be noted that the larger, integrated university continued to admit, in absolute numbers, about as many Indians as had the small all-Indian college; and they received a better education. Also, improvements in the quality of higher education have been accompanied by improvement in other schools attended by Lumbees, so that increasing numbers of young Indians have been able to meet the more difficult standards of the university. From a low point of 10 percent shortly after consolidation, the Lumbee proportion of the student body rose to about 20 percent for the academic year 1975–76.

Furthermore, the location of a campus of the Consolidated University in Pembroke has strengthened the economic position of this overwhelmingly Lumbee town. It has brought new cultural resources to the community and has reinforced the Indian intelligentsia. It appears that Pembroke will be a much more attractive place for high-achievement Lumbee professionals to locate. Already there are indications that the Indian community is beginning to call some of its native talent home.

At the beginning of the 1970s, Robeson County, with some 30,000 Indians, did not have a single Lumbee lawyer and had but one Lumbee physician. By 1977, at least seven Indian lawyers were practicing in the county, and there seem to be good prospects that some of the dozen or more young Lumbees studying at various medical schools will return home to practice.[42] The Lumbee artist–baseball player, Gene Locklear, maintains a studio in Pembroke, where he works during the months he is not playing with the New York Yankees.

There also appears to be a growing interest in Indian history and culture. This may be seen in a number of ways, but especially in Lumbee involvement in the production of the outdoor folk drama *Strike at the Wind,* based on the life of Henry Berry Lowry. Eighth-grade students washed cars to raise money for the production. The amphitheater was built largely with volunteer labor and donated materials. The compensation for actors was often less than their transportation expenses.

The growing interest in the Lumbee heritage also can be seen at the Pembroke "Indian Day" homecoming each July 4, which corresponds with the opening of the tobacco harvest and the beginning of the season for the folk drama. From all over the nation, "exiles" bring their largely assimilated children back to Pembroke to meet relatives, to savor the smell of curing tobacco, to watch the reenactment of the tragic epic of courage and death, to discover or rediscover what it means to be a Lumbee. Especially on these occasions, one sees the painful dilemma in which many Indians are caught: the exile has not been able to resist the economic pressures that disrupt his community. Yet the kinship ties, the legends, the childhood memories that bind that community together constantly draw him back to it.

For the Lumbees, furthermore, their native region has a significance that goes beyond nostalgia, because it is in Robeson County, and in the economic opportunities they can seize for themselves in Robeson County, that the question of assimilation or ethnic survival will be decided. This is a question of consequence since most Lumbees are less interested in becoming brown-skinned Anglo-Saxons than in establishing their own ethnic identity within a society free from ethnic oppression.

Notes

1. Chapman J. Milling, *Red Carolinians* (Chapel Hill: University of North Carolina Press, 1940), p. 213; John Reed Swanton, *Probable Identity of the "Croatan" Indians* (Washington: U.S. Office of Indian Affairs, 1933), p. 2.

2. North Carolina *Constitution* (1835), art. I, sec. 3, par. 3; *Revised Statutes of North Carolina, 1836–1837*, I, chap. 71.

3. Conversation with George Stephenson of the North Carolina Department of Archives and History, August 15, 1977.

4. Especially estates papers and wills.

5. U.S. Bureau of Census, *Eighth Census of the United States* (1860), "Free Population," North Carolina, XII, Robeson County (unpublished reports in National Archives).

6. Adolph L. Dial and David K. Eliades, *The Only Land I Know: A History of the Lumbee Indians* (San Francisco: The Indian Historian Press, 1975), p. 45; cf. Gerald Marc Sider, "The Political History of the Lumbee Indians of Robeson County, North Carolina: A Case Study of Ethnic Political Affiliations" (Ph.D. dissertation, New School for Social Research [New York], 1971), p. 36; George Alfred Townsend, comp., *The Swamp Outlaws: Or, the North Carolina Bandits, Being a Complete History of the Modern Rob Roys and Robin Hoods* (New York: M. DeWitt, 1972), p. 48, quoting "Mr. Leech" (Giles Leitch?).

7. John G. Barrett, *The Civil War in North Carolina* (Chapel Hill: University of North Carolina Press, 1963), p. 30; W. McKee Evans, *Ballots and Fence Rails: Reconstruction on the Lower Cape Fear* (Chapel Hill: University of North Carolina Press, 1967), pp. 6–7, 10–12; W. McKee Evans, *To Die Game: The Story of the Lowry Band, Indian Guerrillas of Reconstruction* (Baton Rouge: Louisiana State University Press, 1971), pp. 34–36; Don Carlos Sleitz, *Braxton Bragg: General of the Confederacy* (Columbia, S.C.: State Co., 1924), pp. 506–7.

8. Evans, *To Die Game*, passim.; Mary C. Norment, *The Lowrie History, as Acted in Part by Henry Berry Lowrie, the Great North Carolina Bandit, with Biographical Sketches of His Associates, Being a Complete History of the Modern Robber Band in the County of Robeson and the State of North Carolina* (Wilmington, N.C.: Daily Journal Printer, 1875), passim.

9. Hamilton McMillan, *Sir Walter Raleigh's Lost Colony* (Wilson, N.C.: Advance Press, 1888). McMillan's theory is elaborated by a trained scholar in Stephen B. Weeks, "The Lost Colony of Roanoke: Its Fate and Survival," *Papers of the American Historical Association* 5 (1891):441–80.

10. This article is an appendix to Orlando M. McPherson, *Indians of North Carolina*, 63d Congress, 3d sess., Senate Document No. 677 (Washington: Government Printing Office, 1915).

11. Swanton, *Probable Identity of the "Croatan" Indians*, and John Reed Swanton, *Siouan Indians of the Lumber River*, House of Representatives Report No. 1752, 37th Congress, 2d sess., 1934.

12. Norment, *Lowrie History*, pp. 5, 7, 27, and John C. Gorman, "Henry Berry Lowry Paper" (MS in North Carolina Department of Archives and History, Raleigh), p. 1.

13. North Carolina, *Public Laws*, 1885, chap. 51.

14. Sider, "Political History of the Lumbees," p. 6.

15. Evans, *To Die Game*, passim.

16. Dial and Eliades, *The Only Land I Know*, pp. 107–8.

17. Sider, "Political History of the Lumbees," pp. 87, 90–91.

18. North Carolina, *Laws*, 1887, chap. 400.

19. Vernon Ray Thompson, "A History of the Education of the Lumbee Indians of Robeson County, North Carolina, from 1885 to 1970" (Ed.D. dissertation, University of Miami, 1973), pp. 44–48; Dial and Eliades, *The Only Land I Know*, pp. 91–98.

20. Abraham Makofsky, "Tradition and Change in the Lumbee Community of Baltimore" (Ph.D. dissertation, Catholic University of America [Washington, D.C.], 1971), p. 28; John Gregory Peck, "Urban Station—Migration of the Lumbee Indians" (Ph.D. dissertation, University of North Carolina [Chapel Hill], 1972), p. 42; U.S. Department of Commerce, Bureau of the Census, *Statistical Abstract of the United States* (Washington: Government Printing Office, 1976), p. 409.

21. Peck, "Urban Station—Migration of the Lumbee Indians," pp. 45, 142–44; *Statistical Abstract of the United States*, p. 871.

22. Peck, "Urban Station—Migration of the Lumbee Indians," pp. 42, 139.

23. Ibid., p. 67.

24. Ibid., p. 138.

25. Sider, "Political History of the Lumbee Indians," pp. 73, 76, 79, 183.

26. Peck, "Urban Station—Migration of the Lumbee Indians," p. 45.

27. Makofsky, "Tradition and Change in the Lumbee Community," p. 30.

28. Sider, "Political History of the Lumbee Indians," p. 84.

29. Thompson, "History of the Education of the Lumbee Indians," p. 45.

30. Peck, "Urban Station—Migration of the Lumbee Indians," p. 42.

31. The problem of Lumbee adjustment to industrial jobs is illuminated by E. P. Thompson in "Time, Work-Discipline, and Industrial Capitalism," *Past and Present* (December 1967), pp. 56–97.

32. Peck, "Urban Station—Migration of the Lumbee Indians," p. 80.

33. Ibid., p. 69; Makofsky, "Tradition and Change in the Lumbee Community," p. 30.

34. Peck, "Urban Station—Migration of the Lumbee Indians," pp. 86, 92, 115. See also Makofsky, "Tradition and Change in the Lumbee Community," pp. 51–52.

35. Lumberton (N.C.), *Robesonian*, Dec. 29, 1970.

36. Peck, "Urban Station—Migration of the Lumbee Indians," p. 120.

37. For example, in 1973 a 17-year-old Lumbee was admitted as a freshman to Harvard as a National Honor Scholar and as a National Merit Scholar. It is significant, however, that this young man grew up in Indianapolis (Lumberton *Robesonian*, July 15, 1973). In parts of Robeson County an Indian has to struggle even to finish high school.

38. Ibid., Jan. 16, 20, 23, 30, 1958; Detroit *Times*, Jan. 20, 1958; *Newsweek*, Jan. 27, 1958, p. 27; *South Atlantic Quarterly* 7 (1958):433–42.

39. Sider, "Political History of the Lumbee Indians," pp. 120ff.

40. Charlotte *Observer*, Mar. 20, Apr. 5, 1973.

41. Interview with Tuscarora leader, Howard A. Brooks, near Maxton, N.C., August 29, 1977.

42. Telephone conversation with Pembroke State University professor, Adolph Dial, October 9, 1977.

4

The Struggle of the Louisiana Tunica Indians for Recognition

ERNEST C. DOWNS

The opposite side of the official policy of removal was an un-official and roughly conceived policy of neglect. The United States' purchase of Louisiana and President Jefferson's avowal that "full rights of possession as well as of property and sov-ereignty" would be guaranteed to the Indians of Louisiana[1] were accompanied by immeasurable federal ignorance of the tribes of the region. The Indian people who had played an important role in French and Spanish colonial enterprises encountered the most severe test of their survival in the American period. The United States ignored the legitimate relationships and formal agreements that former governments had negotiated with these tribes, neglected to ensure proper confirmation of Indian title to Indian lands, and in many instances did not even acknowledge that the tribes existed. Indian affairs in Louisiana entered a deep sleep in 1803.

With the American acquisition of the vast territory, recorded his-tory seems to have skipped from English-founded states on the East Coast to conquests in the West by English-speaking people. The French-speaking inhabitants of the former French colony did not play so active a role in opening the West as they did a passive role in isolating Louisiana from the national experience of the nine-teenth century. French heritage was not added to the acquisitive United States; it was simply overlooked. The Indian tribes which had been friendly to the French and which lived near French settle-ments were, of course, as easily forgotten.

Some historians realized that tribes had disappeared in Louisiana. Brownell, in his 1864 history *The Indian Races of North and South America*, noted that the French "had obtained the hearty good will of [Indian] nations little known to the English."[2] In 1874, Tuttle recalled that no Englishman had dared to venture among "the more remote tribes of the Mississippi."[3] The United States inherited the language and information which the English left behind and this largely accounts for the "disappearance" of England's Indian enemies. As Anglo-Americans began to envision their "manifest destiny," Indians who had befriended France were remembered as being strangely threatening, and that too was reason enough not to look for the lost tribes. Henry Schoolcraft, long after England had forgotten its Indian wars, stirred American readers by calling to mind "that Franco-Indian power, which like a gigantic serpent, coiled its folds around, and for a period, threatened to crush the British colonies."[4] That the tribes which had aided the French had never threatened the United States and that France itself had been an ally in the War for Independence was apparently inconsequential. The penalty for tribal alliances with a colonial government other than the one the United States had rebelled against was consignment to oblivion.

The Tunicas were the southernmost Indian nation to oppose the English, the rattles on the tail of that serpent Schoolcraft found so venomous. The tribe's relationship with France began as early as 1699, when the Tunicas and other small groups along the Yazoo River[5] were struggling to resist English-inspired and English-armed Chickasaw slave traders.[6] On January 11, 1699, a French missionary, Antoine Davion, established a mission in their village, offering the tribe an alternative relationship to a European power. The Tunicas reportedly greeted the French missionary "with joy."[7] A decade later, the Tunicas were so attached to the French that they moved their village halfway to New Orleans, establishing themselves opposite the juncture of the Red and Mississippi rivers.[8] This location not only afforded them a commanding position on trade routes between the two river valleys and New Orleans, but situated them strategically between the French and their Indian antagonists, the Natchez nation. This Grand Tunica Village became a landmark, serving as French headquarters during the long Natchez wars.[9] In those wars, King Louis XV awarded the Tunica chief, Cahura Joligo, the title Brigadier of the Red Armies for his commanding role.[10] Later American histories, apparently unable to recognize or translate *Tonicas*, recorded cursorily that the Choctaws, a tribe Americans had heard of, were responsible for the Natchez defeat.[11] In another episode which American historians also overlooked, the Tunicas participated in the Pontiac uprising and concluded their alliance with France by atttacking an English settlement party in 1764, after France had lost its North American colonies.[12]

As a result of the treaty ending the French and Indian wars, France gave all its territory east of the Mississippi River to England. France then ceded western Louisiana to Spain in the Family Compact between the two Bourbon kings of France and Spain. In this strange governmental display of musical chairs, the Tunicas found that their village, on the eastern bank of the river, was considered English domain; at the same time, they saw their French friends enlist in the service of the Spanish king on the western bank of the river.[13] The Tunicas were inclined to favor the Spanish government, which promised to honor the agreements which had been arranged between France and the Indian nations, in accordance with principles of international law.[14] But at the same time, the tribe needed the assistance of the English government to control the increasing encroachments of English subjects. Both European governments, of course, were wary of Tunica involvement with the other. For fifteen years the Tunicas diplomatically tried to retain their land on the eastern bank and their friendships on the western bank. The difficulty of this effort was concisely demonstrated when an English official reprimanded Chief Lattanache for attending a party at a Spanish post. Lattanache, who saw no reason for the English attitude, explained, "We want to be friends with all the white people near us, as we live among them." Then he pointedly asked, "Are we not free to go to which side of the river we please, are not the lands our own?"[15]

Forces beyond the Tunicas' control finally ended this precarious balance of power in the lower Mississippi Valley. The American Revolution began, and Spain sided with the rebellious colonies. With the Tunicas' help, Spanish Governor Bernardo de Galvez attacked English posts at Manchac and Baton Rouge (September and October 1779) and wrested control of the eastern bank from England.[16] After these skirmishes, the Tunicas decided it was no longer advisable to stay along the embattled Mississippi River. The major portion of the tribe moved to its traditional hunting territory, Avoyelles Prairie,[17] and established themselves where they are to-day, near Marksville, Louisiana. The tribe continued to use the Grand Village site on the Mississippi River occasionally for hunting and trade, and operated as guides in this area well into the nineteenth century.[18]

The Spanish government encouraged the tribe's resettlement in Avoyelles. On November 5, 1779, Governor Bernardo de Galvez formally instructed "all officers and soldiers and inhabitants under His Catholic Majesty to respect and protect the rights of the tribe of Thonicas [sic]."[19] A Spanish post was built nearby to carry out Galvez's order.[20] Indian trade was regulated, Indians held rights before the courts,[21] and in 1796 Governor Miro ordered a Spanish militia officer away from Indian land "because Indians have known rights which ought to be respected everywhere."[22]

This legacy of respect for the Tunicas' rights was not passed on to the United States. Jefferson tried to institute proper conduct of the federal relationship with the tribes of Louisiana. However, his appointee to the position of Indian agent, a doctor from Massachusetts, was unfamiliar with the history, geography, and culture of the territory which became the eighteenth state. Devoting himself to divesting the Caddos of their land which bordered on Spanish territory (Mexico), Dr. John Sibley dismissed the smaller groups in Louisiana. His notation regarding the Tunicas was the only official federal record of the tribe until 1938:

TUNICAS.—These people formerly lived on the Bayou Tunica, above Pointe Coupee, on the Mississippi, East Side, live now at Avoyelles; do not, at present, exceed twenty five men. Their native language is peculiar to themselves, but speak Mobilian; are employed occasionally by the inhabitants as boatmen, &c.; in amity with all other people, and gradually diminishing in number.[23]

Even more irresponsible than the federal negligence in locating and describing the Tunicas was the government's attempt at determining land title in the newly acquired territory. The United States was faced with the task of determining title in a territory already populated with Europeans, an unprecedented situation at that point in American history. Unwilling to create discontent among the

Chief Eli Barbry, shown with a traditional Tunica corn mortar in 1940.
Courtesy of the Barbry family.

former French and Spanish colonists who were now American citizens, federal officials wanted to confirm title to these people generously. Additionally, the government wanted to sell land which was unoccupied in order to offset the federal cost of the Louisiana territory. Everything worked against the Tunicas, who sought the assistance of a lawyer to protect their land.

In 1826, attorney George Gorten presented the tribe's land claims to the federal land commissioners. He pointed out that the Spanish government had recognized Tunica title, and asserted that the tribe owned its land *as a nation*. Calling for "an act of justice and humanity in the office charged with the state of the lands . . . to stop the sale," Gorten commented, "I consider it a misfortune of the Indians that their claims have not been known to the government. It is the duty of the government to inquire into their rights. There are Indian agents appointed for that purpose and I do not think the Indians should forfeit anything by neglect."[24]

The federal official who occupied the position of Indian agent did not take an interest in the case. The officials from the land office, who apparently were unfamiliar with federal laws concerning Indian lands, constructed their own regulations. Ruling that the Tunicas were "*savages*, not merely *Indians*" (emphasis in the original), the officials decided that the Tunicas had not "subdued their original propensities and evinced a determination to live and cultivate the ground as white men do," and therefore could not own the land in question.[25] There was no such requirement in the laws regarding Indian title, but the officials' decision went conveniently unquestioned by local authorities.

The geographer William Darby, who visited the Tunicas in 1813, wrote a description of the tribe which refutes the land commissioners' observation. "The Tonicas," he wrote, "have adopted the manners and customs of the French. One or two white families reside amongst them, and it would puzzle Montesquieu himself, to determine which of the parties has been the most influenced by the other."[26] At this date, the Tunicas were sedentary, lived in cabins, raised cotton and maize, and hunted. These occupations provided livelihood for the white settlers as well as the Tunicas. The commissioners' decision, therefore, was based neither on law nor fact. But "amity" with their neighbors, which Sibley had noted, made it possible for the Tunicas to live on their land, whether or not the federal government recognized their title.

There was never more than a superficial effort by the government to carry out Jefferson's just intentions in Louisiana. By 1851, the commissioner of Indian Affairs candidly bared his hopes that Louisiana could "soon be relieved from the annoyance of an Indian population."[27] Relief would not, however, require removal. Since the Tunicas lived in "amity" with all other people, they could be, and were, ignored. Sibley had reported in 1806 that the Tunicas were diminishing in numbers, so subsequent Indian affairs officials *assumed* that they had died out, that the government had been "relieved from the annoyance" of a Tunica population.

The people in Avoyelles Parish, however, knew the Tunicas were there. Even though the tribe was peaceful, the whites took the precaution of organizing an Indian "patrol" which observed the Tunica village. Celestin Moreau, a French settler, was appointed "Captain of the Patrol." There were never any incidents between whites and Indians which required a patrol, but the position gave Moreau some familiarity with the tribe's situation, and its vulnerability.[28]

In 1841, Moreau moved onto the Indian land and claimed title to it. As he tried to put a fence around "his" property, he drew the ire of the Tunica community. The Tunica chief, Melacon, followed Moreau at a distance and pulled out the fence posts. When Moreau saw that his work had been undone, he walked over to the chief and, in view of most of the tribe, shot him through the head.[29]

Up to that point, there had been no open aggression between the white and Indian communities. The Tunicas had originally been the stronger element in Avoyelles, controlled most of the trade, and knew the best hunting and fishing areas; but by 1841 the situation had changed. The struggling band of Tunicas who had seen their chief murdered had no choice but to seek a legal remedy. They wanted to charge Moreau with murder, but unable to finance a lawsuit, the tribe was forced to wait until 1844, when Moreau charged five of the tribe's old women with trespassing. At that time, Moreau, as plaintiff, was bound for all court costs.

Ralph Cushman, an Avoyelles lawyer, observed that the Tunicas were "extremely poor and unable to pay counsel fees," and decided to represent them "from the motives of humanity." In his argument, he concluded that the tribe was "strictly and justly entitled to a league square around their village," supporting his assertion with Spanish precedents:

The United States promised to execute such treaties and articles as may have been agreed upon between Spain and the tribes and nations of Indians until, by mutual consent of the United States and said tribes or nations of Indians, other suitable articles shall have been agreed upon. It is clear then, if their title was good under the Spanish government, it is good under the government of the United States, and any alienation grant or donation made by the United States is null and void. And it appears to me that no action was required by the Indians to perfect a title which was already perfect under the Spanish government.[30]

The case ended with an arrangement whereby the "Indian village" was left in the hands of the tribe; the larger portion of the tract went to Moreau. This arrangement did not award the Tunicas their full right to the "league square" but it did ensure that the Indian people who were struggling for their livelihood could at least continue to do so.

The Moreau case was not tried before the federal courts, even though questions regarding treaties and Indian law are usually decided in the federal court system. Moreau would not have wanted the case to be tried before a higher court, and would not have paid for such a disadvantage; the Tunicas could not even afford the local court, and appeal was beyond question. The present-day Tunica "reservation" was thus established neither by treaty nor executive order—in fact, with no involvement from the United States government at all.

The murder of Chief Melacon drove the Tunica government underground for approximately twenty years. It did not emerge until the 1870s. At that time, a man of considerable "medicine," Volsin Chiki, reunited the tribe, restored the cemeteries, and rejuvenated the ceremonies. Tribal leaders now recall that Chief Volsin was blind, but even without his sight he cut firewood and hauled it to his home, kept an herb garden, hunted, and startled children of the village when he could find items they playfully hid around his house.[31] Smithsonian ethnologists Gatschet and Swanton first visited the Tunicas during Volsin's lifetime, and recorded some of the Tunica language and stories from him.[32] Swanton's interest gave birth to Mary Haas's study of the Tunica language and tradition, and began a process which has resulted in some scholarly awareness of the tribe's existence.[33]

Volsin's reactivation of tribal life was an answer to increasing outside forces which were threatening Tunica livelihood. By 1870, blacks and whites in Avoyelles Parish had schools, but the Tunicas remained illiterate.[34] The tribal economy depended on hunting, farming, and fishing. Traditional medicine and training, rather than schooling, aided Tunica hunting and fishing ventures and kept the Tunicas alive. Felicien Chiki, one of Volsin's brothers, used herbs to cover his scent and developed the endurance to chase down deer. Fishing was conducted at night, when the large fish fed, and when there was no competition from night-timid non-Indian fishermen. Rituals blessed the first corn every year. Farming produced corn primarily for the tribe's use, but some cotton was grown for sale and pecans were harvested and sold. Women of the village became well known within a fifty-mile radius for their beautiful split-cane baskets, which they sold at grocery stores and along the roads. Traditional skills maintained Tunica livelihood.[35]

There was little friction between the Tunicas and the surrounding white community, partly because they shared difficult economic conditions. During Civil War campaigns, soldiers stationed near the village stole lard and sugar from some of the Tunicas, and during the smallpox epidemic of 1899 whites left their clothes at the village and infected the tribe. So relations were far from cordial, but generally the antagonism expressed itself in non-overt ways.[36] Dances and stickball (racquet) games, even during the ceremony of the first corn, were open to the public, and whites often attended.[37] It was not unusual, however, for whites to find themselves at the tail of the snake during a snake dance, and spun into the trees or cornfields as the momentum of the Indians at the head of the snake increased.[38]

Fights broke out more often between Indians than between whites and Indians, and the Tunicas today use the term "Indian fighter" to describe a belligerent Indian.[39] The roughest of these was Fulgence Chiki, the chief's younger brother, who terrorized his family and local whites with drunken belligerence. On April 25, 1896, according to court records, he allegedly "did wilfully, maliciously, felo-

Tunica woman, Ana Mae Juneau, weaving a traditional pine straw basket, 1975.
Courtesy of Ernest C. Downs and Ana Mae Juneau.

nously cut, stab, strike and thrust, Ernest Pierite [a respected hunter of the tribe] with a dangerous weapon, to wit: a knive, with intent him the said Ernest Pierite to Kill."[40] Members of the tribe wanted Fulgence punished, and approached the local authorities with their allegations. The lawyers argued about jurisdiction over the crime, since it was committed on Indian land, by an Indian, against an Indian. The case was referred to the Supreme Court of Louisiana, which in turn referred the question to the U.S. Department of Interior. The commissioner of Indian Affairs, unaware that Indians were living in Avoyelles, repeated Sibley's 1806 description of the Tunicas and stated that "the Federal government does not have jurisdiction over any Indians in Louisiana."[41]

Congress had specifically extended federal laws regarding Indian affairs over Louisiana in 1804,[42] but lack of implementation and knowledge regarding Louisiana's Indians had buried that fact. Since no one in Louisiana saw any reason to question this statement from the nation's leading Indian "expert," historical errors regenerated themselves. The Louisiana court assumed that the Tunicas were apparently subject to the same laws as citizens of the state.[43] Since the state government had never imagined that it held jurisdiction in Indian affairs, it had never instituted provisions for Indians in the state code.

The authorities in Avoyelles Parish, however, never exercised jurisdiction over the case involving Fulgence Chiki. After the judicial ruminations, Fulgence's body was found sliced to pieces on the railroad tracks near the Tunica village.[44]

Fulgence's sister, Arsene Chiki, often walked along these same tracks to towns where she could sell her baskets and to Indian communities where she could practice her medicine. On May 19, 1915, between 4:00 and 5:00 p.m., she met a fate similar to her brother's. Eyewitnesses recorded this second death on the railroad: "I seen her go up in the air, seen her dress go up, seen her come down . . . she was caught under the wheels of the train and dragged a few yards and cut to pieces."[45] Her son, Chief Sesostrie Youchicant, tried to sue the Texas and Pacific Railway Company for negligence. The railway, which had previously been sued for killing two mules and a cow, managed in this instance to evade the issue of carelessness.[46] After questioning Sesostrie and other witnesses about Arsene's "morality," lawyers for the railway convinced the court that Sesostrie was illegitimate. His parents, Arsene and Sosthene Youchicant, had been married by a formal Tunica ceremony described in court records,[47] but since the Tunica customs were not legally recognized, the court ruled that Sesostrie was illegitimate. According to the Louisiana Civil Code at that time, illegitimate children could not sue.[48] Sesostrie lost the case and returned to the Tunica village haunted by the idea that tribal members could not avail themselves of due process of law.

From that point on, attainment of formal federal recognition of the Tunicas' Indian identity became the major concern of every twentieth-century Tunica chief. The goal required research and letter writing, and since the Tunicas did not yet read or write, they found it necessary to enlist the aid of local lawyers and courthouse authorities. The Tunica objectives enveloped land questions, educational opportunities, financial aid, and legal status—all of which interested local whites, who offered to write letters to the federal government. Sesostrie Youchicant's half-brother, Eli Barbry, was elected chief in 1936, and for a time the two brothers worked to win federal recognition. But all official responses to the chiefs' letters pleaded ignorance. Most of them cited Sibley's 1806 report and repeated that the federal government had no jurisdiction over Indians in Louisiana.[49]

The 1930s brought severe economic difficulties for the tribe, as they did for the rest of the United States. Congressman Numa F. Montet was moved to ask the Bureau of Indian Affairs what services could be provided for Louisiana's Indians, "who, because of the lack of educational facilities, are living in ignorance and deplorably unhealthy conditions."[50] Montet called for federal recognition and federal services. Fifty years before, the federal policy toward Indians had asserted that Indians were wards who had to be cared for, educated, and "civilized" by the federal government. By 1930, it was no longer advantageous to advocate this federal responsibility. BIA Commissioner C. J. Rhoads responded to the congressman, acknowledging—officially for the first time—that there were "a few Tunica Indians" in Avoyelles Parish, and offering a new philosophy which was a strange contortion of wardship policy. "Without federal aid," the commissioner imagined, "the Indians of Louisiana exist, free of the handicaps of wardship . . . we do *not* [his emphasis] believe that for the federal government to assume jurisdiction over the Indians of Louisiana today would be any kindness to those Indians."[51] Tunicas remained in the nebulous legal status of unrecognized Indians, continued to be excluded from public schools, and suffered increasing economic hardships.

After the great Mississippi flood (1927), Tunica impoverishment grew even more desperate. Most of the young men left the Tunica village and followed a path of lumberyards to Texas. Checks were sent home to the village; food and lodging were supplied by the lumber companies. One Tunica man returned after losing a hand in a sawmill; some died violent deaths in Texas. Those who were too young to leave remained in the village with the older men and tried to make a living by more traditional methods. Harvesting swamp moss for mattress stuffing, hunting, and fishing provided subsistence, but even the more familiar environment held horrors. One man died from wounds incurred while wrestling with a deer, another from accidentally eating "bad" berries, another from a sting inflicted by an insect hidden in swamp moss. Women of the village worked "in town," cleaning white people's houses and washing laundry, or "in the fields" picking cotton. A few of them died from pneumonia and tuberculosis.[52] The deaths of young people diminished the future of the tribe. By 1940, only three family names survived: Pierite, Barbry, and Picote.

When John Collier was commissioner of Indian Affairs, some federal attention was directed to the Tunicas. On September 12, 1938, Eli and Sam Barbry and Horace Pierite Sr. visited the Office of Indian Affairs in Washington. Collier was not in his office, but the men met with Assistant Commissioner Fred Daiker, who concluded, "With such a small group it was doubtful . . . whether any official should be sent there to make an investigation and as to whether or not we should endeavor to do anything for these people."[53] But Collier was more interested in the Tunicas' situation, and a month later sent Ruth Underhill to investigate their problems.

Underhill perceived that "all the young people are anxious to move to Houston, Texas, where they will be free of racial discrimination and feel they will have a better chance." She advised the Tunicas, "This would be the best thing to do."[54] But some members of the tribe did not take their community life or their tribal land so lightly. Suspicions about Chief Eli Barbry's interest in selling the land and moving to Texas resulted in the chief's removal from office in 1948. A new Tunica administration, in which Horace Pierite became chief and Joseph Alcide Pierite subchief, was instituted.[55]

The flurry of letters for information, requests for recognition, and responses quoting Sibley's 1806 report began anew under the Pierite chieftainship. In the 1950s the government forgot even its own activities during the 1930s and responded to letters by denying it had any information concerning the Tunicas, other than Sibley's report. Congressman Speedy Long could not excite federal interest in the Tunicas. On March 18, 1965, the assistant commissioner for Indian Affairs wrote the congressman: "Current policy in Indian affairs is to promote the social and economic development of Indian tribal groups now under our jurisdiction so that, as rapidly as possible, they may become independent of their special relationships with the Federal government."[56] Throughout the 1960s, letters requesting loans, land title investigations, educational assistance, medical help, and legal aid were all blocked by a final bureaucratic impasse: the tribe was not recognized by the federal government.

Chief Joseph Pierite, the last chief of the tribe, fought consistently for federal recognition until his death on March 16, 1976. Along with letters to congressmen and federal officials, he sought to tell the story of the tribe to everyone who would listen. On February 7, 1967, he had a literate friend write to Vine Deloria Jr., then executive director of the National Congress of American Indians. The chief described the Tunicas' problems and concluded, "Our people are buried here and it means a lot for us to be able to stay here."[57] Deloria's interest spawned new hope for the tribe. Since that time, the Tunicas have played a significant role in the movement for recognition of the East's "lost" tribes.

Throughout the American period, the Tunicas have met with nothing but negligence on the part of the federal government, irresponsibility in the General Land Office, and disregard in the Bureau of Indian Affairs. In the one instance of federal attention (Ruth Underhill's 1938 visit), the advice of the official spokeswoman was "move."

In the case of the Tunicas, inattention was the favorite policy, removal was the only suggested alternative. The Tunicas, however, have continued to live on their land, and continue to maintain their Indian identity. They defiantly await federal recognition of federal responsibilities.

Notes

1. Annie Heloise Abel, "The History of Events Resulting in Indian Consolidation West of the Mississippi," in *Annual Report of the American Historical Association for the Year 1906* (Washington: Government Printing Office, 1908), 1:241–42.

2. Charles de Wolf Brownell, *The Indian Races of North and South America* (Hartford: Hurlburt, Scranton and Co., 1864), p. 376.

3. Charles R. Tuttle, *History of the Border Wars of Two Centuries* (Chicago: C. A. Wall, 1874), p. 31.

4. Henry Rowe Schoolcraft, *History of the Indian Tribes of the United States* (Philadelphia: Lippincott, 1857), p. 185.

5. John G. Shea, *Early Voyages Up and Down the Mississippi* (Albany: Joel Munsell, 1861), p. 76; John R. Swanton, *Indian Tribes of the Lower Mississippi Valley and the Adjacent Coast of the Gulf of Mexico*, Bulletin 43 of the Bureau of American Ethnology (Washington: Government Printing Office, 1911), p. 308.

6. De Montigny to Monseigneur. Bibliothèque Nationale (Paris), Manuscrits Français, Nouvelles Acquisitions (hereafter cited B.N., Ms. Fr., N.A.), 7485, part 2, ff. 122–122v.

7. Shea, *Early Voyages*, p. 75.

8. R. G. McWilliams, trans., *Fleur de Lys and Calumet* (The Penicaut Narrative) (Baton Rouge: Louisiana State University Press, 1953), p. 129; E. A. Taschereau, *History of the Seminary of Quebec* (Paris, Seminaire des Missions Etrangères, n.d.), pp. 345, 1012–42.

9. See Swanton, *Indian Tribes of the Lower Mississippi Valley*, p. 198; De Richebourg narrative in B. F. French, *Historical Collections of Louisiana* (New York, 1851), vol. 5, pp. 44–56, and Dunbar Rowland and A. G. Sanders, *Mississippi Provincial Archives, 1729–1740, French Dominion* (Jackson: Press of the Mississippi Department of Archives and History, 1927), vol. 3, pp. 202, 206, 360, 364.

10. Le Page DuPratz, *The History of Louisiana* (London, 1774; facsimile reprint, Baton Rouge: Claitor's, 1972), p. 298.

11. Brownell, *The Indian Races of North and South America*, pp. 431–40.

12. Marc de Villiers du Terrage, *Les Dernières Années de la Louisiane Française* (Paris, 1904), pp. 177–83; Journal of M. D'Abbadie, translated in

Clarence E. Carter, *The Critical Period, 1763–1765* (Springfield: Illinois State Historical Library, 1915), vol. 10, pp. 162–215.

13. John W. Caughey, *Bernardo de Galvez in Louisiana* (Gretna, La.: Pelican Publishing Co., 1972), p. 33.

14. O'Reilly to Arriaga, October 17, 1969, Archivo General de las Indias, Audencias, Santo Domingo (hereafter cited AGI, Aud., Sto. Dom.), legajo 80-1-7, translated in Lawrence Kinnaird, ed., "Spain in the Mississippi Valley, 1765–1794," in *Annual Report of the American Historical Association for the Year 1945* (Washington: Government Printing Office, 1949), vol. 2, pp. 101–3.

15. David Knuth Bjork, "Documents Regarding Indian Affairs in the Lower Mississippi Valley, 1771–1772," *Mississippi Valley Historical Review*, 13 (December 1926): 340–98.

16. Caughey, *Bernardo de Galvez*, pp. 153–57.

17. D'Annville, "Carte [map] de la Louisiane," drawn in 1732, printed in 1752, copy preserved in Louisiana Room of the Eugene Watson Library, Northwestern State University of Louisiana, Natchitoches.

18. Paul Wilhelm, duke of Wurttemberg, *Travels in North America, 1822–1824* (Norman: University of Oklahoma Press, 1975), pp. 109–10.

19. Bernardo de Galvez at New Orleans, November 5, 1779, Miscellaneous Papers of the register and receiver, Opelousas, Tunica Indians, Cabinet No. 5, Memo No. 20, recorded in Works Progress Administration, *Survey of Federal Archives in Louisiana*, "Indian Land Claims and Other Documents" (typescript; Baton Rouge: Louisiana State University, 1940), pp. 113–14.

20. Corrine L. Saucier, *History of Avoyelles Parish* (New Orleans: Pelican Publishing Co., 1943), p. 295.

21. Ibid., pp. 432–542.

22. Spanish Governor Miro to Jacques Gagnard, commandant of the Post of Avoyelles, New Orleans, October 6, 1786. Extract recorded in French. Translated and submitted to register and receiver October 6, 1897; included in claims under Act 136–200 (Louisiana Land Claims), Opelousas; reported to Congress April 8, 1816. *American State Papers*, Public Lands, vol. 3, p. 151.

23. John Sibley, "Historical Sketches of the Several Indian Tribes in Louisiana, South of the Arkansas and between the Mississippi and River Grande," *American State Papers*, Indian Affairs, vol. 1 (Washington, 1832): 725.

24. State Land Office, Baton Rouge. Unpublished Pintado Papers, 20: 219–20.

25. Decision of the register and receiver, Opelousas, September 26, 1826. Recorded in Works Progress Administration, Survey of Federal Archives in Louisiana, "Indian Land Claims and Other Documents" (typescript; Baton Rouge: Louisiana State University, 1940), pp. 74–75.

26. William Darby, *Emigrant's Guide to the Western and Southwestern States and Territories* (New York, 1813), p. 70.

27. Report of commissioner of Indian affairs, Luke Lea, November 27, 1851, reprinted in Wilcomb Washburn, *The American Indian and the United States, a Documentary History* (New York: Random House, 1973), p. 55.

28. Works Progress Administration, Survey of Federal Archives in Louisiana, "Transcriptions of Parish Records of Louisiana," no. 5, Avoyelles Parish Police Jury minutes, vol. 1, 1821–43 (Louisiana State University, 1940).

29. Transcriptions of the author's recorded interviews with tribal members (the tapes are cited "tape number, side, page"). The following tapes support the assertion in the text: 4-A-1; 5-A-5; 5-B-4; 9-A-1, 2; 10-A-4; 10-A-7; 17-A-5; 17-B-20; 13-A-6, 7, 8; 18-B-21, 22.

30. Letter of Ralph Cushman, attorney for the Tunicas, to surveyor general of the United States for the state of Louisiana, Marksville, April 29, 1844. Recorded in Works Progress Administration, "Indian Land Claims," pp. 5–7.

31. Tapes 3-B-6, 7; 6-A-9, 10; 17-B-20, 21; 19-B-25, 26.

32. Tape 18-B-17 and John R. Swanton, unpublished annotated copy of A. S. Gatschet's Tunica texts, Bureau of American Ethnology Collections, National Anthropological Archives, Smithsonian Institution, Washington, D.C.

33. Mary R. Haas, "Tunica Dictionary," *University of California Publications in Linguistics* 6 (1953): 179–81.

34. Saucier, *History of Avoyelles Parish*, p. 96.

35. Tapes 13-B-1, 2, 3, 4; 15-A-20; 19-A-20, 21, 22, 23; 19-B-25; 20-A-19; 20-B-1, 4; 21-A-2.

36. Tapes 5-B-10; 13-A-8; Saucier, *History of Avoyelles Parish*, p. 112.

37. Tapes 6-B-7; 12-A-17, 18; 14-B-1, 2; 17-B-22; 19-A-6.

38. Tape 6-B-7.

39. Tapes 18-A-19, 20.

40. *State of Louisiana* v. *Fulgence Chiqui*, 49 La. Ann. 131 (no. 12,288); Avoyelles Parish criminal docket no. 2039.

41. Commissioner of Indian Affairs Browning to the secretary of the interior, December 9, 1896; National Archives Record Group 75, Land, file no. 44916–1896. Printed in *State* v. *Fulgence Chiqui*.

42. Act of March 26, 1804, sec. 15. Recorded in United States Government, *Laws of the United States, Resolutions of Congress under the Confederation, Treaties, Proclamations, Spanish Regulations, and other Documents Respecting the Public Lands* (Washington: Gales and Seaton, 1828), 1:510.

43. *State* v. *Fulgence Chiqui*.

44. Tape 14-A-14.

45. *Sesostris Youchican* v. *Texas and Pacific Railway Company*, 86 South. 551; Supreme Court of Louisiana docket no. 22808; Avoyelles Parish civil docket no. 2915; transcript, pp. 15–16, 72.

46. Avoyelles Parish Courthouse docket nos. 1272, 3517.

47. *Sesostris Youchican* v. *Texas and Pacific Railway*, transcript, pp. 52–56.

48. Ibid., report, 86 South. 551.

49. National Archives, Record Group 75, Bureau of Indian Affairs, Central Files, 1907–39, particularly file nos. 67669-1931-053, 68776-1931-800, and 78634-1925-307.4.

50. Congressman Numa F. Montet to Commissioner Rhoads of Bureau of Indian Affairs, December 11, 1931; National Archives, Record Group 75, 68776-1931-800.

51. Commissioner Rhoads to Congressman Montet, January 4, 1932.

52. Tapes 4-B-3; 6-A-1; 10-A-9; 12-A-18, 19; 12-B-1; 12-A-10, 11, 12, 13, 14; 19-A-33, 34, 35, 36, 37, 38, 39, 40.

53. Memorandum from F. H. Daiker to John Collier, September 15, 1938, National Archives Record Group 75, 68776-1931-800.

54. Ruth M. Underhill (associate director of Indian education), "Report on a Visit to Indian Groups in Louisiana, October 15–25, 1938," National Archives Record Group 75, 68776-1931-800.

55. Conveyance Book A-132, no. 109046, Avoyelles Parish Courthouse, Marksville, La.

56. Assistant Commissioner of Indian Affairs Graham Holmes to Congressman Speedy O. Long, March 18, 1965. Copy kept by the Pierite family.

57. Chief Joseph A. Pierite to Vine Deloria, executive director of National Congress of American Indians, February 7, 1967. Copy from NCAI Papers, Louisiana File, National Anthropological Archives, Smithsonian Institution, Washington, D.C.

5

Southern Louisiana Survivors: The Houma Indians

MAX E. STANTON

For the past 150 years there has been an identifiable Indian community in the swamp and marsh area of Terrebonne and Lafourche parishes in southern Louisiana, living along the bayous which fan out toward the Gulf of Mexico from the cities of Houma and Thibodaux. These people are concentrated in six communities. They are, from west to east, DuLarge, Dulac (the largest Indian settlement in the area), Pointe au Barree, Champs Charles, Lower Pointe au Chien, and Lower Bayou Lafourche (Golden Meadow). In much of the literature these people are referred to as Houma Indians, but apparently the term is used locally neither by the Indians themselves nor their non-Indian neighbors. There is a local designation, Sabine, which is sometimes used in reference to these people, especially by the non-Indians, but it is perceived as derogatory. They prefer to be referred to as Indians, not using the term Houma and resenting, even among themselves, those who use the word Sabine. (The terms Indian and Houma will be used interchangeably throughout this report.)

The contemporary social milieu of the area described above is essentially a triracial community. In Dulac and other nearby communities, whites, Indians, and Negroes live in close spatial propinquity but have limited contacts, usually of a secondary nature, with persons outside their own recognized ethnic group. There seems to be little tension or discord as a result of the limited contact between the groups, but it would be inaccurate to describe the situation as one of full interethnic accord and harmony.

The Indian status is on the middle rung of the socioeconomic hierarchy in the area, with whites in the preeminent station and

Negroes in the socially least preferred situation. A general trend has been operating in the last decade to weaken this rather strict racial trichotomy, but established tradition is difficult to overcome, and so long as the social reality of ethnic separation exists and so long as racist conditions prevail in the community, we must concede the reality of the situation and recognize it for what it is—a powerful social phenomenon which tends to permeate the private and public lives of all persons involved, especially people who find themselves in ethnically subordinate positions within the social structure.

There seems to be a trend toward closer cooperation and association between the Indians and the whites, but in most instances such interaction is initiated by the Indians and the terms of the relationship are dictated by long-standing tradition and convention, which definitely favors those who are in power. Much of the Indian–white interaction is due to the general desire of the Indians to emulate white culture and to eschew association with black people in the community. When it becomes necessary for an Indian to interact with blacks, such behavior is generally not carried on as openly and freely as it would be with whites.

The Indians readily admit to a strong white element in their biological and cultural heritage. All have European surnames (mostly of French origin), and for nearly all of them the local Cajun (French) language and culture type typifies their domestic life. Cajun is a corruption of *Acadien*, which refers to Acadia (New Brunswick), the homeland of most of the French emigrés who arrived in this area after their expulsion from Canada at the conclusion of the French and Indian War in 1763. Apparently there are some regions in the American South where this term (Cajun) has a negative connotation, but in southern Louisiana it is a proper designation, accepted by those of French and non-French origin and used to refer to persons of French ancestry and their culture.

It is interesting that many of the Indians are of fair complexion and cannot readily be distinguished, by phenotype alone, from their non-Indian neighbors. Their Indian identity, therefore, is a phenomenon of their social relations in the community rather than a result of basic physical differences. Because of family connections or surnames which are considered to be Indian (e.g., Billiot, Verdin, Diane, Gregoire, Parfait, and Verret)[1] or of simply being known in the community, the middle-range status in the social hierarchy becomes an ascribed situation over which a particular individual or group has little control. As mentioned above, one's ethnic group identity is a major factor in the network of relationships within the community and the social aspect of racial identification precludes the possibility of avoiding the negative aspects relegated to members of the Indian group by the dominant white element in the area.

Some members of the Indian community bear an unmistakable African ancestry. These persons are often placed in a marginal position within the group of other Indians, but they tend to cling to their Indian connections and identity, emphasizing especially the Cajun aspects of their heritage. By so doing they are able to maintain, at least to the community at large, their Indian status and avoid the even lower position accorded to Negroes.

That there is some element of black ancestry among the Houma seems to be unquestionable. As will be discussed later, the Houma readily admitted strangers into their ranks, among them escaped slaves, but the Indians insist that the Afro-American aspect of their heritage is not significant. Whether or not this is true is irrelevant, except for the social implications.

Some persons who have had contact with the Indians of southern Louisiana have emphasized the triracial nature of the Houma,[2] but this seems to confuse the issue. The conclusion reached by E. Peter Roy, and supported by the author of this report, is that a black element is present in the Houma population, especially in particular families, but only about one Indian in five has any African ancestry. In this same vein, Mr. Roy goes on to state that the term Sabine is used by the Indians to refer to members of their group who have known black progenitors.[3]

In this whole area of interethnic relations it is interesting to note that until the United States Supreme Court ruled against antimiscegenation laws, the Indians of Louisiana enjoyed the unique privilege in the state of being able to marry outside their group. Whites and blacks were prohibited by law from intermarrying, but Indians had no such restrictions on outgroup marriages.

For most Houma, the ethnic-status issue soon disappears when they leave the community. Elsewhere, their social and familial histories are not known and the physical appearance of the person determines one's ethnic status. Since most Houma lack the "classic" Indian phenotype, when they go away from their home communities they readily assume the identity of a Cajun from rural Louisiana. It is not surprising that persons with African ancestry, who might be regarded as blacks outside the area, prefer, by and large, to remain in the Terrebonne-Lafourche parish area, where they are accepted as Indians.

The whole question of race among these people has been summarized by Frank G. Speck:

> The so-called Houma of today include remnants of most of the Louisiana coast tribes, in all degrees of mixture; Indian, White, and Negro. The state recognized about 350 as Indian. They claim over 800 of all mixtures and intermarriages. The wide variation in the estimates of the number of Houma today raises an issue that applies to many modern Indian bands, even to tribe. When do Indians cease to be Indians anthropologically, sociologically or politically? Is classification dependent upon the legacy of a direct tradition under a name identity involving all of these conditions plus forms of separatist behavior and self-consciousness?[4]

Since the problem of racial and ethnic identity in contemporary America is not strictly a biological function but is also very much bound to social realities, this whole question of ingroup identification is critical. The past decade in America has shown a marked rise in ethnic identity, accompanied by an assertion of pride in one's heritage. Because of the heterogeneous nature of the biological and cultural heritage of so many groups in the country (including the Houma), it would be an injustice to demand a "percentage pure" basis of one's genetic makeup to determine racial and ethnic affiliation. Because the actual differences resulting from a person's biological and social heritage are principally expressed in a social context, one's self-identification (when such an option is permitted), along with the recognition accorded by knowledgeable members of the community, should be the overriding factor in determining the ethnic affiliation of an individual. Any arbitrary formula created by a state or federal agency will not suffice, especially in the case of a group such as the Houma, because the social realities of the area often transcend known or presumed biological facts.

Historical Setting to 1840

At the time of first European contact, in the latter part of the seventeenth century, the Houma were living on the eastern bank of the Mississippi River in the area of the present West Feliciana Parish, Louisiana and Wilkinson County, Mississippi. The name, Houma, literally means "red" and is probably an abbreviation of their tribal emblem, *sakti homma*, the red crawfish. They spoke a Muskogean language closely related to Choctaw and shared the cultural lifestyle of their neighbors in the lower Mississippi Valley.[5]

Shortly after their initial contacts with European explorers (La-Salle, Tonti, and Iberville), the Houma were severely affected by a disease described by Iberville as "an abdominal flux,"[6] which reduced the group to about half its former size. A few years thereafter, in the early part of the eighteenth century, the group allowed a large portion of the Tunica tribe to settle in their midst. Sometime between 1706 and 1709, the Tunicas massacred most of their hosts and drove the survivors out of their home territory into what is now southern Louisiana. Thereafter, the Houmas moved south along the Mississippi River, settling on Bayou St. John, not far from New Orleans. A few years later they moved back up the Mississippi River and settled in Ascension Parish, near the present site of Donaldsonville.[7]

The combination of disease, massacre, mass movement, and the general disruption of their traditional way of life had, by the middle of the eighteenth century, greatly reduced the size of the Houma tribe. Also, the disruptive combination of the abovementioned factors had an effect on the operation of traditional norms and values. Throughout the middle and latter part of the 1700s, the tribe readily accepted segments of closely related groups and was one of the few Louisiana Native American bodies which maintained an identity into the nineteenth century.[8]

The Houma Indians remained in their Ascension Parish site for about 100 years. As late as 1836, a village of about 200 persons (60–80 men), presumed to be Houmas, were reported to be living on the shores of Lake Maurepas in Ascension Parish.[9]

During this period the Houma undoubtedly had frequent contact

Thatched-roof Houma house with wattle-and-daub walls, early twentieth century.
Courtesy of Smithsonian Institution National Anthropological Archives, photo no. 244.

with the non-Indians in the area, particularly with the recent refugees from the former French colony of Acadia. Because of the general
disruption of their traditional social structure and the advantageous
nature of European material technology, it is safe to assume that
many foreign influences, especially those of the French, were eventually incorporated in the Houma culture.

The Houma were able to maintain their numbers and identity as
a group by allowing scattered remnants of other Indian tribes and
bands to join them. But at the same time the constant infusion of
new persons and ideas tended to generate a further element of in-
stability in the cultural network, promoting further change.

Most of these newly adopted persons were from closely related
tribes of the Muskogean linguistic group, speaking dialects more or
less mutually intelligible with that spoken by the Houma, so that
the rate or direction of change cannot be fully assessed because of
the inability to determine which practices were traditionally used
by the tribe, as differentiated from items which were later introduced or revived by the infusion of these neighboring Indians.

Later, in the early part of the nineteenth century, as the United
States became more firm and committed to its policy of Indian removal from the southeastern portion of the nation, other scattered
Indian groups undoubtedly sought refuge with the Houma. The condition of most of the tribes in the lower Mississippi River Valley
became quite desperate and disorganized as a result of the syste-
matic policy of the non-Indians to displace the native inhabitants.
Even the Houma, in their semi-isolated camps west of the Mississippi River, were not safe. Probably only a small portion of the tribe
escaped removal to Oklahoma,[10] but enough of the tribe remained
to retain a reasonable degree of group continuity. In fact, they were
one of the few tribes in the area with a population substantial
enough to provide order and security, and thus continued to attract
Indians and non-Indians alike, who for their own reasons desired
to take up residence within the group. This situation is summarized
by Swanton:

   Although they called themselves "houmas" or, rather Homas, it has been
   intimated . . . that remains of other tribes, such as Bayogoula and Acola-
   pissa, have been incorporated with them. To these must be added Biloxi

and Chitimacha . . . who were often introduced (traditionally in the capacity of slaves), and probably the remnants of the Washa and Chawasha, besides individuals from a number of other Louisiana and Mississippi peoples. The family history of the writer's older informant, Felicite Billiout [sic], will serve to illustrate this tribal complexity. Her mother whose Indian name was Nuyun, but who was baptized "Marion" after her removal to Louisiana, was born in or near Mobile: her grandfather Shulushumon, or, in French Joseph Abbe, and more often called "Couteaux", was a Biloxi medal chief; and her mother "an Atakapa from Texas." In addition, she said that Cherokee (Tsalaki), Choctaw, and Alibamu had all married with her people. Among other tribes, she had heard of Chickasaw (Shikasha), Tallapossa (Talapush), and Tunica. Her grandmother, whom she said had moved successively to the Mississippi, "Tuckapaw canal", Bayou La Fourche, Houma and the coast of Terre Bonne, was evidently among the Indians who migrated from the neighborhood of Mobile after 1764, in order to not remain under British rule. It is plain that the remnants of all sorts of tribes joined the Houma before and at this period, though it is certain that most of these were Muskhogean, and that the Houma was always the dominant element.[11]

It is not clear from the historical record when the first Houma settlers arrived in their present home in Terrebonne and Lafourche parishes. However, it is known that by 1795 at least three whites, all bearing French surnames, had settled in the southern portion of Terrebonne Parish, all three married to Indians. Pressures for the better farm and plantation lands in Ascension Parish probably accounted for part of this southward movement. Also, the most isolated and virtually inaccessible marshland of the southern portions of Terrebonne and Lafourche parishes undoubtedly offered an attractive sanctuary for persons resisting attempts to remove the tribe to Oklahoma. By 1820 there were reports of small groups of Indians living in their present-day location, and in 1834 the city of Houma, Louisiana, was founded, taking its name from a group of Indians residing in the vicinity.[12] Swanton reports that only three bands of Houma ever settled in Terrebonne Parish,[13] the main body having left Ascension Parish in 1785, migrating farther up the Mississippi River toward their old homeland. This larger portion of the tribe has become lost in the historical record, but it can reasonably be assumed that they merged with other tribes and suffered their general fate of decimation and removal. By 1840 all the Indians had vacated Ascension Parish, and from this time on the Houma history is confined to Terrebonne and Lafourche parishes.

Years of Isolation: 1840–1930

After the Houma settled in their present location, a trend to break off into isolated camps or dispersed settlements, consisting of a few closely related families, is apparent. The overall ecological nature of the area probably had much to do with this situation. With its maze of channels, bayous, lakes, and ponds, with few high, relatively dry areas, it was impossible for settlements of more than a few dozen persons to exist. Also, the area did not lend itself to the traditional horticultural practices of the people, thus requiring greater dependency upon hunting (including trapping for cash and exchange) and fishing.

The Houma continued in their relative isolation throughout the latter part of the nineteenth century and into the early years of the twentieth century. Descriptions of the group during this period, especially those of Swanton, give evidence that much of their material culture had been adjusted to meet the needs of life in this world of water and marsh grass.[14] Some of their traditional social organization remained, such as marriage practices described by E. Peter Roy as "jumping over the broom,"[15] in which the young couple literally jumped over a broom during a celebration honoring their marriage. There is, however, no evidence that this is purely a traditional Indian practice, and it is popular among the non-Indians in the area as well.

When John Swanton visited the area in 1907, most vestiges of the Indian culture had disappeared and been replaced by that of the rural French-speaking community of the area. It is obvious that the ascendancy of the Cajun cultural type occurred long before Swanton's visit, because of his difficulty in locating persons who had *any* knowledge of the traditional Houma language.[16] This observation is corroborated by a letter written by Harvey E. Meyer, then superintendent of the Choctaw Indian Agency in Mississippi, to John Collier, the United States commissioner of Indian Affairs. It was the intention of Mr. Meyer to establish the possibility of federal monies in the support of a special school catering to the needs of the Indians of the area. In the letter, he states that he had contacted "chief" Victory Naquin, living at Champs Charles (Isle St. Jean Charles), and in the course of discussion Chief Naquin:

informed us that his grandmother spoke "Indian", and that it is his understanding it was "Houma-Choctaw". No others since that date have spoken the Indian language and even *then* their language was Cajun, as it is now (my emphasis).[17]

If we assume that Mr. Naquin was born in 1900 (making him 40 years of age at the time he met Mr. Meyer) and that his grandmother was no less than 40 at the time of Victory Naquin's birth, we can conclude that by the time of the Civil War the French language was already important among the Houma and that their traditional language was rapidly fading into disuse by 1860. Because of this long association with the local Cajun language and culture (most likely dating back to the later part of the eighteenth century), any practice or mode of behavior asserted to be "traditionally Indian" must be carefully examined to ascertain possible French antecedents. Even the "traditional" thatched-roof houses in much of the literature of the earlier part of the twentieth century[18] seem to be an adaptation of the common trapper's hut of the area, utilizing readily available materials.

The major historical event of this period is the visit by John Swanton in April 1907 to make a brief study of the group to determine their future relationship with the federal government. It was the determination of Dr. Swanton that the group had been so intermixed with white and black elements that their traditional culture and Houma biological heritage had been lost, to such a degree that they could no longer have a legitimate claim to Indian status. He thus recommended that the group not be recognized as Indians by the federal government,[19] and by so doing—it is this writer's firm opinion—a major injustice has been done to these people. It seems incredible that Swanton should have so easily dismissed the obvious Indian connections of these people, especially in light of his own statement, when he reports that "it is plain that remnants of all sorts of tribes joined the Houma . . . though it is *certain* that most of these were Muskhogean and that the Houma was always the dominating element" [my emphasis].[20]

In a report written by Frank G. Speck some thirty years later to the U.S. Department of Education, Office of Indian Affairs, the "Indianness" of the Houma was again confirmed:

> There is in the physical type of the group . . . a predominately and distinctly Indian Cargo. The leaders of the Houma people themselves are, in my judgement, capable of satisfactorily evaluating the validity of claims to Houma "raciality", in respect to the blood quantum, when the time arrives for listing and segregating the Indians.[21]

It is the contention of another recent researcher that Swanton was greatly influenced by his principal informant, Bob Verret, who misrepresented the Houma cause and apparently greatly prejudiced Swanton against the basic Indian affiliations of the group's past.[22] In the whole argument, lack of Indian "blood" and their strong acculturation into the rural Cajun culture of southern Louisiana has been an important factor in the nonrecognition of the Houma. Only a few miles to the west, in St. Mary Parish, the Chitimacha Indians, having suffered from just as much cultural and biological "dilution," were recognized as a legitimate Indian tribe and, beginning in 1916, largely as a result of Swanton's visit (also in 1907), began to receive federal aid.[23] If we look at the problem more closely, it seems that had the approximately 2,000 Houma in the early part of the twentieth century lived in compact, easily accessible communities, as did the few hundred Chitimacha, the argument for federal recognition might have been stronger and ultimately more successful. This thesis is substantiated in a report by Roy Nash, special commissioner (investigation) for the Bureau of Indian Affairs, who wrote in June 1931: "If these Indian mixed bloods were concentrated in any one place, it might be possible for the Federal government to afford them school facilities; but they are scattered widely through Louisiana."[24]

Regardless of the many statements made in favor of some type of federal affiliation with the Indian people of southern Louisiana, they entered the twentieth century and remain today outside the often mismanaged but still advantageous sphere of federal recognition.

Exploitation and Awakening: 1930 to the Present

During the third decade of the twentieth century, strong pressure was exerted by the non-Indians in southern Louisiana to get the Houma to again pull up their roots and move elsewhere. One important reason for displacing the Houma was the desire of fur-buying companies in the area to gain exclusive trapping rights. But the principal interest in securing these lands was oil. The oil fields in the area had been shown to be very promising, and there was no desire on the part of persons who sought high profit to share their wealth with the Indians. In a detailed and very pessimistic letter to Dr. Frank Speck in 1938, Ruth Underhill stated:

> Now the land question. My present opinion is that the Indians have been robbed of their property but by entirely legal procedure, hard to upset in court. . . . There *was* some land privately owned by ancestors of some of these Indians and it is that of which they have been dispossessed by legal means. The means are Louisiana law which forbids "bastards" to inherit, even if their father makes a will in their favor. The Indians, who did not go in for white marriage procedure are all technically "adulterous bastards", with no rights of their father's lands.[25]

The communication continues at length, outlining other means that were used to expropriate lands from the Indians, such as failure to file a deed, nonpayment of taxes, inability to show documented proof of birth or parentage, and even harassment by local civil authorities. In view of the virtually nonexistent power base of the Houma and the highly skilled legal expertise of their opponents, it is no surprise that the Indians lost the land struggle and ended up, again, a dispossessed and defeated group.

As a result of the inability to sustain a living from the marshes, and with improved road conditions among the bayous, the Houma began to settle in larger groups. By 1940, Speck estimated, 700 Indians were living within walking distance of Dulac.[26] By this time, mission schools had been established for the benefit of the children: Methodist in Dulac and Baptist in Pointe au Chien. There was now a definite need for schooling among the Houma. The state of Louisiana and the local parishes had made no attempt to educate the children, and as long as they lived in widely dispersed settle-

Houma women in front of their plankboard house, circa 1907. *Courtesy of Smithsonian Institution National Anthropological Archives, photo no. 133A.*

ments it would have been difficult to establish a school in their behalf. But as the nucleated settlements at the termini of the bayou
roads continued to grow, the need for education grew as well. The
problem was made acute by the intermediate status of the Indians in
the social hierarchy. They were not permitted to attend schools
established for white students and they were unwilling to attend
black schools. In 1944 a separate school system was established in
Terrebonne Parish for the Houma, followed by separate schools in
Lafourche Parish.[27] Still, not all Indian children were able to receive
an adequate education, and it was not until 1964 that full integration and satisfactory educational opportunities for all the children of
southern Louisiana were realized.[28]

Interest in the Houma waned considerably during World War II
and for some fifteen years thereafter. During this time (1940–59)[29]
only three references to the Houma appear in the general literature.
The first of these articles[30] is a broad summary of the remnant
Indian groups of the eastern United States, in which the Houma
receive only one paragraph. The second, more complete report is a
seven-page synopsis of the general historical development of the
group,[31] with considerable attention to the biological admixture of
non–Native American genetic stock in the population. This article
also gives some valuable information regarding Houma demography
and population dynamics for the first half of the twentieth century,
but contains little new information on their contemporary culture
which cannot be found more extensively in the earlier writings of
Swanton, Speck, Underhill, and the BIA investigations of the 1930s.
The third reference appears in the voluminous tome related to the
proceedings initiated by the Eighty-second Congress in 1952 to
terminate federal jurisdiction over the American Indians. In this
work (exceeding 1,600 pages), only two brief, one-paragraph passages
appear pertaining directly to the Houma Indians.[32] Both passages are
reiterations of items abstracted out of Parenton and Pellegrin's article of 1950.

The two decades following the Second World War brought increasing pressure for change in the marsh and swamp regions of
southern Louisiana. Relatively high national wages and the need
for able-bodied workers drew many young persons out of the Indian
community into the "mainstream" of American life. The Houma

were no longer isolated, and with the end of isolation came the effects of the rural migration to urban centers. The city of Houma, which in 1950 recorded few resident Indians (there were only 166 urban Indians for the whole state of Louisiana in the 1950 census), reported 333 in the 1970 census.[33] It is safe to assume that most of these Indians were of the Houma group (although some members of the Chitimacha tribe may have been included). In addition, it is virtually impossible to determine how many Indians left the area because of the ease with which most of them are accepted as whites outside their home areas. And because of the social advantages incurred by assuming non-Indian status, it is logical to assume that a large number of persons, when given the option, chose the status which gave them the greatest mobility and freedom of action.

The first detailed field research to be undertaken among the Houma in the twenty-year period following the late 1930s was conducted by Edison Peter Roy,[34] a resident of the city of Houma, Louisiana. (The study was conducted in conjunction with research related to obtaining a master's degree from Louisiana State University under the supervision of Dr. Vernon J. Parenton.) As a longtime resident of the area, Roy had many valuable insights which might have been overlooked by someone not completely familiar with the area. The report's most valuable asset is the fact that it was written at the end of the extended period of semi-isolation for the Houma, when the introduction of all-weather roads, integrated schools, television, widespread usage of English, and other elements of rapid social and technological change had begun to make their full impact upon the people of the area.

The Houma today probably number over 3,000 in Terrebonne and Lafourche parishes (the total in the 1970 federal census for the two parishes was 2,365, with a median age of 17.1 years, indicating a young population and a continuing high birthrate). In the span of one lifetime (three generations) they have changed from scattered, seminomadic trappers and fishers who ranged throughout the swamp and marsh country of the south-central Louisiana Gulf Coast lowlands to permanent residents, living in the "line settlements" along the paved highways that parallel the major navigable bayous of the region.[35] Although most of the adults still look to fishing and the water for their livelihood, today's diesel-powered commercial oyster and shrimp boats are far removed from the hand-powered pirogues and flat-bottom boats of thirty years ago. The highly mechanized canneries, which now employ many of the women, bear no resemblance to the large, open, shrimp-drying platforms of the recent past.

The Houma have long been handicapped by a lack of tribal government—or in fact any locus of central leadership—but a form of affirmative action has been expressed. In the early 1970s a shrimping co-op was organized in Dulac to overcome the unfair buying and selling practices of merchants and suppliers in the area. Because of the seasonal nature of the shrimping industry and the relative unavailability of other types of employment, it was necessary to depend on the local merchants (who also supplied and outfitted the boats and purchased the shrimp catch) for credit to live from season to season. The merchants demanded that eligibility for credit be contingent on the shrimpers' stocking their boats with their merchandise and selling their catch to them as well. There is good reason to believe that this arrangement was abused by the merchants; so after considerable effort the Indians were able to obtain a federal grant which established a shrimping cooperative. This cooperative provided fair credit terms, a source of supplies, and a place to sell the catch through a venture owned and operated by themselves. This has been a successful enterprise and has given a great degree of economic independence to the people.

There are presently Houma Indians in college, and now that the group enjoys full access to good public education, it is reasonable to assume that further access to legitimate means to promote their rights and interests will be pursued.

Although there still is no centralized locus of leadership, there is communitywide respect for the charismatic leader—a man or woman, who is usually prominent in a family, who can influence a large number of fellow Indians. Such a person might well serve as the speaker for all the Indians and Indian-related issues in the area, but thus far such a person has not appeared. In fact, the collective sense of "peoplehood" is still quite weak among the Houma. Except for the fact that they recognize themselves as a group which is socially apart from the whites and blacks in the area, there is no expression of a tribal-type unity. Not one of the six communities with a large number of Houma inhabitants has a formal or informal governing body, and with the exception of the recently organized shrimping cooperative in Dulac, there has been no effort to organize the group for collective interests.

However, such a lack of communal effort is not surprising when one recalls that these people have not experienced a strong sense of tribal belonging since the 1830s. This is not to suggest that their "Indianness" be discounted; their Indian awareness has simply been focused on the extended family and extended only weakly to a common ingroup identity, recognizing the mere presence of other families that share a common heritage. It is not, therefore, surprising to discover that even in Dulac, in which about one-third of all the Indians in the area live, attempts to coordinate activities on a scale larger than the extended family have only recently taken form.

It is to be expected that the Houma will exhibit a more unified group awareness than in the past. There is still a three-way racial stratification in all communities where Indians live in southern Louisiana, and because they are still set apart from whites and blacks, they form a separate group wherein their identity as Indians is emphasized.

Virtually all the Houma families live within easy access of hard-surface, all-weather roads and have an automobile or truck. This allows greater contact and communication within a community and with other communities. However, because of the informal segregation which is still the general rule, the extended network of communication is primarily among other Indians in the area.

The school system should also intensify the sense of community among most of the Houma, at least in Terrebonne Parish. Since the late 1960s, all children from the seventh grade up attend a common junior and senior high school in the city of Houma. This brings students together from five of the six Houma settlements in the area (the sixth community is in Lafourche Parish). By bringing young people together from the various settlements (including children from families which have moved to the city of Houma) within a context which preserves their separate identity (because of the informal sanctions exercised by their non-Indian fellow students), group awareness of their Indian heritage is recognized and their sense of the tribal-like identity should be reinforced.

Despite, or because of, rising standards of education and improved health services since the mid-1950s, many young Houmas have begun to leave the area. This has to some degree weakened the socioeconomic prospects for the Indian community, because some of the most enterprising and promising persons, who might have become leaders, are gone; but this is not a problem unique to the Houma. In fact, such a rural–urban migration pattern is common in most parts of the world today. However, probably enough well-qualified persons remain in their home areas that there is no threat that all potential leaders of the group will be gone.

It is the opinion of the author that the Houma will experience an ever increasing trend toward social and cultural change. However, it is also anticipated that the general sense of "Indianness" will prevail and probably intensify, especially in light of continued strong kinship ties and expanded communication with fellow Houmas in the area. Also, the local classification of "Indian" may continue to hold significance long after any functional need for Indian identification within the community has passed.

It is to be hoped that the tribe will eventually be recognized by the federal authorities for what it really represents: a living, vital link with the past of Native Americans in Louisiana. In 1938 Frank Speck wrote an eloquent plea in behalf of the Houma to Dr. Willard Beatty of the Educational Division of the Bureau of Indian Affairs in which he states:

It is evident that the Houma people are suffering from unwillingness on the part of a certain group of local Administration to grant them recognition as an Indian group. I think that in taking such a stand we should oppose such classification which deliberately or ignorantly does the Houma people an injustice. . . . They have a conscious tradition and sense of their separateness from black and white peoples, and of their direct and continuous lineage with the Houma tribe of Louisiana history. . . . I should rate the Houma as a people possessing Indian blood and cultural characters to a degree about equal to that of the Crook [sic], Choctaw, Catawba, and Seminoles . . . they have been constantly mentioned in Louisiana Indian history . . . and their movements can be traced from the very earliest villages on the Mississippi to the parishes . . . where they are now located. I am sure that an unbiased judgement of their past and present, allowing for changes which affect all the groups of the Southeast, should grant the stature as Indian descendants from the historic tribe whose name they bear.[36]

It is a fact that the above statement, written by Dr. Speck forty years ago, falls now, as it did then, on largely unresponding and inattentive ears. Federal recognition for the Houma and its ensuing benefits (not totally without concomitant headaches) should be granted as soon as possible. These people have been denied their legal rights as Native Americans too long.

Notes

1. Frank G. Speck, "A Social Reconnaissance of the Creole Houma Indian Trappers of the Louisiana Bayous," *América Indígena* 3 (April–July 1943):212–13.
2. Vern J. Parenton and Roland J. Pellegrin, "The Sabines: A Study of Racial Hybrids in a Louisiana Costal Parish," *Social Forces* 29 (December 1950):148.
3. Edison Peter Roy, "The Indians of Dulac: A Descriptive Study of a Racial Hybrid Community in Terrebonne Parish, Louisiana" (M.A. thesis, Louisiana State University, 1959), p. 120.
4. Speck, "A Social Reconnaissance," p. 137.
5. John R. Swanton, "Indian Tribes of the Lower Mississippi River and the Adjacent Coast of the Gulf of Mexico," Bulletin 43, Bureau of American Ethnology (Washington: Government Printing Office, 1911), p. 285.
6. Ibid., p. 288.
7. Parenton and Pellegrin, "The Sabines," p. 149.
8. Swanton, "Indian Tribes of the Lower Mississippi," p. 290.
9. Parenton and Pellegrin, "The Sabines," p. 149.
10. Ibid.
11. Swanton, "Indian Tribes of the Lower Mississippi," p. 292.
12. Parenton and Pellegrin, "The Sabines," p. 149.
13. Swanton, "Indian Tribes of the Lower Mississippi," p. 292.
14. Ibid., pp. 291–93.
15. Roy, "The Indians of Dulac," p. 50.
16. Swanton, "Indian Tribes of the Lower Mississippi," p. 292.
17. Ernest C. Downs and Jenna Whitehead, "The Houma Indians: Two Decades in a History of Struggle," *American Indian Journal* 2 (March 1976):16.
18. Swanton, "Indian Tribes of the Lower Mississippi," p. 293; Speck, "A Social Reconnaissance," p. 134, and a photograph (taken by Speck in 1907) on the cover of *American Indian Journal*, vol. 2 (March 1976).
19. Swanton, "Indians of the Lower Mississippi," p. 291.
20. Ibid., p. 292.
21. Speck, "A Social Reconnaissance," p. 138.

22. Ann Fischer, "History and Current Status of the Houma Indians," in *The American Indian Today*, ed. Stuart Levine and Nancy O. Lurie (Deland, Fla.: Everett/Edwards, 1968), p. 217.

23. U.S. Congress, House, *Report with Respect to the House Resolution Authorizing the Committee on Interior and Insular Affairs to Conduct an Investigation of the Bureau of Indian Affairs*, H.R. 2503, 82d Congress, 2d sess., December 15, 1952, pp. 776–77.

24. Downs and Whitehead, "The Houma Indians," p. 18.

25. Ibid., pp. 13–16.

26. Speck, "A Social Reconnaissance," p. 215.

27. Downs and Whitehead, "The Houma Indians," p. 18.

28. Fischer, "History and Current Status," pp. 222–23.

29. Although Speck's article, "A Social Reconnaissance," appeared in 1943, it contains material gathered earlier, in 1938 and 1939.

30. William Harlen Gilbert Jr., "Surviving Indian Groups of the Eastern United States," in *Annual Report*, Smithsonian Institution (Washington: Government Printing Office, 1949), p. 424.

31. Parenton and Pellegrin, "The Sabines."

32. U.S. Congress, H.R. 2503, pp. 387–88, 1248.

33. U.S. Bureau of the Census, Census of the Population: 1970, *General Population Characteristics*, Final Report PC(1)–B20, Louisiana, p. (20)–73.

34. Roy, "The Indians of Dulac."

35. Max E. Stanton, "The Indians of the Grand Caillou–Dulac Community," (M.A. thesis, Louisiana State University, 1971). The information contained here and throughout the remainder of this report (unless specifically indicated) is from the 1969 fieldwork for this work, (pp. 30–47) and the author's subsequent field research. The author acknowledges the assistance of a National Science Foundation Summer Traineeship grant, and the staff of the Dulac Community Center of the United Methodist Church for its hospitality, free lodging, and research facilities.

36. Downs and Whitehead, "The Houma Indians," p. 11.

6

The Catawba Indians of South Carolina
A Question of Ethnic Survival

CHARLES M. HUDSON

The majority of the people who are known as Catawba Indians live near the city of Rock Hill, South Carolina. Some of them live on a small state-owned reservation on a bank of the Catawba River, others live nearby and in neighboring towns, and a few live in other parts of the United States. The strength of their claim to descent from historic Indian ancestors is intermediate between that of the Choctaws and Cherokees, on the one hand, whose ancestry can clearly be traced back to Indians mentioned by the earliest Spanish explorers in the sixteenth century, and the Lumbees, on the other hand, who had lost both their Indian language and culture when they first entered the historic record in the eighteenth century. Hence the Catawbas have never had to face such agonizing questions about their identity as have the Lumbees, but neither have the Catawbas been as firmly Indian in their identity as have the Choctaws or Cherokees.

Some of the people whose descendants became known as Catawbas were contacted by Hernando de Soto in 1540, when he and his men explored the back country of South Carolina. Here they encountered the province of Cofitachique, as well as lesser societies. From the chronicles of the de Soto expedition it appears that there were substantial linguistic and social differences among these people. And these impressions have since been confirmed by archeological research.

By the eighteenth century, the people who came to be known as Catawbas had been fundamentally transformed by a century of contact with the European invaders. They were refugees from quite diverse societies of the Carolinas who realigned themselves in the face of adversity. In part, this transformation was due to severe depopulation of the various tribes, caused by numerous epidemics of Old World diseases. It was also due to their dependence upon European weapons and goods which they obtained in the fur trade.

Because the white traders held a monopoly on manufactured products, they were able to establish power over the weakened Indians. South Carolina traders wanted not only deerskins but Indian slaves as well. In 1715 the Catawbas joined other Indians in the Yamassee War, a widespread revolt against the increasing power of the white merchants, but within a year the colonists prevailed. After this defeat the Catawbas declined rapidly in numbers, particularly after a severe smallpox epidemic in 1738.

In the eighteenth century the South Carolina colonists made a social distinction between settlement Indians and Indian nations. The settlement Indians were refugees from shattered and displaced Indian groups, or else Indians who had abandoned their own people and had taken up residence in or near the towns and plantations of the colonists. Their origins were various, including Saras, Yuchis, Peedees, Natchez, Cape Fears, and others. They lived a poor existence, mainly by performing petty services for the colonists, such as hunting for game and tracking down and capturing escaped slaves. In contrast, the Indian nations were presumed to be numerous in population, to possess and control land of their own, and independently to conduct their own affairs.

In the middle of the eighteenth century the Catawbas were technically regarded as a nation, but in fact they were perhaps as composite a group as were the settlement Indians. Another smallpox epidemic came in 1759–60 and killed one-half to three-quarters of the population.[1] The Catawbas were thoroughly demoralized after this, and were in fact dependent upon South Carolina for some of their food and clothing. In return for these goods, the Catawbas were subject to the political control of the South Carolinians, who wanted to preserve them as a buffer against hostile forces to the north. Therefore, in 1760–61, during the French and Indian War, the Catawbas reluctantly fought against the Cherokees at the behest of South Carolina. After the close of this war, the power of the

Children of Catawba Chief Samuel F. Blue, 1918. *Courtesy of Smithsonian Institution National Anthropological Archives, photo no. 29b.*

Cherokees was crushed and white frontiersmen from Pennsylvania, Virginia, and North Carolina began moving southward into the piedmont to stake claims to the land. A few frontiersmen had moved in before this, both from the north and from the Carolina lowland, but between 1761 and 1765 the white population in the piedmont increased by 50 percent. They began moving onto land which the Catawbas claimed for their own. Moreover, the Catawbas found themselves in the middle of a boundary dispute between North Carolina and South Carolina. The Catawbas attended the Indian Congress at Augusta in 1763 to complain about white encroachment on their land. In the treaty which was drawn up there, they were granted a reservation measuring fifteen miles square (144,000 acres), with the promise that the whites already living there would be evicted. The Catawbas were also promised hunting rights outside this area.[2]

This reservation, however, turned out to be a piece of real estate which they could not defend against white encroachment, and there is no evidence that the whites were ever evicted. The Catawba population further declined. John Smythe, who visited them just before the War for Independence, describes them as perhaps more docile and servile than the frontier whites who lived among and around them. They had about 60 or 70 warriors at this time, and a total population of 300 or less. They had adopted English surnames, and some of them spoke English as well as they spoke their own language. They told Smythe that they were afraid that the whites were going to seize their land.

In the closing decades of the eighteenth century they began leasing their land to whites in an informal way. Some of the Catawba women were at this time living with or married to white men. After the dislocation caused by the War for Independence, the Catawbas established two towns on opposite sides of the Catawba River. Newtown, the larger of the two, was on the west side of the river, and Turkeyhead was on the east side.[3]

In the opening years of the nineteenth century, the position of the Catawbas became ever more precarious. Here was a tiny group of dispirited Indians, pressed on all sides by white farmers who wanted land at all costs. The very fact that they were able to retain title to their land into the nineteenth century requires explanation. The reason seems to be that effective political power at this time lay not in the hands of the back-country frontiersmen but in the hands of the slaveowning planters in the low country. These planters believed that the Catawbas could be used to terrorize their black slaves and that this would prevent them from running away and escaping into the interior. In the latter half of the eighteenth century the planters had hired Catawbas as well as settlement Indians to track down escaped slaves. The planters used every possible means to hold their slaves in terror. It was divide and rule. The tiny white minority held sway over their pluralistic society by playing one segment against another.

But when the cultivation of cotton was introduced into the piedmont around 1800, everything changed. Many of the planters began moving into the piedmont, taking their black slaves with them. At this point Catawba land became far more valuable than the Indians' potentiality for terrorizing slaves. In 1808 South Carolina passed a law which made it "expedient" that the Catawbas should have the right to lease out their lands. And lease they did. By 1826 the Catawbas had leased out virtually all their land, and some of these leased tracts had been subdivided into smaller tracts, with few or no records having been kept of the transactions. At this time there were about 30 families of Catawbas, numbering about 110 individuals in all. Many of them were so impoverished that they were reduced to moving about from place to place like gypsies, with no permanent place to live. In the 1830s as many as half of the Catawbas moved to North Carolina to live with the Cherokees. Some of them rented or bought land in Haywood County, North Carolina.

In 1840 the Catawbas signed a treaty with South Carolina ceding all their land. For this they were promised (1) a tract of land worth $5,000, to be purchased in Haywood County, North Carolina, or in some other thinly populated region; (2) if no satisfactory land could be purchased, they were to be paid $1,500 in cash; (3) upon moving away from South Carolina they were to be paid $2,500 in a lump sum and $1,500 per year for nine years thereafter. South Carolina made none of these purchases or payments immediately. Most of the Catawbas moved up to live with the Cherokees, a small number moved up to live with the Pamunkeys in Virginia, and two families somehow managed to remain in South Carolina.

The Catawbas who moved in with the Cherokees did not get along with their hosts, and in 1847 they requested that the federal government assist them in moving to the Indian Territory to live with the Chickasaws. Congress appropriated $5,000 to finance their removal, but it was never spent. By 1852 most of the Catawbas had moved away from the Cherokees on their own. About half of them returned to South Carolina, some of them moved to Arkansas and to the Indian Territory, and others apparently moved elsewhere. Those who returned to South Carolina were given back 630 of their original 144,000 acres. This was a poor tract of land around the old site of Newtown, which became known as the Old Reservation and was administered by South Carolina. At about the same time, South Carolina began paying them an annual "pension" of $800, to be divided among them, and a state agent was appointed to administer their affairs.

A few Catawbas served in the Confederate Army during the Civil War. Their motive for serving in the army of a society that had reduced them to the status of abject poverty is not clear. According to one local tradition, the whites came and told them that if they did not serve in the army they would be shot. After the war, attempts by Radical Republicans to reshape southern society had little effect on the Catawbas. When the conservative Democrats regained power after Reconstruction, even the potential for improvement was eliminated.

Whites had a monopoly of power, and a law was passed in 1879 making interracial marriage illegal. This law forbade marriage between white and Indian as well as between white and black. The Catawbas found themselves living in an enforced endogamous enclave on fewer than 700 acres of poor land. They could not hope to sustain themselves with so little land, but if they moved away they faced the possibility of relinquishing their Indian identity and of being categorized as "mixed bloods," a far more ambiguous and troublesome status. Many of them adopted the expedient of going away to sharecrop for a year or two at a time, periodically returning to live on the Old Reservation.

At the same time, they preserved their identity as Indians by retaining the Catawba language, and also by making and selling "Indian" handicrafts, particularly pottery. Unlikely as it seems, pottery was an important source of income for the Catawbas in the late nineteenth century and early twentieth century. They produced it with materials and techniques that were old, but in shapes that largely catered to the tastes of whites. They made pots, pipes, animals, pitchers, flower vases, and various kinds of toys and ornaments. In short, the Catawbas had become artifacts of South Carolina history, making handicrafts for tourists and curio hunters. A few of them became "professional Indians," working in circuses and medicine shows.

In addition to maintaining some claim to an Indian identity in these ways, the Catawbas made themselves distinctive from the whites in another way—they became Mormon converts. The Catawbas requested that a Christian missionary be sent to them as early as 1773, but South Carolina was evidently not much interested in saving Catawba souls. A few attended Methodist, Baptist, and Presbyterian missions and churches, but never in great numbers. They did not want seats in the back of the church. But when two Mormon missionaries visited the Rock Hill area in 1883, Catawbas became their first converts. The whites in the area were openly hostile toward the Mormons, and they were similarly hostile toward the possibility of the Catawbas' becoming Mormon converts. In one episode, some whites went to the Old Reservation at night and seized two Mormon missionaries who were living there. They horsewhipped one of them and slightly wounded the other one with gunshot when he escaped. They threatened to kill them if they caught them on the reservation again. But the Catawbas persisted, and in time the missionaries returned, at first covertly and later openly. With few exceptions, the Catawbas remain Mormons to this day.

By the 1930s the annual appropriation from South Carolina had increased to $9,500 per year. This paid for essential services, and when any money was left over it was divided among the people. The Catawbas instituted a tribal council consisting of a chief, a committee chairman, two councilmen, and a secretary. Most of the effective power resided in the hands of the committee chairman,

Catawba girls selling Indian pottery to tourists, 1941. *Courtesy of Charles Hudson.*

while the chief represented the Catawbas to outsiders. The last of these chiefs was Samuel Blue (1873–1959), the last person who spoke the Catawba language. Above all others, Samuel Blue symbolized the "Indianness" of the Catawbas. Wearing a Plains war bonnet, he periodically made an appearance before the South Carolina legislature to plead for more state assistance to the Catawbas. His argument was that the Catawbas had a "good history"; that with only one exception (the Yamassee War) the Catawbas had been staunch friends of the whites during the colonial period; and that the whites were indebted to them.

By the 1930s the Indianness of the Catawbas was more symbolic than real. They were Indians in a social sense but less so in a genetic sense, and even less so in a cultural sense. For the most part, the last vestiges of Catawba culture existed only in the memory of Samuel Blue and a few other old people. They still retained some of their folk medicine, but even this was largely limited to the use of herbals; scarcely any of the older ceremonial practices remained in use. Aside from this, they retained some old hunting and fishing techniques, including the use of a cane blowgun to kill birds and small game.

Industrialization came to the South Carolina piedmont in the late nineteenth century. Like many other areas in the piedmont, Rock Hill became a textile center. At this time the Catawbas were excluded from most occupations, and this included jobs in the textile mills. The first Catawba was hired in a mill in 1918; some whites protested, but as time went on more Catawbas were hired. Other than this, very few Catawbas were able to find paying jobs until the late 1930s, when some of them were employed by the WPA. With the onset of World War II, more of them found jobs in textile mills.

This is the period the Catawbas remember as the time when their economic and social condition improved most drastically. The Catawbas also say that their membership in the Mormon church, which at first set them apart from the whites, later helped them to assimilate into the larger society. In particular, the Mormons helped them to attain their first formal education. Between 1935 and 1940 they succeeded in gaining admittance to a high school which had formerly been for whites only.

In 1941 South Carolina appointed a committee to negotiate with the Bureau of Indian Affairs and the Federal Farm Security Administration to give economic assistance to the Catawbas. In 1943 the Catawbas signed a memorandum of understanding with South Carolina and the Bureau of Indian Affairs. At this time they became legal citizens of South Carolina, thereby securing the right to attend public schools and other institutions of higher learning. At the same time, the Catawbas came under the administration of the Bureau of Indian Affairs as federally recognized Indians.

In 1944 several tracts of land adjacent to and near the Old Reservation were purchased for the Catawbas. These tracts of land, totaling 3,432.8 acres, became known as the New Reservation. The stated motive of South Carolina in this transaction was to repay the Catawbas "for patriotic service their forefathers had rendered and the financial obligations likewise due them because of the unscrupulous methods employed by white citizens in business transactions with them especially in acquiring title to most of their land."

The intent of this purchase of land was to allow the Catawbas to gain a livelihood as small farmers. Various cooperative enterprises were envisioned, such as a cooperative cattle project, but in the 1950s it became increasingly difficult for small farmers to sustain themselves. Many began abandoning their farms to move to cities in search of work. Moreover, the cooperative enterprises consistently failed. For all these reasons, the Catawbas became increasingly interested in divesting themselves of their Indian status, thereby becoming ordinary citizens.

Finally, in 1959, the Catawbas voted to terminate their status as Indians with the Bureau of Indian Affairs and put the New Reservation up for sale. The final tribal roll, drawn up July 2, 1960, contained the names of 631 Catawbas. Each had the choice of claiming as his own a tract of New Reservation land or being paid a cash sum from the sale of New Reservation land which no one claimed. Their termination was final on July 1, 1962. The Old Reservation, however, still remains, and for this reason, more than any other, the Catawbas still retain some claim to Indian identity.

When I did field work with the Catawbas in the early 1960s, they were not much interested in preserving an Indian identity. It seemed to me, in fact, that they were ill at ease with it. But with the Red Power Movement and Indian activism in the late 1960s and early 1970s, this changed to some degree. Some of the Catawbas became interested in such organizations as the Coalition of Eastern Native Americans, and there has been some discussion about the possibility of reestablishing ties with the Bureau of Indian Affairs. Some of the women have continued making and selling pottery, and during a period of heightened white interest in Indians, they began producing more pottery than in the past. Some of the potters began traveling and staging exhibitions in various places. But with all of this, there are few Catawbas who are actively interested in maintaining an Indian identity.[4]

The Catawbas began their existence as a recognizable group by the eighteenth century, as a coalition of refugees from diverse societies and cultures. Today it is difficult to predict if they will be able to bring about a resurgence of Catawba ethnicity, or if they will finally go the way of some of their aboriginal neighbors and disappear entirely as a coherent ethnic group.

Notes

(Unless otherwise noted, this paper has been drawn from material in my monograph *The Catawba Nation* [Athens: University of Georgia Press, 1970].)

1. Steven G. Baker, *The Working Draft of "The Historic Catawba Peoples: Exploratory Perspectives in Ethnohistory and Archaeology"* (Columbia: University of South Carolina Department of History, 1975), pp. 106–8.

2. Ibid., pp. 136–38.

3. Ibid., p. 143.

4. I am grateful to Steven G. Baker for information used in this paragraph.

II

Remnants of the
Removed Nations

7

Back from Disappearance: The Alabama Creek Indian Community

J. ANTHONY PAREDES

In 1941 the eminent American ethnologist Frank G. Speck rediscovered "the almost 'lost Creeks of Alabama.'"[1] The community is at Poarch, near the town of Atmore in Escambia County, Alabama. Speck's very brief report on these people noted hopeful signs for improvement in the abject poverty and lack of education from which they had apparently so long suffered, yet the anthropologist observed that "no recognized leader possessing energy and experience exists [1941] to direct their efforts, to consolidate their feelings and interests, and to represent the community in the eyes of the people of the county and the state, [which] is in my mind another factor responsible for the loss of prestige and the economic dissipation in which they live."[2] Ironically, in the very year in which Speck's report was published (1947), one of the Creeks, Calvin W. McGhee, initiated a suit against the county school board which would snowball into a full-blown social movement under McGhee's leadership. The movement brought educational reform, social recognition, and a renewed sense of historical pride to the Creeks of south Alabama.

Despite Speck's efforts to direct the attention of anthropologists to this "hitherto unnoticed tribal group in the Southeast,"[3] no detailed studies of the Alabama Creeks were conducted until my research began in late 1971. This research has involved collection of oral history tape recordings and utilization of such standard ethnographic techniques as participant observation, genealogical interviews, and community surveys.[4] The main objectives have been to understand the present-day characteristics of the Indian community and the social and cultural processes which have brought the Creeks to their present situation.

Despite my concern with contemporary problems and the re-membered history of living Creeks, I have increasingly become interested in the more remote past. In part, these historical interests have derived from the genealogical concerns of the Creeks them-selves. Eastern Creek interest in family history was greatly stimu-lated by the necessity for each individual to prove lineal descent from the Creek nation of 1814 in order to share in a land claim brought against the United States government in 1951 (U.S. Indian Claims Commission, docket 21). Although much remains to be done in the documentary study of Eastern Creek history during the nineteenth and early twentieth centuries, the primary purpose of this paper is to trace the major outlines of the evolution of the Creek Indian community from its beginnings in the early nineteenth century to the present. It should be emphasized that this study is concerned with the history and development of the only surviving *community* of Creek Indians east of the Mississippi, and not with the widely scattered, and largely assimilated, descendants of non-removed Creek Indians, who now number in the thousands. Neither does this paper try to detail the history of the many Creeks who at-tempted to remain in the East under various treaty stipulations, following the general removal of the tribe, but were forcibly re-moved or otherwise induced to relocate to Oklahoma during the period 1836–50.

Perhaps no other group of contemporary American Indians came nearer social extinction than did the Eastern Creeks. They are the descendants of only a dozen or so mixed-blood Friendly Creeks who avoided the removal and remained in their former homelands east of the Tensaw and Alabama rivers, only a few miles from the site of the Creek Indian attack on Fort Mims which triggered United States involvement in the Creek War of 1813–14.

Article 1 of the Treaty of Fort Jackson of 1815 (7 Stat., 120), by which the Creeks capitulated to the United States, provided that each Creek chief and warrior who had remained friendly to the United States was entitled to "a reservation of land . . . of one mile square," so long as he or his descendants occupied the tract. On abandonment by the Indian or his descendants, rights to the land would devolve to the United States. However, some of those who received these "reservations," such as David Tate, Josiah Fletcher, and John Weatherford, obtained title to their land by act of Congress as early as 1825 (6 Stat., 323). Descendants of these and other Friendly Creeks still reside in south Alabama, principally in Baldwin and Monroe counties; the famous and venerable Creek name, Weatherford, is still borne by some. Many of these descendants are scattered through much of the Southeast (and elsewhere as well) and assimilated into the general population. Article 1 of the Treaty of Fort Jackson also provided the legal basis for later allotments to certain Friendly Creeks. These later allotments established the land bases for nucleated settlements of Creek Indians which developed during the latter half of the nineteenth century.

The Creek Treaty of 1832 (7 Stat., 366) was designed to remove the Creek Indians west of the Mississippi. Nonetheless, that treaty provided (article 12) that it should "not be construed so as to compel any Creek Indian to emigrate, but they shall be free to go or stay, as they please." Despite this proviso, for the most part those Creeks who attempted to remain in the East on allotments, as provided for in the 1832 treaty, soon lost their lands through fraudulent practices by whites.[5] An outbreak of hostilities by some Creeks in 1836 in response to these depredations provided the rationale for the forcible removal of thousands of Creeks who remained in the East during the 1830s, as succinctly described by Holátte Cvpvkke in a recent article.[6] Concerted effort to remove the few remaining Creeks in Alabama continued through the 1840s; in 1845 an estimated 160, "including slaves," remained in Alabama and Georgia.[7] As late as 1849 the annual report of the commissioner of Indian Affairs stated that "within the last year, forty-four of the few Creeks remaining in Alabama, and five hundred and forty-seven Choctaws from the State of Mississippi, have removed to the country of their brethren west," but, the report noted, "all that can be induced to go will probably be removed within another year, at the end of which all further proceedings and expenses should be terminated, and those that shall then remain, be permitted to do so in the quiet enjoyment of their rights as citizens."[8]

Despite the concerted and persistent efforts of the United States to remove Creek Indians from Alabama during the 1830s and '40s, a few mixed-blood Friendly Creeks were allowed to remain and some were provided with land. In consequence of circumstances and events which are not yet clearly understood, in 1836 an act was passed (6 Stat., 677) "for the relief of Samuel Smith, Lynn MacGhee, and Semoice, friendly Creek Indians," entitling them to select "reservations" of one section of land each, to which they were entitled under the Treaty of Fort Jackson, but for "which lands have been sold by the United States," to be held under the same terms as those stipulated under the 1815 treaty. Likewise, a similar act (6 Stat., 678) was enacted for the relief of Susan Marlow, "only surviving child of James Marlow, a Creek Indian, who lost his life at the destruction of Fort Mimms." Both acts were amended in 1837 (6 Stat., 689) to provide that the grantees were not limited to a single section, but could enter land in legal subdivisions so long as each total did not exceed 640 acres. One of the plots selected by McGhee was a 240-acre tract at the headwaters of Perdido Creek, which flows into the Perdido River, dividing Florida and Alabama. This McGhee "grant land" became the hub around which eventually emerged the three hamlets of Hedapeada (Head of Perdido), Poarch Switch, and Hog Fork, constituting the present-day Indian community of approximately 400 at Poarch, Alabama.

Formerly, another Indian community was located near what is now Huxford, Alabama, and consisted of localities known as Red Hill, the Neal McGhee place, and the Colbert settlement. This community also centered on a portion of the McGhee lands. Today there are only a few Indian families at Huxford, most of the others having moved to the Poarch area (or elsewhere) in recent decades. However, from oral accounts it appears that gradual movements of Indian descendants into the Poarch area from Huxford, Monroe County, and other areas to the north and northwest was a long-standing trend, begun in the nineteenth century.

In addition to providing the initial land base for the Escambia County Creek community, Lynn McGhee and his wife Hettie Semoice[9] were one of that handful of couples who remained in the backwoods of south Alabama following the removal, who were the genetic founders of the contemporary Creek Indian community. Other than the McGhee-Semoice line, the most important founding ancestors of the present Creek community were Betsy Elliot and her husband Dixon Manac, son of Sam Manac (variously spelled Moniac, MacNack, MacNacs). Unlike the somewhat obscure Lynn McGhee, Manac appears often in early accounts of the Creek War (e.g., Woodward, Halbert and Ball).[10] However, in a deposition of August 2, 1813, Sam Manac reported that hostile Creeks had destroyed many of his cattle and burned his houses, "as well as those of James Cornells and Leonard McGee."[11] Perhaps Leonard McGee is Lynn McGhee or his father.

Although much research remains to be done, available evidence indicates that by the time of the Creek War the McGhees and the Manacs occupied private homesteads, rather than practicing the aboriginal pattern of communal farming. Dispersal of the aboriginal Creek towns into individual homesteads along creeks and rivers appears to have been a practice which was explicitly encouraged by agents of the United States government in the period immediately before the Creek War.[12] While informants' descriptions of late nineteenth-century Alabama Creek lifestyles suggest that the founding families must have been fairly acculturated to rural white ways, a few remnants of native Creek language and custom survived even into the twentieth century.[13] Nonetheless, the early decades of the nineteenth century apparently were a period of major cultural change for the ancestors of the Alabama Creeks. Writing of the people of Tuskeegee town at the very end of the eighteenth century, a white observer wrote that they had "some cattle, and a fine stock of hogs, more perhaps than any other town in the nation. One man, Sam MacNack, a half-breed, has a fine stock of cattle. He had, in 1799, one hundred and eighty calves. They have lost their language [English, Dutch, or French?] and speak Creek, and have adopted the customs and manners of the Creeks."[14]

However, by the late 1830s the Creeks who remained in Alabama had been reduced to a mere handful who had lost their original landholdings, although in the case of Lynn McGhee (and a few others) these losses had been at least partially compensated for by the allotments of 1836 and 1837.

Despite their small numbers, intermarriage between the McGhee and Manac lines, plus a few other in-marrying mixed-bloods and whites, through natural increase produced an expanding population

Table 1.

Population for Escambia County, Alabama, and Environs:
1860–1970

	Indian*				White	Black
	Baldwin County	Escambia County	Monroe County	State of Alabama	Escambia County	Escambia County
1860	91	–	38	160	–	–
1870	0	43	17	98	3,047	951
1880	38	23	77	213	4,106	1,590
1890	0	173	3	1,143	5,843	2,650
1900	0	122	21	177	7,683	3,515
1910	4	164	291	979	13,156	5,569
1920	8	292	51	405	15,878	6,293
1930	7	349	38	465	19,056	8,558
1940	13	312	24	574	20,494	9,865
1950	20	373	0	928	20,880	10,190
1960	4	498	16	1,276	22,052	10,960
1970	84	541	60	2,443	23,748	10,601

* For the censuses of 1930, 1940, 1950, the total figures given for "other races" are presented as the Indian population.

of people identified as Indians in south Alabama. Gradually, a large portion of that population became localized on and around the McGhee grant land in Escambia County. Probably in every generation since the removal, numerous individuals have been "spun off" into the general population of whites through outmigration and intermarriage, but by 1900 a core of Creek families, characterized by strong patterns of ingroup marriage, had become firmly established in western Escambia County. Although there appears to be a growing trend toward outmarriage, in 1973–74, of the eighty-nine Indian households in the Poarch community, only twenty-seven included even one individual who was not a Creek descendant.

The growth of the Indian population in south Alabama may be demonstrated by information drawn from United States censuses[15] (as shown in Table 1), questions as to the validity of the data notwithstanding. In the census of 1860, the last census before the creation of Escambia County from parts of Baldwin and Conecuh counties in 1868, only 160 Indians were reported for the entire state of Alabama; of these, 91 were reported from Baldwin County and 38 from Monroe County, which borders Escambia County to the north. By the 1970 census, the Indian population of Alabama had increased to 2,443, with 541 in Escambia County, 60 in Monroe County, 84 in Baldwin County, and the rest widely scattered throughout the state. In 1970, every Alabama county (except two, Choctaw and Lamar) had at least one Indian in its population.[16]

In the first census following the establishment of Escambia County (1870) there were 3,047 whites and 951 "colored" in the county. Since that time the black population has increased in rather even increments, to a maximum of 10,960 in 1960; the largest increase was between 1900 and 1910, when the black population grew from 3,515 to 5,569. The white population of the county has shown similar trends, but an even more dramatic increase in the 1900–1910 period, rising from 7,683 in 1900 to 13,156 in 1910. Earlier, the county's main centers of population had been around Brewton, the county seat, and Pollard. With the opening of the timber and turpentine industries and the founding of Atmore (originally William's Station) in the 1880s, there was a rapid expansion of population in the formerly sparsely settled area where most of the Creek Indians live. Significantly, a few oldtimers who were born in those days are the only living Poarch Creeks who can remember fluent speakers of the native language. Thus at the turn of the century the relative isolation and tranquillity the Escambia County Creeks had apparently enjoyed for much of the nineteenth century suddenly ended, and they were swept back into the mainstream of southern history. Then their real troubles began.

By virtue of the continued occupancy of his descendants, title to the Lynn McGhee land grant remained with the United States government. This fact seems to have been overlooked by local authorities; taxes were assessed against portions of the property, and these taxes were paid by some individuals. Partly on this basis, timber rights were sold to one of the large timber companies in the new town of Atmore in about 1904, and much of the best timber was cut over. Several years later, a United States government "timber cruiser" discovered this fact and initiated a suit against the

Eastern Creek Chief Calvin W. McGhee in 1970, two months before his death.
Courtesy of Buford Rolin and Ray Malinowski.

company. The suit was settled out of court, but the heirs of Lynn McGhee apparently received no benefits. Moreover, the timber issue apparently opened the whole matter of the status of the McGhee lands. In a series of letters to local Indians and whites during the period 1914 to 1922, the United States government finally reasserted the special status of these lands under the Treaty of Fort Jackson and enjoined the county from assessing further taxes against the property. Nonetheless, in 1924, for reasons which are not yet clear, the United States government issued a fee-simple patent to the heirs of Lynn McGhee, thus ending any special protection the Eastern Creeks may have had under federal authorities.

Subsequently, much of the land passed from Indian hands by sale and tax default. Today, only a fraction of the original Lynn McGhee "reservation" remains in Indian ownership—and that by private title. Similarly, in the early twentieth century much of other lands which Creeks acquired by homesteading passed from Indian hands through sale and default on debts to whites. During these years, the Indians shifted from being rather self-sufficient subsistence farmers (supplemented by hunting and fishing) to workers in the booming timber industry, and then to sharecropping and agricultural labor in the 1920s through the '40s. (Today, many Poarch Creeks still work in forest-related industries and some still hire out as agricultural laborers, but none are full-time farmers.)

In 1906, many of the Creeks were apparently duped into paying to register for the Eastern Cherokee claim of that year. In conversation to me, one old man recalled:

There come another man through here—big Indian fellow . . . had a lawyer with him. He charged five dollars to write us up. . . . I had a breech loadin' shotgun; I had to sell that to him to get my five dollars—that signed slip. And, there ain't no money yet.

The claims of the Creeks were rejected, of course, on the grounds that they were not Cherokee. Some of the Creeks, according to oral accounts, were aware of the foolhardiness of attempting to share in the Cherokee claim and advised their kinsmen not to waste their money.

The early twentieth century was also the beginning of marked social discrimination against the Creeks. Although oldsters recall that in the "early days" (1890s) some Indians in the Poarch area attended one-room schools, with whites (Eastern Creeks in other areas always attended school with whites), immediately before World War I the Indians had to operate their own schools, each family paying a fee to hire someone to teach its children (if they received any education at all). About the time of World War I, the county provided salaries for teachers in the Indian hamlets, but school was still conducted in community halls built by the Indians. In 1939, with the help of Episcopal church missionaries (white people who had begun their work in 1929), the county created a consolidated Indian school of six grades near the McGhee grant land at Poarch. The school operated in a building acquired by the Episcopal church and Indian children were bused from all the Indian hamlets (from as far away as Huxford) to that school. The county's consolidation of the Indian schools probably did much to solidify the Indian community of Escambia County, albeit in a negative and indirect fashion. By at least the 1930s, "Indian" had become a pejorative term. As some Creeks say, "They didn't like that word 'Indian.'" Some of that feeling persists today, and pride in ancestry is most often expressed in the more descriptive term "Creek Indian."

The period from the early twentieth century to the 1950s is a time remembered by the Creeks when certain whites were "hard on the Indians," and Indians had even less educational opportunity than blacks. The attitudes of some whites at the time are perhaps exemplified by a statement in a letter of May 8, 1913, concerning the timber lawsuit:

During my residence in Brewton I became acquainted in a general way with the indians [sic] living in the locality in question. While I was a deputy marshal I arrested several of them for timber depredations and after I came to the bar I had from time to time some little legal business with different members of the tribe. As I now remember, aside from the _____ and _____ [families which had "illegally" paid taxes on the grant land] and possibly a few others, all of them were considered as being very worthless, very low and of questionable character. I do not know that I ever heard anything to the detriment of old _____ [the Indian who was the central figure in the timber suit] except that he was just generally good for nothing. I remember that he received more or less indulgence because he had been a Confederate soldier, and for that reason was accorded a position somewhat above the most of his family. The _____ and the _____ were re-

Creek boys performing a stickball demonstration at the 1972 powwow. An effort is being made to revive this traditional Indian game, and teams from the Mississippi Choctaws have been brought in to stimulate interest. *Courtesy of J. Anthony Paredes.*

garded as substantial and useful citizens, but many of the other members of the family, notably a number of the women, had very bad reputations. . . . I mention these matters to show that in this instance, as well as in all others which have come within my personal knowledge, the virtues of the noble red men are confined almost exclusively to works of fiction.[17]

Despite such attitudes, for educational purposes the Indians were technically classed as white. However, in the Poarch and Huxford areas Indians were not allowed to attend local white schools. Generally, the Indians appear to have occupied a social status below that of whites but above that of blacks. Paradoxically, Indians could marry whites but could not go to school with them. A number of older Creeks seem to pride themselves on having "gotten along" equally well with whites and blacks. Two former slaves of a local country doctor are warmly remembered by older Indians for having returned the Indians' cemetery, which had fallen into the doctor's possession and the blacks had inherited. For the most part, however, blacks have not figured importantly in the history of the Alabama Creeks, even though there have been occasional close contacts between Indians and blacks.

Today, many Poarch Creeks hold somewhat ambivalent attitudes about blacks. Many see themselves as having suffered as much as blacks, if not more, from discrimination by whites. Yet they feel their closest ties are with whites and resent any suggestion of identification with blacks. Moreover, many Creeks sometimes seem alarmed at current expressions of black activism, yet understand the sentiments which give rise to such activities, citing the experience of their own people. Privately, a few Creeks have even expressed satisfaction that integration has been just retribution for whites who only a few years ago "didn't even want Indians to go to school with them and now they have to go to school with the colored." Similarly—although Eastern Creeks have been increasingly drawn into the national networks of Indian politics—they see themselves as having a history which is quite distinct from most other Indians'. Many Alabama Creeks understand, but do not expressly endorse, Indian activism in other parts of the country. Understandably, given their small numbers and former isolation from other Indians, the Creeks have adopted a moderate stance in interracial relationships, and their leaders tend to promote their cause through the courts, advantageous political connections with whites, and being "colorfully" appealing to journalists.

For most of their post-removal history the Poarch Creeks were ignored by the federal government, and national Indian policy has had little relevance for them—early twentieth-century problems over the grant land, the timber suit, and the abortive attempts of some to share in the Cherokee claim notwithstanding. Beginning in the 1950s, this situation changed dramatically, but even in the 1970s the local social and political environment continues to be the most immediate and important context for understanding the history of the Alabama Creeks, since they are not "federal Indians."

To return to our historical progression, the people Speck found shortly before World War II had just suffered several decades of overt discrimination, loss of lands, and crushing poverty. But the situation, as Speck noted, was fraught with possibilities. In the preceding ten years, many Indians had found spiritual hope through the work of Episcopal missionaries, who ministered as much to medical and educational needs as to the spiritual. Others were influenced by the Holiness church. Although there were, and continue to be, backsliders, the white Holiness preachers who came to the Creeks (beginning in the 1920s) appear to have been a major factor in moving some away from despair and toward "respectability" (in white terms). Prior to the coming of Episcopal missionaries and Holiness preachers in the 1920s, the Poarch Creeks had been without benefit of regular clergy or pastors, but they subscribed to the Free Will Baptist and the Methodist denominations under the direction of Indian laymen and occasional visiting white preachers. In addition, in 1941 the population of the Creeks (over 300) had reached what might be considered a critical mass for effective political action. Finally, creation of the consolidated Indian school formed a common focus for mobilizing community action. Then came World War II.

During World War II, many Creeks started "getting out into the world more" in the military and in defense work. By 1947 a core of informal community leaders became very dissatisfied with the quality of education at the Indian school and the de facto exclusion of Indian children from schooling beyond the sixth grade. Calvin McGhee, with his suit against the school board to provide public transportation to high school for Indians, spearheaded the drive for educational reform. At times the case came close to violence and many Indians were skeptical that anything would be accomplished, but with the help of sympathetic whites (including the governor) the Indians won. In 1950, for the first time in their history, the Escambia County Creeks had an elementary school built with public funds (though located on 18 acres of land provided by the Episcopal church for a token sum of $1.00) and for the first time their children were allowed to ride school buses to junior and senior high schools in nearby white communities. [18]

Through a set of fortuitous circumstances, the school case led to a land claim against the United States and the formal organization of the Perdido Band of Friendly Creek Indians of Alabama and Northwest Florida, which later became the Creek Nation East of the Mississippi. This organization represented not only the interests of Poarch residents but a much larger and amorphous class of individual, self-acknowledged Creek descendants in the eastern United States. On entering their land claim, the Eastern Creeks found that the Oklahoma Creeks had already entered a claim for remuneration for the same territory, ceded in 1814 (approximately 9,000,000 acres), for which the Eastern Creeks were suing. Though the Indian Claims Commission refused to recognize the Eastern Creek claim, the U.S. Court of Claims ruled that the eastern group should be permitted to intervene in the Oklahoma Creek petition on the grounds that the original injury had been to the Creek nation of 1814, and all descendants of that nation had an equal interest in the claim.

In 1962 the Indian Claims Commission awarded $3,913,000 under this Creek case (docket 21) and Congress appropriated the funds in 1967. However, it was not until 1972 that the judgment funds were dispersed among the Creeks of Oklahoma and the East. With the deduction of attorneys' fees and other costs, each Creek Indian who had applied to share in the claim and was found eligible by the federal government (i.e., "proved up") received a payment of only $112.13. [19]

In 1951 Calvin McGhee was elected permanent chairman of the

"council" of the Eastern Creek organization, and he continued as chairman until his death in 1970. McGhee emerged as a full-fledged charismatic leader and brought publicity and recognition to the Creeks. He established contacts with other Indian groups, and introduced modern powwow dancing and costume making to the Eastern Creeks. However, wearing feathers and beads and putting on Indian dances has met reproval by some Creeks for a variety of reasons. For others, appealing to the stereotyped public tastes for "Indian culture" is seen as critical for gaining outside support for the Indian cause. Indeed, some of the younger Creeks have reached the point where powwow dancing is intrinsically rewarding, and the annual Thanksgiving Powwow (established in 1971) has become a routine part of community life. The organization of the powwow is one of the principal activities of the local Indian council, now that their role in the land-claims case has been effectively completed. Since 1973, the council's responsibilities have been greatly expanded by its administrative involvement in a number of programs for local Indian people, which have been funded by various federal agencies *other* than the Bureau of Indian Affairs.

The land-claims case was the focus of the movement started by Calvin McGhee, and the "Indian money" was the wellspring of contemporary Indian identity for many Eastern Creeks. However, it is important to acknowledge that the real genesis of the social and cultural revitalization of the Alabama Creeks was the successful drive for equal education begun immediately after World War II— and nearly a decade before the 1954 Supreme Court decision outlawing segregation. Ironically, Calvin McGhee did not live to see the successful conclusion of the land claim. Unfortunately, McGhee *did* live to witness the closing of the Poarch school, for which he had fought so hard. The school was closed in 1970 as a result of the implementation of federal rulings designed to promote integration. It was unfortunate in that the schoolhouse had become an important symbol of Indian victories, a focus of community activities, and a source of social solidarity. (The local community still has free access to the school and uses it for meetings of various kinds, and the school grounds have been developed as the site of the annual powwow.) While there seems to be no strong community sentiment to resume classes at the school, in the 1970s the schoolhouse has become an important issue which rekindled community spirit, as momentum of the Indian movement began to lag with the conclusion of land-claims cases.

In part, the annual powwow, instituted by the former chief Houston McGhee (one of Calvin's sons) and other council members, has provided a substitute for the school, as well as the land claims, as a focus for community interest and Indian identity. (The council also has pursued negotiations with state and federal authorities to acquire land and funds for an Indian cultural center.) Nevertheless, in 1973 efforts were begun to transfer title to the school grounds from the county to the Indian community. More recently, the effort has been integrated into the council's bid for full federal recognition, which would entitle the Creeks to federal protection and certain services available to other groups, such as the Mississippi Choctaws, the Eastern Cherokees, the Florida Seminoles and Mikasukis, and most Indian tribes in the western United States. To receive federal recognition, an Indian group must have a tract of tribal land; it is hoped that the school grounds can serve this purpose for the Eastern Creeks.

Although some of the Creeks are uncertain about the impact federalization might have on local autonomy and the structure of community leadership, for the moment, at least, the benefits to be gained by federal recognition are viewed as outweighing any costs that might be involved. In the meantime, the community has begun to receive some federally funded programs through OEO, the Indian Education Act of 1972, and a federal grant to the Coalition of Eastern Native Americans (CENA). CENA represents non-federally-recognized Indian groups throughout the eastern United States and was organized in 1971 with Creek Nation East of the Mississippi as one of the charter members. Since 1975 the council has served as its own "prime sponsor" for a major project under the U.S. Department of Labor's Comprehensive Employment and Training Act (CETA). In 1976 at the Thanksgiving Powwow, in connection with its new responsibilities, the council (the lineal descendant of that first group of individuals, informally elected in 1950 to press the land claim) organized the first secret-ballot general election of a "tribal council" for the Creek Nation East of the Mississippi. By

1978 the variety and scope of state and federally funded programs at Poarch had dramatically expanded, far beyond the level in 1976.

In summary, from the inauspicious beginnings of a handful of Friendly Creek Indian families in the backwoods of Alabama in the 1830s grew a viable modern community of several hundred people with a renewed sense of tribal identity as Creek Indians. Following the lead of the Escambia County Creeks, there are many more Creek descendants who gather at powwows and other meetings to proclaim their identity as Creek Indians. However, it is only at Poarch (Alabama) that historical forces welded many descendants of the McGhees, Manacs, and others into a unique social and geographic community of Creek Indians east of the Mississippi. The trends toward marriage with outsiders and emigration to Pensacola, Mobile, and more distant cities may continue (despite very recent indications of reversals) and the pain of past injustices may be erased, but for now the Alabama Creeks have turned a legacy of hardship and discrimination to their advantage and veered sharply from "the road to disappearance" to gain their long overdue recognition in the ranks of survivors of the removal.

Notes

1. Frank G. Speck, "The Road to Disappearance: Creek Indians Surviving in Alabama, a Mixed Culture Community," *American Anthropologist* 51 (October–December 1949):682.
2. Frank G. Speck, "Notes on Social and Economic Conditions among the Creek Indians of Alabama in 1941," *América Indígena* 7 (July 1947): 196.
3. Speck, "The Road to Disappearance," p. 682.
4. This research has been supported by the Southeastern Indian Oral History Project, Florida State Museum, University of Florida, Gainesville, and by the Council on Faculty Research Support, Florida State University, Tallahassee.
5. Grant Foreman, *Indian Removal: The Emigration of the Five Civilized Tribes of Indians* (2d ed.; Norman: University of Oklahoma Press, 1953), pp. 129–39; Mary Elizabeth Young, *Redskins, Ruffleshirts, and Rednecks: Indian Allotments in Alabama and Mississippi, 1830–1860* (Norman: University of Oklahoma Press, 1961), pp. 73–98.

6. Holátte Cvpvkke (C. B. Clark), "'Drove Off like Dogs'—Creek Removal," in *Indians of the Lower South: Past and Present* (Proceedings of the Fifth Gulf Coast History and Humanities Conference), ed. John K. Mahon (Pensacola: Pensacola Historic Preservation Board, 1975).

7. U.S. War Department, *Annual Report of the Commissioner of Indian Affairs for 1845.* (Washington, D.C.: NCR Microcard Editions, 1959), p. 448.

8. U.S. Interior Department, *Annual Report of the Commissioner of Indian Affairs Transmitted with the Message of the President at the Opening of the First Session of the Thirty-first Congress: 1849–1850* (Washington, D.C.: NCR Microcard Editions, 1960), p. 14.

9. This genealogical section is based on field interviews and copies of documents in the possession of the late Mrs. Calvin W. McGhee. Many of these documents come from the National Archives, but I have not yet had the opportunity to examine the originals personally.

10. Thomas S. Woodward, *Woodward's Reminiscences of the Creek, or Muscogee Indians, Contained in Letters to Friends in Georgia and Alabama* (Montgomery: Barrett and Wimbish, 1859), pp. 6, 16, 42, 49, 89, 91, 94; Henry S. Halbert and T. H. Ball, *The Creek War of 1813 and 1814*, ed. Frank L. Owsley Jr. (University: University of Alabama Press, 1969), pp. 67, 85, 88, 90–95.

11. Ibid., p. 93.

12. Caleb Swan, "Position and State of Manners and Arts in the Creek Nation in 1791," in *Information Respecting the History, Condition, and Prospects of the Indian Tribes of the United States*, vol. 5, ed. Henry R. Schoolcraft (Philadelphia: Lippincott, 1855), p. 693; Halbert and Ball, *The Creek War*, p. 85.

13. J. Anthony Paredes, "The Folk Culture of the Eastern Creek Indians: Synthesis and Change," in *Indians of the Lower South: Past and Present* (Proceedings of the Fifth Gulf Coast History and Humanities Conference), ed. John K. Mahon (Pensacola: Pensacola Historic Preservation Board, 1975).

14. Benjamin Hawkins, *A Sketch of the Creek Country in the Years 1798 and 1799*, Georgia Historical Society Publications, vol. 3, pt. 1 (Reprint; Americus, Ga.: Americus Book Co., 1938), p. 44.

15. All these data were taken from the published U.S. Census reports for 1880, 1890, 1900, 1910, 1920, 1940, 1950, 1960, and 1970.

16. J. Anthony Paredes and Kaye Lenihan, "Native American Population in the Southeastern States: 1960–70," *Florida Anthropologist* 26 (June 1973): 51.

17. T. M. S. (letter to Hon. Joseph F. Johnston regarding *U.S.* v. *W. M. Carney Mill Co.*, U.S. District Court for the Southern District of Alabama, Civil Docket no. 480, filed May 27, 1912, May 8, 1913), General Records of Department of Justice (Record Group 60), U.S. National Archives.

18. J. Anthony Paredes, "The Emergence of Contemporary Eastern Creek Indian Identity," in *Social and Cultural Identity* (Southern Anthropological

Society Proceedings, no. 8), ed. Thomas K. Fitzgerald (Athens: University of Georgia Press, 1974).

19. U.S. Congress, Senate, *Providing for the Disposition of Funds Appropriated to Pay a Judgement in Favor of the Creek Nation of Indians in Indian Claims Commission Docket No. 21, and for Other Purposes*. S.R. 1516, 90th Congress, 2d sess., 1968; Creek Nation East of the Mississippi, *Creek Nation East of the Mississippi: Yesterday, Today, and Tomorrow* (Atmore, Ala.: Creek Nation East of the Mississippi, Inc., 1975), pp. 24–27.

8

Three Efforts at Development among the Choctaws of Mississippi

JOHN H. PETERSON, JR.

The Mississippi Choctaws have been almost completely ignored by students of the American Indian.[1] Choctaw removal from Mississippi has been studied intensively, but post-1830 histories have focused on the Oklahoma Choctaws. Histories of Mississippi and Mississippi counties often describe the Choctaws prior to 1830 but largely ignore them after removal. On the other hand, anthropological studies of the Choctaws have largely concentrated on traditional survivals.

The lack of readily available information about Choctaw post-removal history has to some extent been accepted as indicating that there was no post-removal history. One author states that between removal and the establishment of the Choctaw Agency in 1918, the Mississippi Choctaws were "marking time in a 'no man's land.' . . . Their tribal organization was gone without anything to take its place . . . and time passed them by."[2] This stereotype, of the Mississippi Choctaws' not having a history, is paralleled by descriptions posed largely in negative terms.

The lack of information on Choctaw history and the resulting misunderstanding is matched only by the lack of information on the contemporary Choctaws. Some authors have even grouped them with tribal fragments who "are all strongly suspected of having little Indian blood, and have retained almost nothing of their ancient language and customs."[3]

Yet over 4,000 Choctaws still inhabit their traditional homeland in the sand-clay hills of east central Mississippi,[4] most speaking

their own language and almost all considered legally "full blood."
Currently, under an aggressive tribal leadership, great strides are
being made to strengthen their institutions and improve their educational level and standard of living.[5] Not a leaderless group which
time passed by, the Choctaws have leaders who are reenacting the
dynamic events of Choctaw history. This is the third major effort
by the Mississippi Choctaws to develop their people and adjust to
the white society which surrounds them.

The first effort occurred in the decades preceding Indian removal.
The second effort occurred in the 1880s and 1890s, preceding a
second removal. The third effort began in the 1960s and continues
today, although its ultimate success is threatened. These three efforts of self-development provide the basic theme of Mississippi
Choctaw history.

The prosperity of the Choctaws in the decades preceding removal
was based on an expanded agricultural base which began to develop
in the middle of the eighteenth century. While the dependence of
the aboriginal Choctaws on agriculture may be overemphasized,[6]
it is clear that by the second half of the eighteenth century, traditional subsistence agriculture was supplemented by European grains
and garden vegetables, horses, cattle, hogs, and domesticated fowl.
By the nineteenth century, cattle herds were extensive, and the
Choctaws began to grow cotton and produce their own clothing.[7]
The establishment of a United States trading post at Fort Stevens
on the Tombigbee River (near the Choctaws) in 1802 intensified
trade. Choctaw products, such as bear oil, honey, beeswax, bacon,
tobacco, and furs, were exchanged for cloth, iron tools, arms, ammunition, and plows. As trade increased, public inns were erected
along major travel routes through Choctaw territory, usually under
the ownership of whites or Choctaws of mixed heritage.[8] Under this
influence, Choctaw traditional law was gradually modified.[9] Change
accelerated after 1818, when the Choctaws invited missionaries to
establish schools in their country and, eventually, provided the
primary support for them.[10] By 1830 there were eleven schools
among the Choctaws and twenty-nine teachers.[11]

Missionary efforts contributed to the continued development of
Choctaw law. Punishment by the tribe began to replace the traditional custom of retaliation.[12] A tribal council began to enact formal

laws and a police force was established to preserve public order.[13] While many of these activities stemmed from the efforts of Choctaws of mixed heritage and missionaries, it seems clear that they were supported by more traditional leaders, such as Pushmataha, who felt that by adapting themselves to the way of life of the Americans, it might be possible for the Choctaws to remain in their traditional homeland in Mississippi. This effort was to be cut short by a desire for Choctaw lands at both the state and national level.

Even though the Choctaws were promised under the Treaty of Dancing Rabbit Creek in 1830 the right to remain in Mississippi as individual landowners,[14] this was not to be. The Choctaw agent, William Ward, was responsible for registering Choctaws who wished to receive land grants and remain in Mississippi. The historical record is clear: Ward deliberately ignored the applications of many Choctaws; also, he was frequently drunk and absent from his office. Historical writing[15] on the resulting denial of lands in Mississippi clearly places the blame on Ward's misconduct. Yet what is not asked is the "why" behind Ward's behavior. After all, he had the responsibility of Choctaw agent for a number of years without signs of such misconduct.

One must remember that it was Ward who advised Washington that the greater part of the full-bloods would leave for Oklahoma.[16] One can understand his frustration when Ward was suddenly faced with a great number of Choctaws who wished to remain in Mississippi. (Misunderstanding Indian desires and faulty reporting to Washington seems to be a characteristic of white Indian agents.) Did Ward get drunk through frustration, realizing he was being proved wrong, or did he turn to misconduct in a deliberate effort to force Choctaw compliance with his wishes? We shall never know —but it is clear that this was not a case of simple misconduct on the part of a low officeholder. Ward was acting, or misacting, to ensure the execution of a policy based on false assumptions he helped create.

The approximately 5,000 Choctaws who remained in Mississippi in 1833, after the initial removal efforts ceased, were objects of increasing legal conflict during the next ten years. A Choctaw petition in 1849 describes the situation for the remaining Choctaws: "We have had our habitations torn down and burned, our fences de-

Choctaw sharecroppers, William and Louisa Jim, in front of their home near Philadelphia, Mississippi, 1925. *Courtesy of Smithsonian Institution National Anthropological Archives, photo no. 71-2884-A.*

stroyed, cattle turned into our fields and we ourselves have been scourged, manacled, fettered and otherwise personally abused, until by such treatment some of our best men have died."[17] Under these circumstances, it is no surprise that the number of remaining Choctaws declined as more and more sought refuge in Oklahoma. Even though the Choctaws had been granted the right to remain in Mississippi by the Treaty of Dancing Rabbit Creek, Mississippi political leaders, such as Senator Jefferson Davis, continued to urge the commissioner of Indian Affairs to remove all Choctaws from Mississippi.[18]

While this was never completely successful, the remaining Choctaws were forced to retreat deeper into the hills and swamps of east central Mississippi. Realistically, the Choctaws had little alternative. The expansion of Mississippi law into Choctaw territory brought with it a social system based on two mutually exclusive groups: landowning whites and black slaves. Not owning land, but not being slaves, the Choctaws were forced to become squatters on land not occupied by the incoming whites. There was no place in the local economy for the Choctaws, who were not slaves but who did not own land.[19] As such, they remained geographically and socially separate from both whites and blacks. As Claiborne observed in 1844, "They camp near the school house, and within the sound of the church going bell; but their children are never taught."[20] Soon, the nation was too absorbed in events that were leading to the Civil War to remember the Choctaws, who remained behind in the red-clay hills of home.

Yet the Choctaws were not sufficiently forgotten for their neighbors to call upon them in the Civil War. Almost the only report of Choctaws in Mississippi between the 1850s and the 1870s was the formation of a Mississippi Choctaw battalion as a Confederate army unit during the Civil War.[21] (The fate of the men of this unit remains unknown.) In the 1860s, major Civil War campaigns were fought in northeast and central Mississippi. During and immediately following Reconstruction, there was considerable violence by whites against both whites and blacks in the Choctaw area.[22] Under these circumstances, it seems probable that during the 1860s and much of the 1870s the Choctaws simply retreated deeper into unoccupied land which was still available in east central Mississippi.

During the late 1870s, two factors gradually brought the Choctaws into increasing contact with non-Choctaws. The first of these was the development of the sharecropping system as a new means of organizing farm labor. The second was a marked increase in clearing forests and bringing additional land into agricultural production. A significant portion of the lands made available by Indian removal was purchased by speculators, not practicing farmers.[23] These lands remained largely unoccupied by white farmers until after the Civil War. Agricultural expansion proceeded more rapidly in the flood plains of the Mississippi River, resulting in heavy recruiting of black labor from other areas of Mississippi. The migration of blacks from east central Mississippi to the expanding plantations created an acute labor shortage in the Choctaw area. To a great extent, the Choctaws were forced to become part of the sharecropping system, as the demand for their labor increased at the same time marginal lands available for squatters came under cultivation by white owners.[24]

The sharecropping system increased contact between Choctaws and whites, but this was less true of contact between Choctaws and blacks. The Choctaws had been concentrated in marginal farmland, away from the better farms with their black slaves. The Choctaws' change to a sharecropping economy usually took place without geographic movement: they simply began to work as sharecroppers for the whites who had purchased and occupied the land. As a result, black and Choctaw rural communities tended to be geographically separate, although white landowners lived in or near both. As late as the 1960s it was unusual to see black people in Choctaw communities, though this is less so in the 1970s. Most contact between Choctaws and blacks was limited to visits to local market towns, where, under the Jim Crow laws, Choctaws were forced to use facilities designated for blacks. This pattern also continued into the 1960s, when it began to lapse with the decline of segregated facilities.[25]

In spite of the discrimination the Choctaws faced under the sharecropping system, new opportunities were created which had not existed since the destruction of the tribal government in 1830. Now living in stable sharecropping farm communities, the Choctaws developed their own system of churches, headed by Choctaw preachers,[26] and used the Choctaw Bible which had been partially translated in Mississippi some fifty years earlier. Choctaw schools gradually developed as part of the public school system, created during Reconstruction. Some of the teachers were Choctaw and some were white,[27] and several schools offered bilingual instruction in Choctaw and English. By 1900, the majority of Choctaws in Mississippi lived in stable farming communities, centered around their school and church, much like their black and white neighbors. But they preserved their language and traditions, even while increasing their contact with the rest of Mississippi society.

Then, for the second time, the stability and progress of the Choctaws were unintentionally disrupted through action by the federal government. Partly related to the process of granting statehood to Oklahoma, Indian lands there were divided.[28] Major efforts were made in 1903 by lawyers and real estate agents to remove the Choctaws from Mississippi to take part in this division.[29] It is doubtful if this second removal would have been pursued on a large scale

Choctaw farmers, Cephus McMillan and his sons, near Tucker, Mississippi, 1945. *Courtesy of National Archives, Bureau of Indian Affairs photo no. 75-N-Choctaw-Miss-8.*

without strong persuasion from whites. (A longtime teacher in the Choctaw schools, who was also a speaker of the Choctaw language, believed that the majority of Choctaws were opposed to going to Oklahoma.)[30] Many of the Mississippi Choctaws who went to Oklahoma did not receive land, or were cheated of the land they received, and filtered back to Mississippi, only to find their school system abolished, many of their churches disbanded, and the accomplishments of the preceding decades largely destroyed.[31] The personal cost of this disruption of family and community life can scarcely be imagined. In 1918, only fifteen years after this disruptive second removal, a nationwide influenza epidemic proved particularly disastrous to the remaining Choctaws because of their poor housing. The wife of a local doctor, who worked as his nurse, vividly remembers this time: "They were dying like flies, often without any medical attention."[32]

Fortunately for the remaining Choctaws, the investigations that followed the second removal brought the condition of the remaining Mississippi Choctaws to the attention of the federal government, and with the support of the senators and representatives from Mississippi a bill passed Congress that recognized them as an Indian tribe entitled to services through the Bureau of Indian Affairs.[33] As a result, the Choctaw Agency was created in 1918. During the following decades, a small land-purchase program gradually established what was to be the basis of the current reservation. A hospital was built in Philadelphia, and small elementary schools were built in each of the seven major Choctaw communities. Throughout most of its history, however, the Choctaw Agency has been poorly funded. Elementary schools were not available in all communities until 1930, and it was not until 1964 that a high school was available for the Mississippi Choctaws. A modern hospital was completed only in 1976. As recently as 1968, less than 5 percent of Choctaw families lived in standard housing with modern bathroom facilities.

Most of the progress for the Choctaws in Mississippi has come in the past ten years. With the completion of the high school in 1964, an increasing number of Choctaws have been attending college each year, many of whom return to serve as teachers and administrators on the reservation. A tribally owned construction company embarked on an ambitious housing program which by 1974 had over half the population in sound, well-heated homes with indoor plumbing. Programs in adult education are making dramatic changes in the educational level of the population.[34]

More important than the growth in physical facilities and even the educational level is the reemergence of self-government among the Mississippi Choctaws. Under the Indian Reorganization Act of 1934, the Mississippi Choctaws adopted a constitution in 1945 which created a popularly elected tribal council. Thus Choctaw government was reestablished in Mississippi after 115 years. For the first twenty years the tribal council was weak, meeting infrequently and not directly affecting activities on the reservation. But by the mid-1960s the tribal government had begun developing and operating its own programs in manpower training, education, housing, and health and community development.[35] Today, the tribal government is a strong voice in all matters affecting improvement of the way of life of the Choctaws in Mississippi. In 1975, under a modern tribal constitution, the Choctaws re-created the position of Choctaw tribal chief, and through a general, popular election Calvin Isaac assumed this position.

Equally important, Mississippi Choctaws are entering the top level of national Indian leadership. In 1974, then Tribal Chairman Phillip Martin failed by only a few votes to be elected chairman of the National Tribal Chairman's Association. Martin and former Tribal Chairman Emmett York assisted in the creation of the United Southeastern Tribes and served as chairmen of its board. At the same time, Mississippi Choctaws are rising to leadership positions in the federal agencies on the Choctaw reservation. The superintendent of the Choctaw Agency, the head of the Choctaw school system, two school principals, and the director of the Choctaw hospital are all Mississippi Choctaws.

The developments of the past ten years are certainly cause for pride, but it must be remembered that, twice previously, the Choctaws in Mississippi made rapid progress in improving the way of life of their people, and twice the results of decades of work were largely destroyed through no fault of the Mississippi Choctaws.

Two examples indicate the concerns that face the Choctaws today. Most threatening was a ruling by the Fifth U.S. Circuit Court of Appeals which denied the legal existence of the tribal government.[36] Fortunately, the U.S. Supreme Court agreed to review the case, and ruled in favor of the Choctaws.[37] A potential problem is completion by the U.S. Army Corps of Engineers of preliminary plans for a reservoir which would flood some 2,700 acres of Choctaw land. While there is no indication that this project will be developed in the immediate future, the potential impact of the reservoir on the tribe is unclear and adds a note of uncertainty to tribal plans.[38]

Regardless of the outcome, and in spite of progress in housing and education, the Choctaws still have a major unemployment problem and the tribal government has a limited base from which to stimulate economic development. Additionally, although federal assistance has been an important factor in recent tribal progress, marked changes in federal Indian policy have occurred in the past and can be expected in the future.

The Choctaws have fared best when they had the active support of their fellow Mississippians and the federal government. In 1972, Tribal Chairman Phillip Martin addressed non-Choctaws: "Your acquaintance is something we seek. Your friendship we desire. And your support we need."[39] Certainly as non-Choctaws become better acquainted with Mississippi Choctaw history, they will see that support for the Choctaws has been long overdue and is well deserved. With this support, and the efforts of the Choctaws themselves, the current effort at self-development will not suffer the disruption that past efforts experienced.

Notes

1. The only detailed presentation of Mississippi Choctaw history since 1830 is in unpublished theses and dissertations, the most recent of which is John H. Peterson Jr., "The Mississippi Band of Choctaw Indians: Their Recent History and Current Social Relations" (Ph.D. dissertation, University of Georgia, 1970), based on field work among them in 1968 and 1969. Many of the points made in this paper are based on more extensive documentation in the above source.

2. Thelma V. Bounds, *Children of Nanih Waiya* (San Antonio: Naylor Co., 1964), pp. 51, 53.

3. Brewton Berry, *Almost White* (New York: Macmillan, 1963), p. 33.

4. Barbara G. Spencer, John H. Peterson Jr., and Choong S. Kim, *Choctaw Manpower and Demographic Survey, 1974* (Philadelphia, Miss.: Mississippi Band of Choctaw Indians, 1975).

5. Mississippi Band of Choctaw Indians, *An Era of Change* (Philadelphia, Miss., 1972).

6. William S. Willis, "The Nation of Bread," *Ethnohistory* 4 (Winter 1957): 125–49.

7. Bernard Romans, *A Concise Natural History of East and West Florida* (New York, 1775), as cited in John R. Swanton, *Source Material for the Social and Ceremonial Life of the Choctaw Indians* (Washington, D.C.: Bureau of American Ethnology [Bulletin 103], 1931), pp. 46–47; anonymous, "Relation de la Louisiane" (unpublished French manuscript, ca. 1755), published in Swanton, pp. 243–58; and H. B. Cushman, *History of the Choctaw, Chickasaw, and Natchez Indians* (Greenville, Texas: Headlight Publishing Co., 1899), pp. 44, 250.

8. William E. Myer, "Indian Trails of the Southeast," *Forty-second Annual Report of the Bureau of American Ethnology* (Washington: Government Printing Office, 1928), pp. 824–26.

9. *Niles' Register* 3 (1812): 166, as cited in Angie Debo, *The Rise and Fall of the Choctaw Republic* (Norman: University of Oklahoma Press, 1934), p. 40.

10. Cushman, *History*, p. 145.

11. *Indian Affairs, Annual Report* (Washington: Government Printing Office, 1830), Table B, as cited in Debo, *Rise and Fall*, p. 45.

12. Cushman, *History*, p. 150.

13. *Niles' Register* 37 (1829): 181, as cited in Debo, *Rise and Fall*, p. 47.

14. Arthur H. DeRosier Jr., *The Removal of the Choctaw Indians* (Knoxville: University of Tennessee Press, 1970), pp. 174–84.

15. Franklin Riley, "Choctaw Land Claims," *Publications of the Mississippi Historical Society* 8 (1904): 345–50.

16. William Ward to Hon. William Haile, January 29, 1827, as cited in Mary E. Young, *Redskins, Ruffleshirts, and Rednecks* (Norman: University of Oklahoma Press, 1961), p. 27.

17. Petition of "one hundred red men" to George S. Gaines, December 6, 1849, as quoted in Grant Foreman, *The Five Civilized Tribes* (Norman: University of Oklahoma Press, 1934), p. 75.

18. Davis to Brown, March 27, 1850, as quoted in Foreman, *The Five Civilized Tribes*, p. 75.

19. John H. Peterson Jr., "The Indian in the Old South," *Red, White, and Black: Symposium on Indians in the Old South* (Southern Anthropological Society Proceedings, no. 5), ed. by Charles M. Hudson (Athens: University of Georgia Press, 1972), pp. 125–26.

20. J. F. Claiborne, "Choctaw Indians, Memorial," House of Representa-

tives, 28th Congress, 1st sess., Document 137 (Washington: Government Printing Office, 1844), p. 4.

21. A. J. Brown, *History of Newton County, Mississippi, from 1834–1894* (Jackson, Miss.: Clarion-Ledger Co., 1894), p. 96.

22. James Wells, *The Chisolm Massacre: A Picture of "Home Rule" in Mississippi* (Washington, D.C.: Chisolm Monument Association, 1878).

23. Young, *Redskins*, pp. 125–37.

24. Vernon L. Wharton, *The Negro in Mississippi, 1865–1890* (New York: Harper and Row, 1965), pp. 104–9; Peterson, "Mississippi Band," pp. 39–45.

25. Based on the author's observations over the past nine years.

26. Eugene Farr, "Religious Assimilation: A Case Study of the Adoption of Christianity by the Choctaw Indians of Mississippi" (Th.D. dissertation, New Orleans Baptist Theological Seminary, 1948).

27. H. S. Halbert, "Indian Schools," *Biennial Report of the State Superintendent of Public Education to the Legislature of Mississippi for the Scholastic Years 1895–1896 and 1896–1897* (Jackson, Miss.: Clarion-Ledger Co., 1898), p. 24.

28. Debo, *Rise and Fall*, pp. 246, 273–76.

29. John W. Wade, "The Removal of the Mississippi Choctaws," *Publications of the Mississippi Historical Society* 8 (1904): 397–426.

30. H. S. Halbert, "The Mississippi Choctaws," *Biennial Report of the State Superintendent of Public Education to the Legislature of Mississippi for the Scholastic Years 1897–1898 and 1898–1899* (Jackson, Miss.: Clarion-Ledger Co., 1900), p. 36.

31. Farr, "Religious Assimilation," pp. 32–41; Peterson, "Mississippi Band," pp. 98–105.

32. Personal interview by the author with Mrs. Claude Yates of Philadelphia, Miss., October 1968.

33. Act of May 25, 1918, 40 Stat. 573.

34. John H. Peterson Jr., *Socio-Economic Characteristics of the Mississippi Choctaw Indians*, Social Science Research Center Report 34 (n.p.: Mississippi State University, 1970); and John H. Peterson Jr., "Assimilation, Separation, and Out-Migration in an American Indian Group," *American Anthropologist* 74 (October 1972): 1286–95.

35. Mississippi Band of Choctaw Indians, *An Era of Change* (Minutes of the Choctaw Tribal Council) (Philadelphia, Miss.: Choctaw Agency 1972).

36. Fifth U.S. Court of Appeals, Case C. A. 5, no. 76-1518.

37. Supreme Court of the United States, Case no. 77-836.

38. John H. Peterson Jr., *Reservation, Reservoir and Self-Determination: A Case Study of Reservoir Planning as It Affects an Indian Reservation* (n.p.: Mississippi State University, Water Resources Research Institute, 1975).

39. Mississippi Band of Choctaw Indians, *An Era of Change*, p. 23.

9

Acculturation and Persistence among North Carolina's Eastern Band of Cherokee Indians

SHARLOTTE NEELY

If most historical accounts are taken at face value, the Eastern Cherokees appear as an insignificant society compared with their Western Cherokee kinsmen. Most histories chronicle the group's steady acculturation during the early nineteenth century and trace the events leading up to the 1838 removal. Thereafter, the thread of Cherokee history is traced as events unfolded in Indian Territory, now Oklahoma. Only about 1,000 Cherokees were left in the East, who became the nucleus of the Eastern Band of Cherokee Indians, centered on the Qualla Boundary in western North Carolina.

Today their population has increased eightfold and they comprise the largest federally recognized reservation in the Southeast. Even today the Eastern Cherokees are a culturally and racially heterogeneous group of people, and this was also the case before and during the removal years. Any outline of Cherokee history would be incomplete without an understanding of these differences.

The roots of this cultural and racial heterogeneity can be traced back before the removal. By the early nineteenth century, a considerable number of whites lived within the boundaries of the Cherokee nation. Since the Cherokees observed matrilineal descent, the offspring of white male/Cherokee female marriages were full members of Cherokee society. It is probable that most of the children of such unions, brought up in biethnic households, were raised within two cultural traditions. In adulthood, some of these people lived mainly a Euro-American lifestyle but as residents and members of the Cherokee nation.

The early years of the nineteenth century saw the beginning of intense efforts by whites and by some factions of Cherokees to change Cherokee culture. The Cherokee factions were largely composed of people with a culturally heterogeneous background, id est, those Cherokees most familiar with Euro-American customs because they had been raised in households where one of their parents was white. Efforts at acculturation centered in the more accessible hill country of Georgia, Alabama, Tennessee, and extreme southern North Carolina. This was the area into which streamed the traders, missionaries, and church-affiliated educators, where the acculturation-minded Cherokee faction largely resided. In the hill country, efforts were made to accommodate the dominant white society by remodeling Cherokee society after that of the new United States. The goal of such efforts was the preservation of Cherokee lands and society by convincing nearby whites that the Cherokees were not "savages" but civilized neighbors.

The factionalism that exists today between "full-bloods" and "mixed-bloods" (sometimes called "white Indians") can be traced back to the nineteenth century, when these factions had a geographical correspondence. Most so-called "mixed-bloods" lived to the south in the hill country, while most "full-bloods" lived to the north in the mountains. The racial terms *full-blood* and *mixed-blood* also carried cultural connotations. "Full-bloods," or "conservatives," rarely came into contact with whites, and represented Cherokee cultural traditionalism. "Mixed-bloods," or "progressives," frequently had whites as kinsmen, and were associated with acculturation.

The Snowbird Mountain range in southwestern North Carolina provided an ecological barrier, separating preremoval northern Cherokee conservatives from southern Cherokee progressives. South of these mountains, at what is now the town of Andrews, North Carolina, were the northernmost permanent, preremoval missions and schools: the Valleytown Baptist and Methodist missions.[1] North of these mountains and continuing into the Smoky Mountains were the homes of Cherokee conservatives, near the present-day Qualla Boundary and Snowbird settlements.

In the hill country to the south, a so-called Golden Age of Cherokee history developed during the early nineteenth century as the progressive Cherokees attempted to remodel Cherokee society after that of white Americans. A constitution, patterned after that of the United States, provided for executive, legislative, and judicial branches of government. The Cherokee nation was divided into eight districts (Amohee, Aquohee, Chattooga, Chickamauga, Coosawatee, Etowah, Hickory Log, and Taquohee) and each sent representatives to a council at the newly established capital of New Echota, near present-day Calhoun, Georgia. Buildings at New Echota were patterned after Euro-American architectural styles, and nearby, at Spring Place, stood the columned mansion of the Cherokee progressive Vann family, slaveowners who operated a large plantation.[2]

By 1835, hill-country Cherokees owned 1,553 slaves, whereas Cherokees in North Carolina owned 37 (only 12 of which were owned by people classified as "full-bloods"). Throughout the Cherokee nation, only 10 percent of the people classified as "full-bloods" owned slaves, and their slaves numbered only 4 percent of the total slave population.[3]

By the time of the removal of 1838, the Cherokees were a culturally heterogeneous people. The removal re-created a nearly homogeneous society by draining off the progressive Cherokee faction and leaving behind the conservative faction. When the removal became a reality in the fall of 1838, it is ironic that most of the acculturated "mixed-blood" population was removed, while most of those Cherokees who remained were "full-bloods" and conservatives. The irony lies in the fact that many progressive leaders had assumed that adapting to Euro-American lifestyles would demonstrate that the Cherokees were not dangerous savages and, therefore, not candidates for removal. Whether or not the Cherokees were acculturating was never really a factor in the removal question.

The basic reasons for the removal of 16,000 Cherokees were economic and environmental: the hill country where progressives lived was fertile for farming and rich in gold; the mountains where conservatives lived were deficient in gold and farming bottomlands. Because of the poorer quality of their land, about 1,000 Cherokees in North Carolina remained behind, to form the nucleus of the 8,000-member Eastern Band of Cherokee Indians.

The circumstances by which Cherokees remained in the Southeast were similar to the circumstances by which other southern Indians remained. Throughout the Southeast, Native Americans who survived the removal period have preserved their landholdings precisely because of the lands' marginal value.

Yonaguska, an Eastern Cherokee chief, clearly perceived that it was the marginal nature of some Cherokee land which had spared his people's being removed. The late nineteenth-century anthropologist, James Mooney, having interviewed people who knew Yonaguska, concluded:

Although frequent pressure was brought to bear to induce him and his people to remove to the West, he firmly resisted every persuasion, declaring that the Indians were safer from aggression among their rocks and mountains than they could ever be in a land which the white man could find profitable, and that the Cherokee could be happy only in the country where nature had planted him.[4]

For the 1,000 Cherokees who managed to remain in the East, removal was avoided by either of two methods. Nearly all of them resided on marginal lands in the mountains of North Carolina, but these lands were divided politically. Some of the North Carolina Cherokees lived on lands that had been ceded to the United States in an 1819 treaty. Many of the conservative Cherokees there, concentrated along the Oconaluftee River Valley in present-day Swain and Jackson counties, were not pressured by white settlers and remained undisturbed after 1819. They were legally no longer part of the Cherokee nation, and nearly 400 of them became citizens of North Carolina and, later, were thereby protected from removal.[5]

In 1849 the Quaker *Friend's Weekly Intelligencer* recounted the process by which these Oconaluftee Indians became citizens:

No law of the United States forbidding such a course, and North Carolina giving full assent . . . and inviting not only the half-blood Cherokees, but the full-blood Indians, who chose to remain in the land of their fathers, to take protection under the aegis of her laws, nothing more was necessary to make them citizens, but a continued residence within her limits twelve months agreeably to the laws of the state.[6]

The petition of the Oconaluftee Indians to become North Carolina citizens had been accompanied by certificates from local whites describing the Cherokees as "a sober, temperate, and industrious people, improving in civilization . . . [and] qualified to make useful citizens."[7]

Although legal status as state citizens aided some North Carolina Cherokees in remaining, even a favorable Supreme Court decision had not saved the Cherokees in Georgia from being removed from their valuable lands. This different treatment demonstrates the dominance of land values over acculturation rates as the motivating factor behind the pressure for removal. In short, whites in 1819 did not want those marginal lands of western North Carolina nearly so much as others wanted the valuable lands of north Georgia in 1838.

Other North Carolina Cherokees, residing within the boundaries of the Cherokee nation, experienced a very different fate. Indians of these areas, in present-day Graham and Cherokee counties, were subject to removal, and concentration camps were built in rounding up these Indians to move them west. Several hundred Cherokees, mainly from Euchella's and Tsali's bands, hid in the Snowbird Mountains. Only after Tsali and his sons, leaders of the resistance who had killed some United States soldiers, gave themselves up for execution did the army abandon its search for the escapees. It was 1842, however, before the United States government officially ended its attempt to remove these people.[8]

Since there was no great onslaught of white settlers into these marginal lands of North Carolina, in contrast to Georgia, some Cherokees managed to collect enough money to buy back some of their lands. However, North Carolina had recently enacted a new state constitution which made it difficult for non-whites to own land. Therefore, land had to be purchased in the names of friendly whites. One group of buyers were Cherokees in the Graham County area, who, within mere weeks of removal, purchased over 1,200 acres of land in the names of three white men. According to the Cherokee census of 1835, over 550 Indians resided in the Graham County area. Many of the land purchases were made in the name of William Holland Thomas, a local trader, tribal attorney, fluent Cherokee speaker, and adopted son of Chief Yonaguska. In 1839, after Yonaguska's death, Thomas acted as the leader of the remnant Cherokees.[9]

The first Cherokee census taken in the east after removal was

Cherokee men performing the traditional Eagle Dance, 1932.
Courtesy of Smithsonian Institution National Anthropological Archives, photo no. 44.368-S.

the Mullay Roll of 1848, which described the post-removal population as

a moral and comparatively industrious people—sober and orderly to a
marked degree—and although almost wholly ignorant of our language
(not a single full-blood and but a few of the half-breeds speaking English)
advancing encouragingly in the acquirement of a knowledge of agriculture,
the ordinary mechanical branches, and in spinning, weaving, etc.[10]

This description testifies to how less acculturated the Eastern
Cherokees were, compared with the pre-removal Georgia Cherokees. This long period of isolation after removal afforded an opportunity for "cultural resynthesis" and stability.[11] The picture that
emerges during the post-removal years is of a traditionalist people
acculturating. Technological changes, particularly relating to farming, were filtering in with rapidity. Some changes in social organization were also occurring; Cherokee men, for example, replaced
women in their traditional role as farmers. The women, like their
white counterparts, began to concentrate primarily on household
duties. Also, Christianity was spreading among the Cherokees,
although Indian, not white, ministers were the rule.

An 1848 traveler's account by Charles Lanman gives another view
of the early post-removal Eastern Cherokees:

They manufacture their own clothing, their own ploughs, and other farming utensils, their own axes, and even their own guns. . . . They keep the
same domestic animals that are kept by their white neighbors, and cultivate
all the common grains of the country. . . . They are chiefly Methodists and
Baptists. . . . They have their own courts and try their criminals by a regular
jury. . . . Excepting on festive days, they dress after the manner of the white
man, but far more picturesquely. They live in small log houses of their own
construction, and have everything they need or desire in the way of food.[12]

Lanman estimated the North Carolina Cherokee population at
1,000, with 100 Catawba Indians residing with them. His account
reveals that few changes had occurred in use of the language or the
traditional clan system. It *does* reveal changes in Cherokee material
culture, political organization, and religion.[13] After years of re-
searching and translating documents of the period, written in the
Sequoyah syllabary, the Kilpatricks have concluded that

the Eastern Cherokee were much more highly acculturated than we had
surmised, that township government was a flourishing organism, and that

economic problems were solved with much ingenuity. . . . Over the Wolftown documents there hang the unspoken distrust of the White man and
the constant fear of eviction. No great spiritual wind sweeps across these
pages; rather is there a stubborn, grubbing tenacity to persevere and en-
dure.[14]

Beyond allowing the Eastern Cherokees to remain, North Carolina did little for the group. The state did not recognize their right,
or that of any non-whites, to own land until 1866, and periodically
disfranchised them.

Between the removal of 1838 and the Civil War in 1861, the
Eastern Cherokees were able to extend assistance to another southern tribe in jeopardy of being removed, the South Carolina Catawbas. In 1840 the Cherokees generously invited the Catawbas to live
with them on their North Carolina lands. Mooney records that
about 100 Catawbas, "nearly all that were left of the tribe," accepted
the invitation and lived with the Cherokees until 1848, when
mutual "tribal jealousies" convinced the Catawbas they should
leave. After many difficulties, the Catawbas were able to take up
residence in South Carolina again. In 1852 only about a dozen continued to live with the Cherokees, and by 1890 only one intermarried woman remained.

The effects of the Catawbas on Cherokee life were not significant,
but the Catawba type of pottery making, special knowledge of Indian medicine, and leadership role in ceremonials influenced the
Cherokees.[15] These influences indicate that Eastern Cherokee culture change was due not only to whites, and that contact with other
Indian groups has continued to the present.

After the majority of the Catawbas returned to South Carolina,
the next major event to affect the Eastern Cherokees was one of
national importance: the Civil War. William Thomas viewed the
approaching war as not an appropriate concern of the Cherokees,
and he did not want them to become involved. After all, North
Carolina still did not recognize the Cherokees' right to own land.
Confederate General Kirby Smith felt differently, however, and sent
Washington Morgan, whose father had commanded the Cherokees
in 1814 at the Battle of Horseshoe Bend during the Creek War, to
enlist them. Faced with the prospect of having someone else lead
them, the aging Thomas himself recruited four companies of Chero-

kees within the Thomas Legion. Nearly 400 Eastern Cherokees served, which meant that in a population of less than 2,000, "about every able-bodied man in the tribe" must have enrolled for the Confederacy (most as home guards).[16]

According to Mooney, the war offered the Cherokees opportunities to engage in traditional practices, including a minor scalping episode in 1862. He wrote:

The war, in fact, brought out all the latent Indian in their nature. Before starting to the front every man consulted an oracle stone to learn whether or not he might hope to return in safety. The start was celebrated with a grand old-time war dance at the townhouse on Soco, and the same dance was repeated at frequent intervals thereafter, the Indians being "painted and feathered in good old style," Thomas himself frequently assisting as master of ceremonies.[17]

Although few Cherokees died in battle, the war brought hardships and factionalism to the group. About a year after enlisting in the Confederate army, a group of Cherokees was captured by Union troops near present-day Bryson City, North Carolina. Dissatisfied with the Confederacy, this group, and others they influenced, joined the Union army, making about thirty Cherokees who fought for the Federal government. As with much of white Appalachia, there were pro-Confederate and pro-Union factions among the Cherokees. After the war, the Union Cherokee soldiers returned home to find their friends and relatives "so bitterly incensed against them that for some time their lives were in danger." Moreover, one of the Union soldiers returned home in 1866 with smallpox, and over 100 Eastern Cherokees died from this disease.[18]

Thus the same year that North Carolina recognized the Cherokees' right to own land, other tragedies struck, first in the form of the smallpox epidemic. In addition, William Thomas's health failed, and with it his business interests. Those to whom he owed money sued, and they made no distinction between Thomas's property and what he held in trust for the Cherokees.

During the following years the major task of the Eastern Cherokees was to clarify the nature of their relationship to the land on which they lived and organize themselves into a legal political unit.

In 1868 the North Carolina Cherokees met in general council, the first since removal, at Cheoah in present-day Graham County, to draw up a constitution and reassert their legal status to their lands. The constitution went into effect in 1870 with the election of the first official "principal chief" of the Eastern Band of Cherokee Indians. During the removal years, Yonaguska had generally been recognized as the major chief among the North Carolina Cherokees. After his death in 1839, leadership of the group passed to Yonaguska's white, adopted son, William Holland Thomas. Although Thomas identified closely with the Indians and served effectively for many years as tribal attorney, his health and financial problems by the late 1860s necessitated choosing other leaders. The following list gives the names and terms of office of all the Eastern Cherokee principal chiefs after Thomas's retirement.

1870–75	Flying Squirrel (Saunooke, Salonitah, or Kalahu)	1919–23	Joe Saunook
1875–80	Lloyd Welch	1923–27	Sampson Owl
1880–91	Nimrod Jarrett Smith	1927–31	John Tahquette
1891–95	Stillwell Saunook	1931–47	Jarrett Blythe
1895–99	Andy Standing Deer	1947–51	Henry Bradley
1899–1903	Jesse Reid	1951–55	Osley Saunooke
1903–7	Bird Saloneeta (Young Squirrel)	1955–59	Jarrett Blythe
		1959–63	Osley Saunooke
		1963–67	Jarrett Blythe
1907–11	John Goins Welch	1967–71	Walter S. Jackson
1911–15	Joe Saunook	1971–73	Noah Powell
1915–19	David Blythe	1973–	John Crowe[19]

In subsequent court cases the Eastern Cherokees were established as a legal corporation; this was confirmed in 1889 by North Carolina and a new Cherokee charter was granted. The federal government was invited to be a trustee for their land, since the Cherokees feared that Indian landowners might again become a doubtful entity to the state.

The lawsuits filed by Thomas's creditors, establishing the Cherokees' rights to the lands held in trust for them by Thomas, were complicated by the fact that Thomas had lent some Cherokees the money to buy lands held in his name. Finally, the courts decided upon a sum of money the Eastern Cherokees had to pay in order to possess their own lands. However, most of this amount was paid by the federal government from funds owed the Eastern Cherokees as a result of the removal. The funds had been held for the Eastern Cherokees since 1842, when the federal government recognized the

right of the group to remain in North Carolina, but the money had
not been given to the Cherokees because of North Carolina's refusal
to recognize the right of Indians to own land. After 1866, when the
state recognized the right of non-whites to own land, the funds were
available for use by the Eastern Cherokees.

In the 1890s Mooney described the Eastern Cherokees' confusing
legal position:

The exact legal status of the East Cherokees is still a matter of dispute, they
being at once wards of the government [since 1875 as a result of the lawsuits relating to Thomas], citizens of the United States [as a result of the
1819 treaty], and (in North Carolina) a corporate body under state laws
[culminating in an act passed in 1889]. They pay real estate taxes and road
service, exercise the voting privilege [although disfranchised in a 1900 elec-
tion] and are amenable to the local courts, but do not pay poll tax or receive
any pauper assistance from the counties; neither can they make free con-
tracts or alienate their lands.[20]

By 1869 the Swetland Roll enumerated the Eastern Cherokee
population at over 1,700. Over 800 Cherokees, nearly all "full-
bloods," resided on the Qualla Boundary, and almost 400 "full-
bloods" lived in Cheoah. The 500 Cherokees who resided near
Murphy were described as "mixed-bloods." Two schools may have
operated temporarily. However, by 1875 there were no schools, and
"very few full-bloods could speak English, although to their credit
nearly all could read and write their own language."[21]

Significant changes began during the 1880s. Two white travelers
who visited the Cherokees, Wilbur Ziegler and Ben Grosscup, re-
marked that "the Indians have no towns, nor does their manner of
life differ in many particulars from that of the white people among
whom they reside. . . . The fields, originally of average fertility, are
worn out by bad farming."[22]

They reported that the main food was corn, supplemented by
fruits. Some cattle and horses were raised for cash sale, but the
Cherokees produced most of their own necessities. Except for moc-
casins, their home-made clothing was similar to that worn by
whites.

In 1881 the Eastern Band received an invitation from their kins-

Since the 1940s tourism has formed a major part of the Eastern Cherokee economy. This 1974 photograph shows the "Honest Injun Trading Post," a white-owned store with a Plains-style tipi on the roof and Northwest-style totem poles as pillars. *Courtesy of Walter L. Williams and Sharlotte Neely.*

men in Indian Territory to join them, and 161 people moved west. But five years later the United States Supreme Court ruled that the two groups were separate entities, thus ending further migrations.

By 1884, a new census, the Hester Roll, enumerated 1,881 Eastern Cherokees in North Carolina, 758 in Georgia, 213 in Tennessee, 71 in Alabama, 11 in Kentucky, and 22 in seven other states. It is doubtful that those who lived outside North Carolina participated in tribal government.[23]

The Hester Roll is the first evidence that the composition of the Eastern Band was changing dramatically, as a result of a white influx. Regarding the Hester Roll, Mooney wrote in 1900 that "a large portion of the band still refuse to recognize it as authoritative, claiming that a large number of persons therein enrolled have no Cherokee blood."[24]

By the end of the nineteenth century, United States government policy was committed to allotment, or the dividing of Indian reservations into individually owned tracts. Rumors of allotment of Eastern Cherokee lands caused many whites to hope they might obtain a tract. Indeed, oral traditions claim that these whites paid bribes to the government enrolling agents to be included on tribal rolls, and their descendants are derogatorily referred to as Five-Dollar Indians.[25] According to Cherokee writer Henry Owl, concerning the 1931 Baker Roll, "enrollment took a sudden spurt in 1929 because of the plans for allotment, and many names on the list will not stand too close scrutiny for eligibility."[26] Almost half of the more than 3,000 names enrolled were contested by the tribal council.[27]

Thus increasing population pressures on the land, among both Indians and non-Indians, resulted in conflicts that damaged the good relations between the two ethnic groups. The inclusion of whites on the tribal rolls, plus an increase in white–Indian intermarriage, drastically changed the formerly homogeneous "full-blood" Cherokees into a heterogeneous population with a significant number of "white Indians" of dubious Indian ancestry. This pattern operated not only in biological terms but in cultural aspects as well, especially in education.

Formal education, begun in 1880 by the Society of Friends (the Quakers), seems to have played an important role in disrupting cultural homogeneity among the Eastern Cherokees. Robert K. Thomas asserts that formal education "upset the previous tendency in the community to 'level' culturally."[28] In other words, before 1880 the tendency had been to assimilate the children of white/Cherokee marriages into Cherokee culture. After 1880, through the influence of the schools, the tendency was to assimilate these children into a Euro-American cultural system. Children who did not live with a white parent and those who avoided the schools and white teachers tended to grow up in a traditional Cherokee subgroup.

In 1892 the Quakers ended their mission to the Cherokees and turned their schools over to the U.S. Bureau of Indian Affairs. During the first two decades of the twentieth century, the role of the BIA bordered on the dictatorial. This was especially true in the schooling of Cherokee children. Under the direction of Quakers during the 1880s, schools had operated voluntarily and successfully in training Indian teachers.[29] However, with the establishment of BIA schools, the white teacher became the ideal, and attendance was made compulsory.

In the BIA schools, children who repeatedly ran away were chained to their dormitory beds.[30] Attendance at faraway schools was encouraged, and letters from Cherokee students who begged to return home were often answered with a harsh reply from the superintendent: "You really have no home."[31] Cherokee adults tell of having their mouth washed out with soap or being beaten every time they dared to speak the Cherokee language in the presence of teachers. Acculturation had degenerated into heavy-handed force, and the schools were often successful in wiping out the Cherokee language.

Much of this changed, however, in the 1930s under President Franklin D. Roosevelt's New Deal. The newly appointed commissioner of Indian Affairs was John Collier, who opposed forced acculturation and upheld efforts to keep traditional cultural traits from disappearing. Out-of-state boarding school education was deemphasized, and among the Eastern Cherokees efforts were made to revive the Cherokee language, which was dying out as a result of previous BIA efforts. So thorough had been the earlier efforts to discourage the language, however, that some Indians opposed teaching Cherokee in the schools because it marked a return to "savagery."[32] But the "Indian New Deal" did not last beyond Roosevelt's death, and many of its policies were reversed throughout the nation, especially during the termination era of the 1950s. The Cherokees' federal services and reservation status were not terminated, but the threat hung over all Indians on federal reservations.

During the twentieth century, Eastern Cherokee history has been characterized by depressing economic trends, which have themselves contributed to acculturation. In the mid-nineteenth century, before population increases placed excessive demands on the limited land base, most Cherokees adequately provided for their needs by farming. Yet by 1908 most Cherokees were reported as living in poverty, because, as a government official stated, "there are few opportunities in that part of North Carolina where they live for them to earn money, and they are obliged to depend upon their sterile little farms."[33]

As the population steadily increased, with no corresponding increases in the size of the reservation, the Eastern Cherokees have been able to depend less and less on farming as a means of livelihood. By the 1950s, only about 10 percent of the people supported themselves by farming, and by the 1970s not one Cherokee family received its livelihood from that source.[34]

This decline in farming has meant that more Cherokees have turned to other occupations, which have often taken them off the reservation into wage labor. World War II and subsequent wars have taken numerous Cherokee men away from North Carolina and exposed them to the larger world. Many of these veterans later left the reservation for jobs, or commuted to neighboring areas by automobile.

If the automobile has had a significant acculturative role by providing transportation for Cherokees going off the reservation, it has also had a tremendous effect on the economy of the reservation itself. During the post–World War II prosperity decades, more and more Americans began vacationing by car. Due to their location near the Great Smoky Mountains National Park, the Cherokees experienced an inpouring of tourists eager to see "real Indians."

By the 1950s, tourism provided more income to the reservation than any form of regular employment, but it was not adequate. Tourism provided many jobs, so that unemployment during the summer dropped to 1 percent, but most of these jobs were low-paying and limited to the summer months. During the winter, unemployment soared to 20 percent, and the average yearly income for most Cherokees was only one-fifth of the national average.[35] In 1958 the local BIA superintendent wrote that because of the "dire need" among the Cherokees, there was "much actual hunger."[36]

By the 1970s, some economic progress had been made, and Cherokee incomes had increased to 60 percent of the national average, but most families needed more than one employed family member to make ends meet.[37] The impact of the tourist trade has been diluted because one-third of the tourist enterprises, comprising the largest money-making shops (complete with fake Indian crafts made in Japan, Taiwan, or Haiti), are owned by non-Indians. The reservation's dependence on tourism has also been hurt by gasoline shortages and recessionary trends.

Despite economic problems and pressures for acculturation, Cherokees have retained a strong hold on their ethnic identity.

This is primarily the result of a strong, continuing cultural tradition, especially among the "full-bloods," that refuses to disappear. No matter the "blood degree" or cultural outlook of an individual Cherokee, however, there are advantages to identifying ethnically as a Cherokee Indian, and many of the advantages are economic. The most basic economic advantage for members of the Eastern Band of Cherokee Indians is access to reservation land.

Still legally a corporation under North Carolina laws, the band's assets consist of its lands, with the band's members functioning as stockholders. Although reservation lands cannot be owned, individual band members have "possessory rights" to tracts of land which can be sold to, bought from, willed to, or inherited from any other band member. Inherited reservation land compares favorably with expensive off-reservation land in nearby towns. Many Cherokees survive more inexpensively by living on the reservation and commuting long distances to work than by moving closer to their off-reservation jobs.

In recent years another major economic advantage has been provided to those who possess reservation tracts. In 1962 a housing authority was formed, and since 1965 over 400 houses have been built or significantly improved, reducing substandard housing from nearly 90 to less than 60 percent.[38] To qualify for a new house under this program, at least one member of a household must have possessory rights to a tract of land upon which the house can be built. The houses, ranging from two to four bedrooms, include a living–dining area, kitchen, bathroom, and carport, and have electricity, hot water, and indoor plumbing. (In addition to possessing a house site, to qualify for a low-cost housing loan a family must put many hours of labor into building the semiprefabricated home.)

Many Indians and whites in the southern Appalachians are not well off economically, and low-cost, good-quality housing encourages many (who can qualify) to establish band membership. There are other economic lures to identifying ethnically as Cherokee Indian, most notably the band's successful suit for a government land-claims payment for all Cherokee lands that have been permanently lost to whites.

The current attraction of band membership can be illustrated by the recent efforts of a peripheral Cherokee community to reassert its Cherokee identity. Located more than eighty miles from the main reservation and comprised largely of people phenotypically white, the community has not always been so eager to assert its Indian identity. In 1950 the U.S. Census Bureau numbered only twenty-four Indians in the community, and not for the previous seventy years had the community numbered more than forty people. But in 1970 the community numbered seventy-one Indians, and in 1973 it was able to get enough people to the polls to defeat a neighboring Indian community of nearly 350 "full-blood" Cherokees, thereby winning two seats in the tribal council.

Though an entire Cherokee community rarely chooses between emphasizing or deemphasizing its Indian identity, some Cherokee individuals are continually confronted with the choice. Most of them are the so-called "white Indians," people with minimal Cherokee "blood degree." Because they look white, speak English fluently (and rarely any Cherokee), and conform to Euro-American cultural standards, these individuals can usually be accepted as white simply by ignoring their Cherokee background. Cherokees with maximal "blood degree" do not have this choice. Phenotypically, they appear Indian, often speak Cherokee, or English with a Cherokee accent, and frequently conform to Indian behavior patterns. These "full-bloods" often resent "white Indians," who can alternate between two ethnic identities as occasion demands. Although "full-bloods" are not burdened with the personality conflicts inherent in an unstable ethnic identity, they are not afforded the social and economic advantages of a shifting identity.

Today there is a slowly growing awareness of Indian identity among the Eastern Cherokees. For many it is an effort to maintain a simultaneous identity as "real Americans" and "real Indians." Each autumn, after the tourist season, the Eastern Cherokees hold their Fall Festival. Other Indians from as far away as New Mexico, Florida, Oklahoma, and New York attend, further reducing the Eastern Cherokees' isolation, not only from the world of white Americans but other Native Americans as well. After the 1972 Fall Festival the *Cherokee One Feather* ran an article which said:

The old fair has become a festival, and "festival" means "sharing, celebration, and ceremony". . . . The major attractions at the Fall Festival were ethnic: Indian customs, culture and self image. Perhaps one bumper sticker summed it up: "Brothers rejoice! It's *in* to be Indian!"[39]

Traditional stickball games and booger dances, thought to have been acculturated out of existence, are performed alongside ferris wheels and cotton candy concessions, but they *are* performed. Also, each year the tiny Snowbird community in Graham County hosts a "Trail of Tears Singing" at which Western Cherokees from Oklahoma are the special guests. The Cherokee language is spoken and traditional foods (e.g., bean bread) are consumed.

Cultural traditionalism may be on the upswing, perhaps as a result of the Red Power Movement, but the Eastern Cherokee economy is not doing as well. Perhaps because of economic conditions, in 1972 the Eastern Band of Cherokee Indians voted to accept an offer from the Indian Claims Commission of nearly $2 million for all Cherokee lands permanently lost to whites. For two decades the Eastern Band struggled with this government commission over a settlement. A general council, the first since 1868, was held to take the vote and the council accepted the government's offer of money —but one young man urged that the land be returned to the Cherokees. His comment received a round of applause.[40] That is not surprising, since the major issue confronting the Eastern Cherokees today, as during the removal period, is land: how to hold onto it, how to use it, how to increase it, and who should have access to it.

Notes

1. Henry Malone, *Cherokees of the Old South* (Athens: University of Georgia Press, 1956), pp. 107–9; Mattie Russell, "William Holland Thomas: White Chief of the Cherokees" (Ph.D. dissertation, Duke University, 1956), pp. 35–36.

2. Malone, *Cherokees.*

3. Douglas C. Wilms, "Cherokee Slave Ownership prior to the Removal," paper delivered at the Symposium on New Directions in Cherokee Studies, Meeting of the Southern Anthropological Society, Blacksburg, Va., 1974.

4. James Mooney, *Myths of the Cherokees*, Bureau of American Ethnology Nineteenth Annual Report (Washington, D.C.: Smithsonian Institution, 1900), p. 163.

5. Duane King, "The Origin of the Eastern Band of Cherokees as a Social and Political Entity," paper delivered at the Symposium on New Directions in Cherokee Studies, Meeting of the Southern Anthropological Society, Blacksburg, Va., 1974.

6. *Friend's Weekly Intelligencer*, Philadelphia, 6, no. 1 (1849): 2–3. Copy at University of North Carolina Library, Chapel Hill.

7. Ibid.

8. King, "Origin"; Mooney, *Myths*, pp. 130–133, 157–58.

9. King, "Origin"; Mooney, *Myths*, pp. 158–164; Russell, "Thomas"; Margaret W. Freel, *Our Heritage: The People of Cherokee County, North Carolina, 1540–1955* (Ashville, N.C.: Miller Printing Co., 1956), p. 400.

10. Gaston Litton, "Enrollment Records of the Eastern Band of Cherokee Indians," *North Carolina Historical Review* 17 (July 1940): 207–8.

11. Raymond Fogelson, "A Study of the Conjuror in Eastern Cherokee Society" (M.A. thesis, University of Pennsylvania, 1958), p. 36.

12. Charles Lanman, *Letters from the Alleghany Mountains* (New York: G. P. Putnam, 1849), p. 95.

13. Ibid.

14. Jack and Anna Kilpatrick, eds. and trans., *The Shadow of Sequoyah: Social Documents of the Cherokees, 1862–1964* (Norman: University of Oklahoma Press, 1965), p. 10.

15. Mooney, *Myths*, pp. 159–72.

16. Ibid., pp. 165–69.

17. Ibid., p. 170.

18. Ibid., p. 171.

19. This list is from the files of the tribal offices, Eastern Band of Cherokee Indians, Cherokee, N.C.

20. Mooney, *Myths*, p. 180.

21. Ibid., p. 174.

22. Wilbur Zeigler and Ben Grosscup, *The Heart of the Alleghanies, or Western North Carolina* (Raleigh, N.C.: Alfred Williams Co., 1883), pp. 36–37.

23. Mooney, *Myths*, p. 176; Litton, "Enrollment Records," p. 222.

24. Mooney, *Myths*, p. 176.

25. Harriet Kupferer, *The Principal People, 1960: A Study of Cultural and Social Groups of the Eastern Cherokee*, Bureau of American Ethnology Bulletin 196 (Washington, D.C.: Smithsonian Institution, 1966), p. 232.

26. Henry Owl, "The Eastern Band of Cherokee Indians before and after the Removal" (M.A. thesis, University of North Carolina, 1929), p. 142.

27. Litton, "Enrollment Records," p. 231.

28. Robert K. Thomas, "Eastern Cherokee Acculturation" (unpublished typescript, 1958), p. 16.

29. Sharlotte Neely, "The Quaker Era of Cherokee Indian Education, 1880–1892," *Appalachian Journal* 2 (Summer 1975): 314–22.

30. Owl, "Eastern Band," p. 160.

31. Eastern Cherokee BIA superintendent's letter, November 2, 1919, Eastern Cherokee Agency Files, Bureau of Indian Affairs, Federal Regional Records Center, East Point, Ga., as quoted in Sharlotte Neely-Williams, "The Role of Formal Education among the Eastern Cherokee Indians, 1880–1971" (M.A. thesis, University of North Carolina, 1971), p. 34.

32. Neely-Williams, "Role of Formal Education," pp. 39–42.

33. Frank Churchill letter, May 20, 1908, as quoted in Litton, "Enrollment Records," p. 225.

34. John Gulick, *Cherokees at the Crossroads* (Chapel Hill: Institute for Research in Social Science at the University of North Carolina, 1960), p. 22; Eastern Band of Cherokee Indians, *Cherokee Progress and Challenge* (Cherokee, N.C.: Eastern Band of Cherokee Indians, 1972), p. 39.

35. Gulick, *Cherokees at the Crossroads*, pp. 18–19; Eastern Band, *Cherokee Progress*, p. 39.

36. BIA Superintendent Richard Butts letter, November 25, 1958, Eastern Cherokee Agency Files, Bureau of Indian Affairs, Federal Regional Records Center, East Point, Ga., as quoted in Neely-Williams, "Role of Formal Education," p. 48.

37. Eastern Band, *Cherokee Progress*, pp. 33–35.

38. Ibid., p. 47. The remainder of this article, except for specific quotations, is drawn from the author's direct observation of the Eastern Band of Cherokees during field work from 1971 to 1976.

39. *Cherokee One Feather*, Cherokee, N.C., October 4, 1972, p. 3.

40. Sharlotte Neely-Williams, "Epilogue: Cherokees at the Crossroads, 1973," in 2d ed. of Gulick, *Cherokees at the Crossroads*, pp. 177–94.

10

Those Left Behind: The Seminole Indians of Florida

HARRY A. KERSEY, JR.

The Seminole Indians of Florida were unique among the southeastern tribes in their protracted and bitter resistance to the intransigent removal policies of the federal government during the nineteenth century. In three Seminole wars, spread over half a century between 1818 and 1858, the Florida Indians developed hit-and-run guerrilla warfare to a fine art. Inexorably, they were forced to retreat ever southward from their north Florida homeland; nevertheless, they were masters of tactics and terrain in a theatre which rarely allowed the use of traditional military maneuvers. Only the massive infusion of regular army forces, augmented by volunteer units from several southern states as well as Creek Indian mercenaries, could bring the Seminoles to bay. The Second Seminole War (1835–42) alone cost the federal government over $40 million and 1,500 casualties. At the conclusion of the hostilities, all but a handful of the Seminole people were incarcerated in camps, then transported by steamers across the Gulf of Mexico, to be relocated on lands in the Indian Territory (present-day Oklahoma). Although an unknown number of Seminoles were still at large, the U.S. Army officially declared the wars at an end in 1858. The remnant group which remained in Florida faded away into the fastness of the Everglades.[1]

With the coming of the Civil War, those Seminoles who had eluded capture, numbering only a hundred or so at most, were no longer of concern to the military. Because of their isolation, the Indians in Florida played no role in the national conflict of the 1860s, thus escaping many problems which befell those Seminoles in the West who chose sides.[2] For the better part of two decades the Florida Seminoles were to live in virtual isolation from the outside world, sequestered in a watery wilderness at the tip of the peninsula. There they displayed great cultural flexibility which enabled them to make a successful transition to life in a harsh environment. They soon learned to substitute loose-fitting, lightweight clothing for the buckskins and leggings they had worn in northern Florida and Georgia. The open-sided "chickee," with its thatched roof and elevated platform to keep persons and goods dry, was a perfectly climate-adapted dwelling. Subsistence farming was carried on with crops of corn, beans, pumpkin, squash, and bananas raised on small hammock plots. The shallow-draft dugout canoe, fashioned from cypress logs, provided the Seminoles great mobility for hunting and traveling throughout the Everglades; some were even fitted with sails and used on Lake Okeechobee or in coastal waters as far as the Bahamas. For the most part, the Seminoles were an independent and economically self-sufficient group, with minimal dependence on trade well into the last quarter of the nineteenth century.[3]

Along with their physical adaptations to life in a new region, the Seminoles made similar adjustments in their social and political organization. Cut off from the main body of their people, they maintained much of the traditional culture, though adapted to meet the demands of their lifestyle. They divided into three bands based upon language: two spoke Miccosukee and the other Creek. Each had its own council of elders and chief, much as the Seminole towns had prior to the wars, though now the Seminoles lived in widely dispersed camps dotting the swamp and sawgrass country. If they were separated geographically and linguistically, the bands retained unity through a common religious observance of many southeastern Indians, known as the Green Corn Dance. The clan or sib system also cut across the bands and served as another unifying bond among the people. By the end of the last century, the Seminoles were concentrated in three south Florida locations. The East Coast band of Miccosukee speakers occupied camps from the New River southward to the vicinity of Miami. There were Miccosukee-speaking settlements throughout the Big Cypress Swamp on the western edge of the Everglades, with Creek-speaking camps around the northern shore of Lake Okeechobee in the vicinity of Cow Creek. In these locations the Indian people would face the challenge to their way of life, posed by the influx of traders, missionaries, land developers, and settlers who began to descend on Florida after the 1870s.[4]

As long as the small bands of Seminoles remained isolated in their Everglades enclaves there was no conflict with the non-Indian majority, most of whom resided in the upper portion of the state. In fact, during the Reconstruction Era the constitution of 1868 extended to the Seminoles the right of representation in each chamber of the state legislature.[5] These seats were never filled, possibly because the Indians were unaware of the provision, although it is unlikely that any Seminoles of that period would have participated in the white man's government. In any event, this entitlement was omitted from the Florida constitution of 1885.

When the first settlers began pushing south of the Lake Okeechobee–Caloosahatchee River line, however, a less kindly visage was turned toward the Indian. By 1869 the secretary of the interior made public letters calling for removal of all remaining Seminoles,[6] and during the 1870s the commissioner of Indian Affairs felt compelled to investigate further complaints against the Indians in Florida. It was not until 1879 that a young army officer, Lieutenant Richard H. Pratt, was sent to conduct a study of the condition of the Seminoles and see if they could be persuaded to leave peacefully; that approach failing, he was to render recommendations for a future course of action by the government vis-à-vis the Seminoles. Pratt's reward for this service was to be command of Carlisle Barracks in Pennsylvania, where he would establish an industrial school for Indian youths.[7]

Pratt enlisted the aid of F. A. Hendry of Fort Myers, one of the largest cattle owners in the state and a close friend of the Seminole people, to secure entrée to the Indian camps. During his limited visits to a few of the camps, Pratt developed the first sketches of Seminole life in Florida as it had developed since the wars. He also found the Indian leaders unyielding in their refusal even to talk about leaving their homeland; thus it was suggested that the government undertake to help them develop agricultural and industrial pursuits, as well as provide medical and basic educational assistance.[8] He held that any attempt to force the Indians to leave against their will would only lead to bloodshed and public outrage. The federal bureaucracy apparently accepted this assessment, for there were no further attempts to effect forced removal of the Seminoles.

Although the government in Washington was to bring no additional pressure on the Seminoles, neither did it immediately take steps to protect their rights or provide the services suggested by Pratt. This left the Seminoles to the vagaries of frontier justice at a time when Indians had few friends. According to Pratt, most of the disputes between settlers and Indians concerned livestock on the open range, with each claiming that the other had taken cattle or hogs illegally. Similar incidents in which there was potential for conflict were noted by Clay MacCauley, who conducted an intensive study of the Florida Seminoles for the Smithsonian Institution during the winter of 1880–81.[9] MacCauley's report was more comprehensive and assumedly more reliable, due to his prior experience with native peoples in Alaska. He managed to visit all of the Seminole camps and, with the aid of a bilingual guide, gained many insights into the organization of the bands. The census which MacCauley compiled revealed that only 208 Seminoles remained in Florida at the time of his visit. Like Pratt, he noted that only a few individuals of Negro lineage were living among the Seminoles; however, the two observers disagreed over the status which blacks were accorded by the Indians. The reports of Pratt and MacCauley were the first meaningful studies of early post-removal Seminole culture, and remain as useful benchmarks for historians and anthropologists who would explore the period more fully.

Prior to the arrival of the railroads in south Florida and the drainage projects which opened the land for farming, groves, and ranches, the population between Tampa and Key West was almost negligible. Mostly, the pioneers clustered near the sites of old forts from the Indian wars: Fort Dallas on the Miami River, Fort Myers on the Caloosahatchee, Fort Lauderdale at the New River inlet, and Fort Pierce on the Indian River. The interior was left to the Seminoles, and they came to the settlements only when they needed to obtain supplies, trading the products of their hunting and trapping at the stores, or selling foodstuffs to the citizenry. During the last quarter of the nineteenth century, the international fashion industry developed an insatiable demand for the items the Indians provided:

plumes for fine millinery, pelts for collars and coats, and alligator hides for luggage and men's accessories. The frontier trading posts prospered as the volume of these items increased and prices soared.

Over the years a symbiotic relationship developed between trader and Seminoles. The storekeepers on the Florida frontier had long depended on the Indian trade for a substantial portion of their business, due to a paucity of population, and now their trade items were increasingly profitable. The Seminoles, in turn, had looked to the trading posts as their only source for guns, ammunition, and other manufactured goods; with the growing value of their pelts, plumes, and hides, they were now able to acquire additional and better items from the stores. High on their list of priority purchases were firearms and traps, hardware of all types, canned foods, coffee, sugar, lard, and grits (from which they made the gruel "sofkee," a staple of the Seminole diet). The women were particularly fond of bright beads, bolts of cloth, appliqués, and hand-cranked sewing machines, with which they made the colorful costumes. On their buying sprees the Seminoles often sought ready-to-wear items, so it is not uncommon in old photos to see Indian men clad in traditional knee-length shirts and barefooted, yet sporting vests, watch chains with fobs, and a new derby! [10]

The relationships which developed between the Seminoles and traders transcended economic necessity. Indians frequently visited in their homes, and it was not uncommon for them to share in family meals, then camp near the house or even sleep on the premises. During these stays some Indians learned a bit of reading and writing, attended church services and other social gatherings, or honed their skills on the family sewing machine. [11] In return, the Seminoles taught their white friends such useful knowledge as herbal medicine, the preparation of native plants for food, and how to thatch a roof for shelter or pole a dugout canoe through sawgrass trails. At remote trading sites, such as W. H. Brown's "Boat Landing" deep in Big Cypress Swamp, white children learned to speak the Seminole language, hunted and trapped alongside their Indian contemporaries, and often established lifelong friendships. [12] The respect and understanding born of such interactions fostered empathy for the Seminoles among many influential Floridians.

Moreover, long before the Seminole hunting grounds played out,

Charlie Billie and family, in front of their Seminole chickee home, circa 1922.
Courtesy of Smithsonian Institution National Anthropological Archives, photo no. 1178-F.

various organizations had tried to transform these seminomadic
hunters and subsistence growers into farmers, all in the name of
"civilizing" or even "Christianizing" the race. In 1891 the Women's
National Indian Association of Philadelphia bought 400 acres of
land and established a mission station at Immokalee, some forty
miles southeast of Fort Myers. The mission was soon turned over to
the Episcopal church, and under the leadership of Bishop William C.
Gray a medical mission was conducted at various locations until
1914.[13] The U.S. Indian Service, not to be outdone, obtained 80 adjacent acres and opened a station with an agent's quarters and store,
schoolhouse, sawmill, and various outbuildings, thus belatedly following through on Lieutenant Pratt's suggestions of a decade earlier.
The government agent was also a medical man, Dr. J. E. Brecht,
who served the Seminoles until the station was abandoned in
1899.[14] Neither the Episcopal missionaries nor the government
agents of that period enjoyed great success in reaching the Seminoles or changing their lifestyle. There would be no significant
conversions of Seminoles to Christianity until Indian Baptist missionaries from Oklahoma began their work among the Florida tribe
in 1907.[15]

   The decade of the 1890s was the zenith of the trading period, and
the Indians could not foresee its ultimate demise. Moreover, as long
as the older Seminoles who had suffered the ordeal of the wars and
removal lived, there was great resistance to accepting any of the
white man's culture—especially if his largess was associated with
the national government. Occasionally an individual Indian would
risk tribal censure and seek to learn new ways, as was the case with
Billy Conapatchee who lived with the F. A. Hendry family for three
years and attended the Fort Myers Academy during the 1870s.[16]
Billy served as the interpreter for Clay MacCauley during his survey
for the Smithsonian, and was well thought of by the townspeople
of Fort Myers, where he was a frequent visitor.[17] Nevertheless, he
was a rarity, for Seminole children avoided both mission and government schools until reservations were established in Florida during the 1920s and '30s.[18] This same resistance made it difficult to
deliver health services or provide vocational skills training. Only as
the old leaders passed away and tribal prohibitions began to erode
in the face of changing social and economic conditions did the Semi-

noles embrace the more materialistic values of the outside world. Their gradual adoption of modern modes of dress and transportation and their entry into a wage economy were sure signs of Seminole acquiescence to a society which had engulfed them. Only a hard-core band of conservatives, living deep in the Everglades, avoided acculturation until well past mid-century and developed their separate tribal entity.

The end of Seminole economic independence could be foreseen before the turn of the century, when organized groups of white hunters began to work the Everglades. Their motivation was economic gain, and they ruthlessly overhunted the region; this was especially true of the "plumers," who could shoot an entire rookery in a single day, destroying sitting birds and chicks alike for the plumage, which was most brilliant during the hatching season. Such wanton destruction was anathema to the Indians, who rarely secured more game than was needed to meet their survival/cash needs. Likewise, alligator hunters, using high-speed boats and hunting at night with electric lights, took many more hides than their Seminole counterparts. White trappers also came to dominate the otter market, with their superior equipment and method of curing the pelts. Even so, the Seminoles still took their share of the goods to the trading posts until the trade lost its profitability. By the time of World War I, the market for pelts, plumes, and hides had all but collapsed, due to the loss of European demand and state and federal laws prohibiting traffic in bird plumes. When the markets recovered during the Roaring Twenties, much of the Everglades game had been lost due to the drastically lowered water table, resulting from state drainage projects inaugurated in 1907. In the competition for the remaining game, Seminoles were at a severe disadvantage against the organized white hunters. Ultimately, many of these Indians began guiding white sportsmen to supplement their meager income from pelts and hides. By 1931 it could be authoritatively reported to the United States Senate that "the Indian is a minority factor in the Florida fur trade."[19]

As the Seminoles found their hunting and trapping economy ruined by a combination of economic and political variables over which they had no control, they began to lose lands they had occupied for generations. Areas that had been inaccessible prior to the drainage projects now became valuable farm and grove property, and a growing Florida cattle industry required vast acreage. Railroads and development companies which owned large tracts of south Florida land began marketing it cheaply, and settlers responded from all parts of the nation. Towns grew up along the Florida East Coast Railway right-of-way as the line pushed southward and reached Miami by 1896. Without legal title to their camp sites, the Seminoles were systematically dispossessed and became wanderers, moving throughout the region. This problem became particularly acute during the Florida land boom of the 1920s, when even sub-marginal land demanded premium prices. Many Indian families were forced to live on the property of farmers for whom they worked, or to become squatters in territory where they had once roamed at will. In desperation, some Seminoles moved into shoddy tourist camps, where they earned a few dollars by selling handicrafts and staging "traditional ceremonies" for northern visitors. Clearly, unless steps were taken to settle the Seminole people on land of their own, they ran the risk of fragmentation and dissolution as a tribal entity.

Fortunately, before this juncture a number of prominent Florida citizens had banded together in societies to assist the Seminoles. The earliest was the Friends of the Florida Seminoles, organized at Kissimmee in 1899. Originally founded to secure the Indians' legal rights, the group was led by James M. Willson and his dynamic wife, Minnie Moore-Willson, whose book *The Seminoles of Florida* (1896) attracted national attention. The society had its greatest success in legislative lobbying, which led the state to set aside 100,000 acres for a Seminole reservation in 1917. The group also purchased a small tract of land, known as Polly Parker's Camp (named for a Seminole heroine who escaped federal troops during removal and returned to her homeland near the Kissimmee River), which was held in trust for the Cow Creek band of Seminoles. The second of these societies, the Seminole Indian Association, was founded at Fort Myers in 1913 through the effort of Dr. W. J. Godden, the last of the Episcopal medical missionaries in Big Cypress Swamp. This group devoted its efforts primarily to assisting the Seminole people in the southwest region of the state. Perhaps the best-known benefactor of the Seminoles was Mrs. Frank Stranahan of Fort Lauderdale, whose husband

By the late 1940s the Seminoles were beginning to produce crafts for the tourist trade. Annie Osceola is making Indian dolls on her sewing machine, while watching her infant under a chickee. *Courtesy of Smithsonian Institution National Anthropological Archives, photo no. 45,216-K.*

ran the local trading post. From 1899 until her death in 1971, Mrs. Stranahan worked unceasingly to improve the conditions of the Seminoles who lived near her home, and was influential in having the new Dania Reservation established there in the 1920s. Her major emphasis was education, having taught Indian children in her home and at their camps for a quarter century. She helped found the Friends of the Seminoles, which carries on her work to this day. Each of these private societies played an important role at a time when the state and federal governments provided minimal assistance to Indians in Florida.[20]

As early as the 1890s, the federal Indian Service, through agent Dr. J. E. Brecht, began to purchase parcels of land in southwest Florida to be held in trust for the Seminoles. In 1911 most of this acreage was combined as the Big Cypress Reservation, but was not occupied until the 1930s. During those depression years, various tracts of state and federal land near Lake Okeechobee were acquired for the Brighton Reservation, and a number of Creek-speaking Seminole families began moving there during the 1940s. On the lower East Coast, the small Dania Reservation, later renamed Hollywood Reservation, had been opened in 1926, primarily as a refuge for sick and indigent Seminoles, but both Miccosukee- and Creek-speaking families settled there as they were uprooted by an expanding and persistent population. A permanent U.S. Indian Service agent for the Seminoles was appointed in 1913;[21] this marked the beginning of a continuous agency operation, delivering various federal services to the reservation populations. Improvement in housing, education, roads, and utilities, as well as technical assistance in establishing cattle herds and other tribal programs, resulted from this government involvement in later years. With the Seminoles ensconced on their own land and government assurances of support and protection, it appeared that the Florida Indians had once again averted catastrophe at the hands of the dominant culture.

However, one more major threat to Seminole integrity as a people was yet to come. In the 1950s the federal government embarked upon a policy of "termination" of Indian tribes, an ill-conceived attempt to remove a number of Indian groups from affiliation with the Bureau of Indian Affairs. The result was disastrous for many tribes, such as the Menominee and the Klamath, which saw their lands dissipated, their economic gains wiped out, and their people reduced to the lowest rung on the socioeconomic ladder—in their own land. The Florida Seminoles were placed on the list of tribes to be terminated, even though no knowledgeable observer would have contended that they were anywhere near ready to protect their own interests. There was only a handful of high school graduates, and none had completed college. Government agents negotiated practically every tribal commitment with the surrounding communities, and no Seminoles had been trained to assume these functions. Only a small percentage of the people spoke English, or could hold outside employment if their lands were lost by government sale, as had occurred elsewhere.

Only the intervention of Mrs. Stranahan's society and other Florida civic leaders, with the support of the state's congressional delegation at Washington hearings, averted having the tribe terminated.[22] Instead, the Seminoles were given the opportunity formally to organize themselves as a legal entity under the terms of the Indian Reorganization Act of 1934.[23]

The so-called Indian New Deal was designed to slow the process of assimilation and give Indian peoples a greater voice in controlling their lives. It recognized the value of communal organization for social control and progress, and allowed tribes to reorganize their governments and run their own business affairs. There was also recognition of the need for expanded government services in education, health, and land development. Much of the Seminole land on the Big Cypress and Brighton reservations was acquired under the provisions of the act, and the beginning of their cattle enterprise stemmed from the same source.

In 1957 these people voted to establish the Seminole Tribe of Florida, Inc., and they received their charter as promised. The first elected leaders of the tribe were elders who had converted to Christianity and were Baptist lay preachers.[24]

Today, after more than twenty years of operation, the Seminole Tribe of Florida has made tremendous strides and is rapidly approaching the day when it can operate without the support of a resident government bureaucracy. An elected tribal council, led by a chairperson and representatives from each reservation, sets general policy. A similar, elected board of directors supervises all business enterprises which produce revenue (although the tribe is still heavily dependent on federal funds for day-to-day functioning). Each year, more young Seminoles complete high school or college, and most return to work in some level of tribal government. Great progress has been made in bringing business development and job opportunities to the outlying reservations, in upgrading education at the reservation school, and in having state reservation lands converted to federal trust status. The Seminole land-claim award has been set by the Indian Claims Commission,[25] and its settlement could ultimately enrich tribal coffers by several million dollars, which would underwrite further development programs. Seminole leadership is becoming politically sophisticated, and is well aware of challenges and opportunities in establishing tribal economic and social independence in an increasingly complex and interdependent south Florida community.

Still, there were conservative Indians who did not accept the course the majority of the tribe and its leaders had chosen. In 1961, several hundred of these dissidents organized as the Miccosukee Tribe of Indians, and a federal Indian agency was established at Homestead.[26] The Miccosukees claim a separate cultural origin from the Seminoles and are generally more traditional in their lifestyle; many families still live in chickee camps, wear tribal garb, and observe the old religious rites. Most of these Indians live along the Tamiami Trail between Miami and Naples or occupy camps deep in the Everglades. Much of their income is derived from tourist-oriented business, such as airboat excursions and the sale of handicrafts. The tribe currently controls a small strip of land along the northern boundary of Everglades National Park under a long-term lease, where it operates a restaurant and service station for travelers. Nearby are the tribal headquarters complex and an elementary day-school. In 1971 the Miccosukee Tribe achieved almost complete self-determination when it began contracting all services directly with the Bureau of Indian Affairs in Washington, and the Homestead agency was closed permanently. The people, through their tribal council, have the final voice in all decisions affecting tribal welfare.

Negotiations are currently under way with the state of Florida for control of 143,000 acres of Everglades land as a permanent preserve for the Miccosukee people. If this is achieved, it will bring the Miccosukees closer to parity with the Seminole Tribe. Although the two Florida tribes disagree on many policy issues, there are many more common bonds which unite them. Both groups lobby at the state and national level and are members of United Southeastern Tribes.

A century ago, two traders were doing business on the Miami River. The Seminoles sold them egret plumes for a quarter and alligator hides for 10 cents a running foot; in return, they received guns and sewing machines, beads and grits. There was mutual trust and respect between independent and resourceful individuals of both races who had met the challenge of the Florida frontier and survived. Perhaps once again it will be possible for the white and the red man to work together to solve those pressing problems of environment and economics which today confront both south Florida and the nation.

Notes

1. John K. Mahon, *History of the Second Seminole War, 1835–1842* (Gainesville: University of Florida Press, 1967), pp. 324–27; U.S. House, Congress, *Report of the Secretary of War*, Exec. Doc. 2, 35th Congress, 2d sess., 1858, pp. 241–42.

2. Edwin C. McReynolds, *The Seminoles* (Norman: University of Oklahoma Press, 1957), pp. 289–330; and Grant Foreman, *The Five Civilized Tribes* (Norman: University of Oklahoma Press, 1934; reprint 1970), p. 278.

3. Alan K. Craig and Christopher Peebles, "Ethnoecologic Change among the Seminoles, 1740–1840," in *Geoscience and Man* 5 (June 1974): 83–96; Wilfred T. Neill, "Sailing Vessels of the Florida Seminole," *Florida Anthropologist* 9 (December 1956):79–86.

4. William C. Sturtevant, "Creek into Seminole," in *North American Indians in Historical Perspective*, ed. E. B. Leacock and N. O. Lurie (New York: Random House, 1971), pp. 96–98; John R. Swanton, "Social Organization and Social Usages of the Indians of the Creek Confederacy," *Forty-second Annual Report of the Bureau of American Ethnology, 1924–25* (Washington: Government Printing Office, 1928), pp. 561–64; William C. Sturtevant, "The Medicine Bundles and Busks of the Florida Seminoles," *Florida Anthropologist* 7 (May 1954):31–70; Clay MacCauley, "The Seminole Indians of Florida," *Fifth Annual Report of the Bureau of American Ethnology, 1883–84* (Washington: Government Printing Office, 1887), pp.

507–8; Alexander Spoehr, "Camp, Clan and Kin among the Cow Creek Seminoles of Florida," *Field Museum of Natural History, Anthropological Series*, 33, no. 1 (1941): 1–27; and Alexander Spoehr, "The Florida Seminole Camp," *Field Museum of Natural History, Anthropological Series*, 33, no. 3 (1944): 115–50.

5. Florida Constitution, 1868, sec. 7, 8; *Florida Statutes Annotated*, 26:465; John Wallace, *Carpet-Bag Rule in Florida, the Inside Workings of the Reconstruction of Civil Government in Florida after the Close of the Civil War* (Jacksonville, 1888; facsimile edition, Gainesville: University of Florida Press, 1964), pp. 271–72.

6. U.S. Congress, Senate, *Report of the Secretary of the Interior*, Exec. Doc. 35, 40th Congress, 3d sess., 1869, p. 4.

7. William C. Sturtevant, "R. H. Pratt's Report on the Seminole in 1879," *Florida Anthropologist* 9 (March 1956): 1–5.

8. Ibid., pp. 14–15. Pratt's report originally appeared in 1888 as one of a number of documents concerning the Seminole Indians in Florida. U.S. Congress, Senate, *Message from the President of the United States Transmitting a Letter of the Secretary of the Interior Relative to Land upon Which to Locate Seminole Indians*, Exec. Doc. 139, 50th Congress, 1st sess., 1888, pp. 10–15.

9. MacCauley, "The Seminole Indians of Florida," pp. 475–531.

10. Mary Douhit Conrad, "Homesteading in Florida during the 1890's," *Tequesta* 17 (1957): 1–15; Alan K. Craig and David McJunkin, "Stranahan's: Last of the Seminole Trading Posts," *Florida Anthropologist* 24 (June 1971): 45–49; Charlton W. Tebeau, *The Story of the Chokoloskee Bay Country* (Miami: University of Miami Press, 1955), pp. 56–59; Emily Lagow Bell, *My Pioneer Days in Florida, 1876–1898* (Miami: St. Lucie County Historical Society, 1928), pp. 46–47; Harry A. Kersey Jr., *Pelts, Plumes and Hides: White Traders among the Seminole Indians, 1870–1930* (Gainesville: University Presses of Florida, 1975); Harry A. Kersey Jr., "Pelts, Plumes, and Hides: White Traders among the Seminole Indians, 1890–1930," *Florida Historical Quarterly* 52 (January 1973): 250–66; on clothing, see Hilda J. Davis, "The History of Seminole Clothing and Its Multi-Colored Designs," *American Anthropologist* 52 (1955): 974–80; "Interview with J. D. Girtman [leading Miami trader, 1890s–1915], December 10, 1938," Typescript by WPA Writers' Project, Florida Collection, University of South Florida Library, Tampa; Charlton W. Tebeau, *Florida's Last Frontier: The History of Collier County* (Miami: University of Miami Press, 1966), p. 196.

11. August Burghard, *Watchie-Esta/Hutrie (The Little White Mother)* (Fort Lauderdale: by the author, 1968); Harriet Randolph Parkhill, *Mission to the Seminoles* (Orlando: by the author, 1909), p. 15.

12. Tapes and transcripts of trader interviews at the University of Florida Oral History Archives. Among the best are W. Frank Brown, September

24, 1971; Rose Brown Kennon, September 24, 1971; Kirby Storter, September 15, 1971; Niels W. Jorgensen, February 8, 1973.

13. U.S. House of Representatives, *Report of the Commissioner of Indian Affairs*, Exec. Doc. 1, 53d Congress, 2d sess., 1893, p. 356; Women's National Indian Association, *The Indian's Friend* (March 1899), p. 8; Harry A. Kersey Jr. and Donald E. Pullease, "Bishop William Crane Gray's Mission to the Seminole Indians in Florida, 1893–1914," *Historical Magazine of the Protestant Episcopal Church* 42 (September 1973): 257–73.

14. U.S. House of Representatives, *Report of the Commissioner of Indian Affairs*, Exec. Doc. 5, 55th Congress, 2d sess., 1897, p. 125; Charles H. Coe, *Red Patriots: The Story of the Seminoles* (Cincinnati, 1898; facsimile edition, Gainesville: University of Florida Press, 1974), pp. 228–37.

15. First Seminole Indian Baptist Church, *Souvenir Brochure, Dedicatory Service*, May 29, 1949; James O. Buswell, "Florida Seminole Religious Ritual: Resistance and Change" (Ph.D. dissertation, St. Louis University, 1972).

16. MacCauley, "The Seminole Indians of Florida," pp. 492–94. Sturtevant, "R. H. Pratt's Report," p. 17; Harry A. Kersey Jr., "Educating the Seminole Indians of Florida, 1879–1970," *Florida Historical Quarterly* 49 (July 1970): 19–21.

17. MacCauley. "The Seminole Indians of Florida," p. 492.

18. Kersey Jr., "Educating the Seminole Indians," pp. 16–28.

19. Charles M. Brookfield and Oliver Griswold, *They All Called It Tropical* (Miami: Data Press, 1949), pp. 60–72, Tebeau, *Story of the Chokoloskee Bay Country*, pp. 44–47; James C. Nicholas, "The Economics of the Indian Trade in Florida," typescript, Department of Economics, Florida Atlantic University, Boca Raton, 1971; U.S. Congress, Senate, *Seminole Indians in Florida*, Senate Doc. 42, 63d Congress, 1st sess., 1913, p. 36.

20. Harry A. Kersey Jr., "The 'Friends of the Florida Seminoles' Society, 1899–1926," *Tequesta* 34 (1974): 3–20; Florida, *General Acts and Resolutions Adopted by the Legislature of Florida at Its Sixteenth Regular Session (April 3 to June 1, 1917) under the Constitution of A.D. 1885*, ch. 7310 52 (Tallahassee, 1917), p. 131; W. Stanley Hanson to Dr. Hamilton Holt, September 3, 1933, Seminole Indian Association File, Florida Collection, University of South Florida Library, Tampa; Burghard, *Watchie-Esta/Hutrie (The Little White Mother)*, pp. 26–30. The Friends of the Seminoles were chartered as a Florida corporation on November 28, 1949 (*Corporation Book 13, Broward County*, pp. 616–22), office of the Comptroller, Broward County, Fla.

21. U.S. Senate, *Seminole Indians in Florida*, pp. 65–66.

22. S. Lyman Tyler, *A History of Indian Policy* (Washington: Government Printing Office, 1973), pp. 161–89; U.S. Congress, *Joint Hearings before the Sub-Committees of the Committees on the Interior and Insular Affairs. Termination of Federal Supervision over Certain Tribes of Indians,*

Part 8, Seminole Indians of Florida, S. 2747 and H.R. 7321, 83d Congress, 2d sess., 1954.

23. Sar S. Levitan and Barbara Hetrick, *Big Brother's Indian Programs—with Reservations* (New York: McGraw-Hill, 1971), pp. 16–17, 100–101; Tyler, *A History of Indian Policy,* pp. 125–36.

24. U.S. Department of Interior, Office of Indian Affairs, *Constitution and Bylaws of the Seminole Tribe of Florida, Ratified August 21, 1957* (Washington: Government Printing Office, 1958); *Corporate Charter of the Seminole Tribe of Florida* (Washington: Government Printing Office, 1958); R. T. King, "Clan Affiliation and Leadership among the Twentieth-Century Florida Indians," *Florida Historical Quarterly* 55 (October 1976):138–52.

25. Harry A. Kersey Jr., "The Economic Prospects of Florida's Seminole Indians," *Florida Planning and Development Journal* 20 (December 1969): 1–2, 8; James C. Nicolas and Harry A. Kersey Jr., *Recommendations Concerning Employment, Income, and Educational Opportunities for the Seminole and Miccosukee Tribes in Florida (1971),* National Technical Information Service, PB 231943-AS; U.S. Indian Claims Commission, *Docket No. 73, The Seminole Indians of the State of Florida v. The United States,* and *Docket No. 151, The Seminole Nation of the State of Oklahoma v. The United States, May 8, 1964,* 13 IND. CL. COMM. 326.

26. U.S. Department of Interior, Office of Indian Affairs, *Constitution of the Miccosukee Tribe of Indians of Florida, Ratified December 17, 1961,* with amendments adopted in 1964 and 1965 (Washington: Government Printing Office, 1965); Sturtevant, "Creek into Seminole," pp. 117–22; Harry A. Kersey Jr., *A Brief History of the Seminole and Miccosukee Tribes, 1959–1970* (1971), National Technical Information Service, PB 233052-AS.

Conclusion

11

Patterns in the History of the Remaining Southeastern Indians, 1840–1975

WALTER L. WILLIAMS

This collection has been designed to bring together a survey of the history of the various groups of Native Americans who remained in the South after the Removal Era of the 1830s. Each author emphasizes the need for more research on the history of his group. Other southern Indian peoples have not even had *any* historical research devoted to their recent past. For example, chapters on the Koasati (or Coushatta) of Louisiana and eastern Texas; the Waccamau-Siouan, Haliwa, and Coharie of eastern North Carolina; small groups of Shawnee-Cherokee descendants in eastern Kentucky and Tennessee; and others could not be included in this collection simply because their histories have remained largely uninvestigated.

That remnant native peoples have disappeared from the white-written histories of the South is perhaps an indication of perceptions of Indians in general. Indians have become so thoroughly associated with the frontier, in historical writing, that they are assumed to have simply disappeared once the frontier era ended. Thus southern Indians were in the center of the great drama of expansion, but once their lands were occupied by whites, they were no longer of concern for scholars, even if they still live in the South.

This ignorance of Indian history of the last century and a third may indicate another perception of Indians: the inability of many whites to conceptualize historic change among Indians. The descendants of aboriginal Americans are somehow seen as outside the historical processes of change, with their Indian cultures and lifestyles being stereotyped as static. For example, many tourists come away from Oconaluftee Village, an eighteenth-century reconstruction in Cherokee, North Carolina, thinking that modern-day Cherokees live like that. No one would tour reconstructed colonial Williamsburg and equate its lifestyle with modern Virginians.

The difference is an inability to recognize that Indians have a history and go through historic changes just like other people. If Indians are seen as changed, according to this stereotype, they cease to be "real Indians." Such a double standard is based upon an unrealistic concept of cultural identity in defining Indians, and has placed a burden upon modern descendants of the first Americans to prove that they are in fact *real* Indians. As has been emphasized in the foregoing chapters, the necessity of continually proving their Indianness has been a major theme of recent southern Indian history.

This need to insist on recognition as Indians has been so important because of whites' tendency to lump all non-whites in the South into a "colored" category. Ironically, such a policy, begun in the early nineteenth century, was a major change in southern thought. The traditional pattern had been "divide and rule"—by separating Indians and Afro-Americans as much as possible in order to prevent their coalition against the whites. But after the main Indian population was removed from an area, it became much easier to force remnant Indians to merge with the black community so that they could be legislated into the subordinate caste. There could be no way to break out of the non-white status, if the biracial society were to survive.

This pressure to merge with blacks was felt to some extent by all southern Indians, but there was great variation. Partly this was due to the size of the black population in an area. The relatively small number of Afro-Americans living in the Appalachian Mountains near the Cherokees, or near the Florida Seminoles, has meant that these Indian groups have avoided some of the most disruptive attempts by whites to classify them as "colored." Probably the biggest factors that account for their acceptance as Indians, however, are their treaties with the government and the amount of aboriginal culture they have preserved.

Such varied responses to southern Indians of the early nineteenth century are indications of the diversity of these native peoples.

The isolation of nineteenth-century southeastern Indians is typified by this Cherokee home in 1888, photographed by James Mooney. *Courtesy of Smithsonian Institution National Anthropological Archives, photo no. 1000-B.*

The most obvious difference was a legal one, depending on their recognition in treaties with the United States government. From the time of its founding, the national government had been directly involved with the large Indian nations remaining in the South. Treaties had been made with these nations, in order to obtain trade privileges, assistance in war, land cessions, or removal. Even if the remnant groups in the East (like the Cherokees, Choctaws, Creeks, and Seminoles) did not have formal relationships with the federal government, connections with the recognized removed elements in Oklahoma provided a degree of acceptance. Even those Indians with legal relations to state governments, like the Pamunkeys and Mattaponies of Virginia and the Catawbas of South Carolina, received some acceptance, based upon their legal status on state reservations.

In contrast, other Indians in the South of the early nineteenth century were unrecognized. Their lack of recognition by the United States government was because of their history during the colonial era. Most of these unrecognized Indians were in areas of early white settlement, like the Atlantic coastal area and French Louisiana. Their populations were most severely hit by the European diseases, and they had been further depopulated in the colonial era by enslavement, wars, and outmigration. Even if they managed to obtain treaties with the colonial governments, to preserve a small parcel of their homeland, such treaties were usually ignored by the new United States government. Because their lands had been passed by in the settlement of the frontier, their small numbers on small tracts of land were of no concern to the federal government. So there was no pressure to recognize them formally and deal with them by treaties.

Besides differences in the response by whites, southern Indians were diverse because of their varied lifestyles. Here again their historical past determined their degree of acculturation to Old World society. Indians who had been in close contact with whites for the longest time, again on the Atlantic Coast and in Louisiana, had gradually absorbed elements of the new way of life. Of course, this influence was not a one-way process, and all three racial groups shared an emerging southern folk culture which included elements of European, African, and Native American lifestyles. Some Indian groups, like the Lumbees, did not have a specific tribal heritage, and their lifestyle was very similar to that of their white and black neighbors.

The remnants of the removed interior nations, in contrast, had not had as long or as intensive cultural contacts with the whites, and they were less acculturated. It is ironic that the most acculturated elements of the interior nations cooperated with the removal policy. Those who were least acculturated, who had no faith in the white government, were the ones most likely to resist removal and escape to the forests, mountains, or swamps. Thus the claim that removal was effected in order to rid the South of "uncivilized savages" simply did not accord with the facts.

Still, the vast majority of members of the large nations *did* have to remove, and many unacculturated Indians also ended up in Oklahoma. Moreover, some of these unacculturated people advocated moving west to get away from whites and thereby preserve more of their culture. A few sympathetic whites agreed, and acquiesced in removal plans because they felt that Native peoples could not survive against land pressures in the East. Nevertheless, it is hard to accept the argument of some historians that the main motivation for removal was to protect Native Americans. The Indians themselves realized the exploitative nature of removal, which is why so many of them resisted even after they had been hopelessly overpowered by the United States.

The removals left behind in the Southeast two very different groups of southern Indians: those who were most acculturated, sometimes even to the point of having lost their tribal heritage or aboriginal culture, and those who were least acculturated. Within this pattern of legal and cultural diversity, we are left with two questions. 1. Why were some groups removed, while others were not? 2. Why were certain remnants of the removed nations allowed to remain? In answering these questions, we can shed considerable light on the reasons for removal itself.

The main distinction between removed and non-removed people was the amount of land that remained in the hands of each tribe. By 1830, white settlement had advanced west of the Mississippi, so that southern Indian lands were surrounded by whites. If an Indian nation occupied a large territory of land that was desired by whites, that nation was subjected to pressures for removal. If, however, the Indian remnant was small, and occupied small amounts of economically marginal land, they were not subjected to removal.

It is this pattern of land control that was most important in determining removal, not the degree of acculturation. This thesis is verified by the fact that non-acculturated individuals were not disturbed in the Southeast, if they fled to lands of marginal value in which whites were not interested. If Indians melted into the mountains or swamplands, it did not much matter to whites, who were primarily interested in more valuable lands.

This does not mean, however, that marginal land status in 1840 would guarantee continued preservation of such land. In later years, as the southern population and economy expanded, previously ignored lands became of economic interest to whites. Locally, the frontier pattern continued to operate in terms of more land loss for Native peoples. Moreover, through every era racism against Indians continued strong, and it was used to justify further encroachment on non-white lands. In some cases the relationship of land hunger and racism assumes a kind of "chicken and egg" causation, in which it is difficult to distinguish which motive was stronger among whites.

After the removal, all remaining Indians were officially unrecognized, except for a few state reservations in Virginia and South Carolina. Even these states, however, moved to terminate their recognition of remnant Indians. Thus the dominant theme of the post-removal era was isolation from white society. While the plantation economy became consolidated, and while sectional tensions flared in the South, the remnant Indians remained demographically isolated. The white South essentially ignored them, except where their small remaining lands were desired for settlement. In those cases, state and local governments consistently tried to deny any "Indianness" in the remnant peoples, in order to force them into the subordinate "colored" caste. By such means they could be reduced in socioeconomic status and more easily be dispossessed of their remaining lands. The only response the Indians could make was to create more social distance between themselves and blacks. As intermarriage with non-Indians decreased, the Indian communities became more and more isolated.

This isolation was not a total protection for the Indians, because

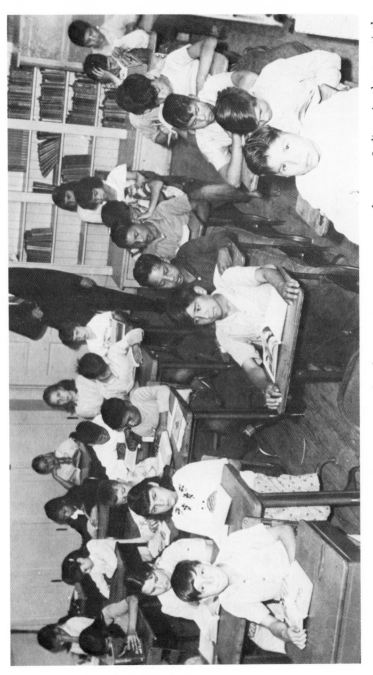

The role of education as an acculturative agent has been important among southeastern Indians in the twentieth century. This class of Eastern Cherokee students, in 1950, was in a Bureau of Indian Affairs school. Note the ethnic diversity of the students. *Courtesy of National Archives, Bureau of Indian Affairs photo no. 75-N-Cherokee-26.*

they could be subjected to further land losses. If they held their lands by individual ownership, whites could use the threat of violence to pressure them to sell or lease their lands, or could use the white-dominated court system to confiscate lands in payment of real or fraudulent debts. If the Indians held their lands communally, then—because they were not legally recognized as having title to the land by the government—they could be easily dispossessed by white settlers. Some states passed laws against landownership by illegitimate heirs or those who had not paid land taxes. Since the Indians did not participate in the white legal system, such stipulations could be disastrous for them. Such methods indicate that treaties and removals were not the only means of dispossessing Indians from their lands.

For white and black Southerners, the 1860s were a major turning point. But because of their isolation, most southern Indians were relatively unaffected by the ravages of civil war. A few Cherokees, Choctaws, Creeks, and Catawbas were persuaded to join the Confederate army, but more research needs to be done to determine their motivation for participating. However, their participation in the war was minimal, compared to that of the removed nations in the western Indian Territory. The main southeastern group that was affected by the war was the Lumbees, who revolted against Confederate attempts to force them to do military labor with black slaves. Such a move was further indication of the attempt to reduce their status to the level of blacks.

By and large, the era of Reconstruction after the Civil War did not greatly affect southern Indians. Even though the new Republican state governments had made a commitment to improve the status of black people in the South, no such comparative policy emerged relating to Indians. This whole era, with its overtones of racial controversy, deserves much further scholarly investigation concerning white–Indian and black–Indian ethnic relations.

Within this pattern of isolation from white society in the mid- to late nineteenth century, the various Indian peoples kept to themselves and developed their own subsistence economy: growing or gathering their own food, supplemented by fishing, hunting, and other activities adapted to their marginal and agriculturally poor environment. Their few outside needs were supplied by trading with whites, especially among groups like the Seminoles, with their trade of pelts, plumes, and hides. In this situation, they remained relatively undisturbed by whites, and may have developed a fairly stable lifestyle. Up to this point, their way of life had not drastically changed from the pre-removal period: those who were acculturated continued to follow their southern folk culture, like that of other Southerners, while the unacculturated Indians remained committed to their aboriginal ways.

This isolation was not to last, as the non-Indian population continued to expand into lands previously considered undesirable. This process occurred at different times, during the late nineteenth and early twentieth centuries, for the various Southern Indian peoples; but it affected all of them. As agriculture and a new timber industry expanded in the South, more Indian-occupied lands were lost. Without legal recognition or clear title to the land, the same processes of land dispossession continued. More and more Indians became sharecroppers for whites (on lands they had previously owned) or were thrown off their lands altogether.

With no land upon which to base a subsistence agriculture, Indians were forced into wage labor within the white cash economy. Even among groups like the Cherokees, who managed to gain federal recognition and hold their lands, increasing population on a nonexpanding land base meant a decline in living standards. In general, the transformation to the cash economy marked a further impoverishment for southern Indians.

For the first time, the remnant groups of Indians began to operate as communities within the white-dominated society. It is at this point, whether in the 1870s for the Choctaws or the 1920s for the Seminoles, that we find the most dramatic acculturation rates. Indians suddenly expressed great interest in Christianity and education, with the church and the school becoming the foci for Indian communities. The struggle to obtain their own schools sometimes continued until the mid-twentieth century, because whites would often not admit them to white schools and insist that they attend black schools. Indian resistance to this pressure sometimes meant that they had no school, and grew up illiterate. A separate Indian school and church, therefore, became a source of pride for the local Indian community. Not only did these institutions provide a focus for community organizing, they represented recognition (at least in the local area) of Indian distinctiveness.

Forced to participate in the white-dominated economic structure yet denied access to white social institutions, Indians took advantage of the only institutions that could receive even minimal white recognition and support but were left to Indian control. Black Southerners also were developing such institutions, mainly centered around the church and the school. Yet such parallel tendencies did not result in the merger of Indian and black communities. These two non-white groups remained separate, even though they felt many of the same discriminations, because of Indian attempts to prevent their being further reduced in status, to the level of Afro-Americans. Indians hoped for at least a halfway social status between blacks and whites, and such inclinations allowed whites to formulate a new divide-and-rule policy. By keeping Indians and blacks from uniting, the white minority could more easily retain its power. As long as the black community remained powerless and subordinated, there were no incentives for Indians to identify with them. So it is not surprising that intermarriage and social interchange with Afro-Americans was discouraged by southern Indians. Indians who married blacks were generally ostracized by the former, and merged into the black community.

Meanwhile, there was more intermarriage with whites. Through this process of outgroup marriage, certain individuals in each generation were "spun off." Usually such Indian-white families who wanted to merge into the white community would move to another area, where there was no Indian community. But whites who intermarried with Indians and remained in their home area would usually merge into the Indian community. Thus, even though each generation was losing and gaining individuals, and some offspring were defined as "mixed bloods," a strong Indian ethnic identity continued.

The Norwegian anthropologist Fredrik Barth, in his 1969 book *Ethnic Groups and Boundaries*, identified similar trends in non-assimilating ethnic groups around the world. Barth's predictions about ethnic persistence hold true for southern Indians, whose lifestyles were becoming more and more like that of other Southerners, despite their continuing identification as Indians. Some southern

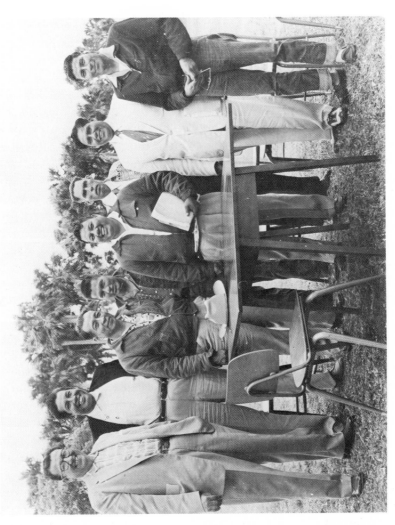

In the twentieth century more southeastern Indian groups became federally recognized and set up official tribal councils. This 1957 photograph shows the Seminole representatives who drafted a tribal constitution, with the advice of the local Bureau of Indian Affairs official (on the left). *Courtesy of Smithsonian Institution National Anthropological Archives, photo no. 45,217-J.*

Indian groups continued to emphasize their distinctiveness through physical appearance and by revitalization of Indian cultural traits (language, music, mythology, clothing style, or crafts), but other groups had lost these traits through intermarriage and acculturation. In that case, Indian identity was retained by kinship relationships and by a sense of a shared past. Often this tradition focused on a past hero, like Henry Berry Lowry of the Lumbees. But whatever the means, the group itself remained homogeneous.

An exception to these trends of the last century is the Cherokees. Unlike any other southeastern group, the Cherokees became a heterogeneous people by the early twentieth century. Such a trend is a result of their particular history, in that they were the only southeastern Indian group that was recognized by the United States government before 1900. The late nineteenth century was marked by a federal government policy known as "allotment," in which the government tried to divide reservations into individually owned land tracts. Allotment was carried out among many western Indians, and there were rumors that the Cherokee reservation would also be divided among all enrolled members of the tribe. Land-hungry whites, even if they had no intention of identifying with Cherokee culture, bribed their way onto the tribal roll so that they might stand a chance of getting part of this land. Even though this allotment never took place, Indian-white intermarriage during this era created a different class of "white Indians" among the Cherokees, which broke the homogeneous nature of the tribe. Consequently, the Cherokees have experienced a factionalism that is common among Indians of the West but unique to southern Indians.

Southern Indians who have been recognized by the federal government in the twentieth century (including the Seminoles, Choctaws, Catawbas, and Chitimaches) have also experienced the problems of forced acculturation which marked past policies of the Bureau of Indian Affairs. Even such problems, however, have not been as harmful as no recognition at all. Accordingly, for nonrecognized groups, a central theme of their history in the twentieth century, in the face of continued land loss and impoverishment, has been to get recognition of their Indian status.

The twentieth century has seen a steady increase in acculturation, with intermarriage continuing to play a role, but the most significant acculturative aspect since 1940 has been in terms of employment. As the American economy continued to grow since World War II and as transportation became more readily available, more and more southern Indians have migrated from their local communities to take jobs elsewhere. The armed forces and industry have had major impact in the geographical mobility of these once isolated peoples. Like rural Southerners of other ethnic groups, Indians have migrated to large cities to join the urban labor force. Faced with poverty and continued discrimination at home, it is not surprising that many Indians—especially those with light skin who could merge into a white community—migrated from their local area. Many of these migrants have lost an Indian identity, but some retain family and ethnic connections by visiting relatives in their native communities. Acculturative trends have also operated on Indians who have remained in their homeland. Connections with kinsmen who have migrated from the area but return for visits have had an effect.

The automobile has had a dramatic impact upon various Indian communities because of the growth of tourism. On the Cherokee and Seminole reservations, in particular, much of their economy has developed around tourist interests. Modern communications, especially television, have made the Indian communities less isolated. Also, increasing education has continued its acculturative role.

Yet with all of these trends toward greater acculturation, and with the loss of individuals through outmigration, the ethnic identity of southern Indians seems not to be in danger. Better education, even though it is acculturative, has also produced an increasing awareness of the methods by which the community can be organized and can act for its interests. This trend has promoted group identity, especially in relation to government programs. Federally recognized tribes organized the United Southeastern Tribes and nonrecognized groups joined the Coalition of Eastern Native Americans. Legal settlements for land losses have also promoted group identity.

Black activism has also had an effect on southern Indians, not only by the example of the black civil rights movement but also by the favorable impact civil rights legislation has had for Indians. As the system of racial discrimination began to break down, increased political power among Afro-Americans has caused some southern

Indians to consider allying with them for the mutual benefit of both groups. School integration, in the short run, was disruptive of Indian communities because the Indian school was an institution central to the group, but in the long run it provided better educational opportunities and promoted other forms of community organizing.

As Indians became more accepted and more popular in the mass culture of the 1960s, southern Indians began to witness a new trend: some whites who had Indian ancestry began to claim an Indian identity. Such a trend is probably harmless, and may be beneficial by attracting more attention to the problems Indians face in modern America, but the insistence of such people that they be accepted by Indians has sometimes produced discord. Especially with the Cherokees, who remember the claims of an earlier group of whites to Indian status in order to get their land, there is understandable distrust of outsiders who expect acceptance as part of the tribe. In a time when federally recognized Indians do not always accept non-recognized Indian groups (who have a long history of Indian identity), such a response is not surprising.

In a most dramatic way, the end of the isolation of southern Indians from the larger society has increased their Indian identity, simply because they are becoming more involved with Indian tribes outside the South. Pan-Indianism, as it arose by the late 1960s, has had a strong effect in reinforcing their ethnic awareness. Even though each isolated Native American group in the South had always used the term Indian in describing itself, this term defined only a single tribal identity. Pan-Indianism provided a means for preserving their identity by attaching themselves to the larger Indian movement, and transformed their ethnic status by giving acceptance and contacts with Indian peoples from all over America. Though the attempt to gain treaty payment funds and federal assistance is part of this resurgence, it must be explained primarily within their historic context of the struggle for preservation of ethnic identity.

Modern-day Indians in the South do not have the same lifestyles as their aboriginal ancestors, and many of them have been acculturated to the white way of life. But neither are southern Indians a "vanishing race." The more than 75,000 Indians in the South, who are generally increasing in ethnic awareness, can no longer be ignored.

Historical studies of southern Indians, such as this collection, are valuable to Indian peoples themselves, as part of their ethnic identity. The biggest threat to their ethnic survival, now as in the past, is the loss of their land base. As long as they can keep a group together on a particular area of land, no matter how small, their ethnic status seems secure. Of course, there is more to being Indian than holding common title to a piece of land, but with no geographical basis at all, small groups tend to disperse and lose their sense of community. Land loss continues to be a threat to southern Indians, particularly those groups without federal recognition. It is notable that Indian land dispossession has continued in the twentieth century; it was not limited to the distant frontier past.

Nevertheless, among several groups which have managed to secure their lands, a new sense of optimism about their ethnic survival has emerged. This recognition extends beyond Indians, to other Southerners as well. The South, an area of three cultural and racial groups, cannot really be understood without a knowledge of the Indian experience in the region. Southern Indians are not on a "road to disappearance," and it is time to ask if they ever were.

Bibliographic
Essay

Bibliographic Essay

WALTER L. WILLIAMS AND THOMAS R. FRENCH

Southeastern Indians before 1840

There has been quite a bit more scholarly study of Native Americans in the southeastern United States before 1840 than there has been of the remnant groups which managed to remain in the area after the removals. This has been true even of the prehistoric periods. The findings by archeologists about southeastern Indians of the pre-European epochs are summarized in James Griffen, ed., *Archeology of Eastern United States* (Chicago: University of Chicago Press, 1952); Jesse Jennings, *Prehistory of North America* (New York: McGraw-Hill, 1974); and Gordon Willey, *An Introduction to American Archaeology: North and Middle America* (Englewood Cliffs, N.J.: Prentice-Hall, 1966), vol. 1. An excellent chapter on the Mississippian Natchez Indians, before they felt the impact of Europeans, is contained in Wendell Oswalt, *This Land Was Theirs: A Study of the North American Indian* (3d ed.; New York: Wiley, 1978). Many prehistoric artifacts are pictured in Emma Fundaburk and Mary Foreman, *Sun Circles and Human Hands: The Southeastern Indians' Art and Industry* (Luverne, Ala.: Emma Fundaburk, 1957).

An encyclopedic study of aboriginal society at the time of European contact is John R. Swanton, *The Indians of the Southeastern United States*, Bureau of American Ethnology Bulletin 137 (Washington: Smithsonian Institution, 1946), but it has recently been partly superseded by an excellent synthesis written by Charles Hudson, *The Southeastern Indians* (Knoxville: University of Tennessee Press, 1976). Although Hudson covers all time periods from the Paleo-Indian to the present, his major focus is on the ideology, world view, and social organization of southeastern Indians in the seventeenth and eighteenth centuries.

The effects of European contact on Native Americans after 1492 were revolutionary. The biological impact, especially of food crops, domesticated animals, and diseases, is well covered in Alfred Crosby, *The Columbian Exchange: Biological and Cultural Consequences of 1492* (Westport, Conn.: Greenwood Press, 1972). Not only does this book incorporate much recent research, but it has an outstanding bibliography. Other important works are Eleanor Leacock and Nancy Lurie, eds., *North American Indians in Historical Perspective* (New York: Random House, 1971); Wilbur Jacobs, *Dispossessing the American Indian: Indians and Whites on the Colonial Frontier* (New York: Scribner's, 1972); Verner Crane, *The Southern Frontier, 1670–1732* (Ann Arbor: University of Michigan Press, 1929); Hale Smith, *The European and the Indian*, Florida Anthropological Society Publications, no. 4 (Gainesville: University of Florida Press, 1956); Alvin Josephy, *The Indian Heritage of America* (New York: Knopf, 1968); Nancy Lurie, "Indian Cultural Adjustment to European Civilization," in *Seventeenth Century America*, ed. James Smith (Chapel Hill: University of North Carolina Press, 1959); William Willis, "Divide and Rule: Red, White, and Black in the Southeast," *Journal of Negro History* 48 (1963): 157–76; and James O'Donnell, *Southern Indians in the American Revolution* (Knoxville: University of Tennessee Press, 1973).

The crucial role of white missionaries in changing southeastern Indian societies by the early nineteenth century is explained in Robert Berkhofer, *Salvation and the Savage: An Analysis of Protestant Missions and American Indian Response, 1787–1862* (Lexington: University of Kentucky Press, 1965). The impact of the acculturated faction of the Cherokees, along with government policies, is emphasized in Henry Malone, *Cherokees of the Old South* (Athens: University of Georgia Press, 1956). Other studies of early nineteenth-century United States policies, as they applied to Native Americans in the South, are Reginald Horsman, *Expansion and American Indian Policy, 1783–1812* (East Lansing: Michigan State University Press, 1967); Francis Paul Prucha, *American Indian Policy in the Formative Years* (Cambridge, Mass.: Harvard University Press, 1962); and Bernard Sheehan, *Seeds of Extinction: Jeffer-*

sonian Philanthropy and the American Indian (Chapel Hill: University of North Carolina Press, 1973).

There has been more historical research devoted to the 1830s removals than to any other era of southern Indian history. The removal story is well told in Grant Foreman, *Indian Removal* (Norman: University of Oklahoma Press, 1953); George Harmon, *Sixty Years of Indian Affairs* (Chapel Hill: University of North Carolina Press, 1941); R. S. Cotterill, *The Southern Indians* (Norman: University of Oklahoma Press, 1954); Annie Abel, "The History of Events Resulting in Indian Consolidation West of the Mississippi River," *Annual Report of the American Historical Association* 1 (1906):235–450; and Mary Young, "Indian Removal and Land Allotment: The Civilized Tribes and Jacksonian Justice," *American Historical Review* 64 (1958):31–45. Among the best studies of particular groups are Angie Debo, *The Road to Disappearance* (Norman: University of Oklahoma Press, 1941), on the Creek Indians; Arthur DeRosier, *The Removal of the Choctaw Indians* (Knoxville: University of Tennessee Press, 1970); Arrell Gibson, *The Chickasaws* (Norman: University of Oklahoma Press, 1971); Malone, *Cherokees of the Old South*; Edwin McReynolds, *The Seminoles* (Norman: University of Oklahoma Press, 1957); John Mahon, *History of the Second Seminole War* (Gainesville: University of Florida Press, 1967); and William Sturtevant, "Creek into Seminole," in Leacock and Lurie, eds., *North American Indians*, pp. 92–128.

For an understanding of general United States Indian policy since the 1840s, there are numerous survey texts. Among the most important are D'Arcy McNickle, *Native American Tribalism* (New York: Oxford University Press, 1973); William Hagan, *American Indians* (Chicago: University of Chicago Press, 1961); Wilcomb Washburn, *The Indian in America* (New York: Harper and Row, 1975); Wilcomb Washburn, *Red Man's Land, White Man's Law* (New York: Scribner's, 1971); Wilcomb Washburn, *The Assault on Indian Tribalism: The General Allotment Law (Dawes Act) of 1887* (Philadelphia: Lippincott, 1975); Oswalt, *This Land Was Theirs*; Leacock and Lurie, *North American Indians*; Stuart Levine and Nancy Lurie, eds., *The American Indian Today* (Deland, Fla.: Everett-Edwards, 1968); and Vine Deloria, *Custer Died for Your Sins* (New York: Avon, 1969). Recently, the American Indian Policy Review Commission, established by the United States Congress, has compiled a comprehensive summary of current United States Indian political status, with recommendations for reform, in the form of twelve *Task Force Reports* (Washington: Government Printing Office, 1977). Task Force Ten focuses on unrecognized tribes and contains many data on Indians in North Carolina and Louisiana.

General Sources about Indians Remaining in the Southeast since 1840

Primary source collections of Indian reflections about their past are rare, but for the twentieth century an outstanding collection is being compiled by the Center for the Study of Southeastern Indians, Gainesville, Florida. Over 500 transcribed interviews, housed at the Florida State Museum, have been collected among Seminoles, Lumbees, Creeks, Catawbas, Choctaws, and Cherokees.

Given the scarcity of Native-authored accounts, much more research needs to be done in searching documents for writings of individual Indians who were literate, for recorded speeches given by Native leaders, and for interviews of Indians by white authors. Certainly the best accounts written by whites which provide source material for Indian views of their past are the writings and field notes of anthropologists. Beginning in the late nineteenth century, professional ethnographers have gathered many data on Native peoples of the South, and their papers have become a valuable historical source. Major collections exist for several southern Indian groups in the National Anthropological Archives, Smithsonian Institution, Washington, D.C. (James Mooney Papers, John Swanton Papers, Photograph Collection); in the American Philosophical Society Library, Philadelphia (Frank Speck Papers, John Gillespie Papers); in the library of the Field Museum of Natural History, Chicago (Alexander Spoehr Papers); and in the Newberry Library, Chicago (Ayer Collection).

In government records, federally recognized groups like the Cherokee, Seminole, Choctaw, and Chitimacha have much more documentation than other groups. In the National Archives in Washington, D.C., see the Bureau of Indian Affairs Papers (Record Group

75: general correspondence, office records, removal records, and audiovisual records). For southeastern agencies' records of the Bureau of Indian Affairs, see their papers in the Federal Regional Records Center, East Point, Georgia.

Much searching of state and local government records remains to be done, but leadership in organizing sources on their remaining Indian populations has been taken by the North Carolina Division of Archives and History, Raleigh, North Carolina, in its publication of Donna Spindel, *Introductory Guide to Indian Related Records (to 1876) in the North Carolina State Archives* (1977). See particularly the governors' papers, legislative papers, adjutant general papers, superintendent of public instruction papers, supreme court papers, and county records. These deal mainly with Cherokees and Lumbees.

Much attention has been devoted to the collection of manuscripts on the removed Indians in Oklahoma, but some scattered references exist within those collections about tribal remnants in the Southeast (Cherokees, Choctaws, Creeks, and Seminoles). At the Western Historical Collection of the University of Oklahoma Library, Norman, see the tribal papers, Patrick Hurley Papers, and C. R. Hume Papers. At the Oklahoma Historical Society, Oklahoma City, see the Grant Foreman Papers. The Thomas Gilcrease Institute of American History and Art, Tulsa, contains the Five Civilized Tribes Papers, which have some material on southeastern remnants.

The best bibliographies that apply to southeastern Indians are George P. Murdock, *Ethnographic Bibliography of North America* (4th ed.; New Haven, Conn.: Human Relations Area Files Press, 1975), and Frederick Hodge, ed., *Handbook of American Indians North of Mexico*, Bureau of American Ethnology Bulletin 30 (Washington, D.C.: Smithsonian Institution, 1907–10). This series of bulletins and annual reports, under the auspices of the Smithsonian Institution, represents some of the most valuable anthropological writings in the field (hereafter cited BAE). Hodge's *Handbook* is being updated and expanded under the direction of William Sturtevant.

There is no major synthesis of the history of Native peoples in the Southeast since the removal era, but several works suggest interpretations of this history. Classics in the field are four volumes by

John R. Swanton, *The Indians of the Southeastern United States*,
BAE Bulletin 137 (1946), *Indian Tribes of the Lower Mississippi
Valley and Adjacent Coast of the Gulf of Mexico*, BAE Bulletin
43 (1911), *Myths and Tales of the Southeastern Indians*, BAE Bulletin 88 (1929), and *Indian Tribes of North America*, BAE Bulletin
145 (1952). See also James Mooney, *The Siouan Tribes of the East*,
BAE Bulletin 22 (1895). Even though his focus is on earlier centuries, Charles Hudson, *The Southeastern Indians*, provides valuable insights about the cultures of Native peoples in the South since
1840. See also his edited works, *Red, White, and Black: Symposium
on Indians in the Old South* (Athens: University of Georgia Press,
1971), and *Four Centuries of Southern Indians* (Athens: University
of Georgia Press, 1975), which bring together original essays on various aspects of southern Indian history. A popularized survey of
value is Jesse Burt and Robert Furguson, *Indians of the Southeast,
Then and Now* (Nashville: Abingdon Press, 1973). The Bureau of
Indian Affairs has compiled brief histories of various groups in three
booklets, all published in 1968 by the U.S. Department of the
Interior: *Indians of the Eastern Seaboard, Indians of the Gulf
Coast*, and *Indians of North Carolina*. For a focus on land problems, see Sharlotte Neely and Walter Williams, "Detour down the
Trail of Tears: Southern Indians and the Land," *Southern Exposure*
2 (1974):94–98.

For the mid-nineteenth century, there are statistics about various
groups in Henry Schoolcraft, *Information Respecting the History,
Conditions and Prospects of the Indian Tribes of the United States*
(6 vols.; Philadelphia: Lippincott, 1853–57). Scott Sutton, "Some
Accounts of Confederate Indian Affairs," *Gulf States Historical
Magazine* 2 (1903):137–54, mentions eastern groups in the Civil
War. Except for the Lumbees, the situation of Indians in the Southeast during the crucial 1860s has been almost totally neglected by
scholars.

There is more material which relates to recent Indians in the
South. *Indian Claims Commission Reports* (New York: Clearwater
Publishing Co., 1975) covers Eastern Cherokees, Eastern Creeks,
Florida Seminoles, Alabama-Coushattas in Texas, and other small
groups such as the Pascagoula, Biloxi, Mobile, and Quapaw. For a
survey of the status of Indians in the 1940s, see William H. Gilbert,

"Surviving Indian Groups of the Eastern United States," *Smithsonian Report for 1948* (Washington: Government Printing Office, 1949), pp. 407–38. A more comprehensive update is J. Anthony Paredes and Kaye Lenihan, "Native American Population in the Southeastern States, 1960–70," *Florida Anthropologist* 26 (1973): 45–56. The *1970 Census of Population*, "Subject Report PC (2)-IF: American Indians" by the U.S. Bureau of the Census, is more complete than any previous census on southeastern Indians.

For understanding the recent resurgence of Indian identity among Native peoples of the South, see Alfred Tamarin, *We Have Not Vanished: Eastern Indians of the United States* (Chicago: Follett Publishing Co., 1974); "Those Non-Indian Indians," *Akwesasne Notes* (Spring 1971), p. 15; and Ernest Schusky, "Pan-Indianism in the Eastern United States," *Anthropology Tomorrow* 6 (1957): 116–23. A most interesting panel discussion by some present-day southeastern Indians, which reveals the bitterness they feel about white racial and cultural biases that have affected their self-perception, is in John K. Mahon, ed., *Indians of the Lower South: Past and Present* (Pensacola: Gulf Coast History and Humanities Conference, 1975). To explain this growing identity, specialists studying ethnicity and ethnic boundary maintenance have increasingly accepted the perceptions of the group itself in defining ethnic status. See Fredrik Barth, ed., *Ethnic Groups and Boundaries* (Boston: Little, Brown, 1969); Everett Hughes and Helen Hughes, *Where Peoples Meet: Racial and Ethnic Frontiers* (Glencoe, Ill.: Free Press, 1952); and John H. Peterson, "The Effects of Historical Indian–White Contacts on Contemporary Indian Studies," in Mahon, ed., *Indians of the Lower South*.

An almost separate field of study analyzes those groups on the fringe of "Indianness," the red-white-black *mestizo* populations scattered over the eastern United States. These groups, which usually formed in the colonial era and have varied degrees of genetic mixture and cultural identity, are surveyed in Brewton Berry, *Almost White* (New York: Macmillan, 1963). See also William H. Gilbert, "Memorandum Concerning the Characteristics of the Larger Mixed-Blood Racial Islands of the Eastern United States," *Social Forces* 24 (1946): 438–47. Edward T. Price, "A Geographic Analysis of White-Indian-Negro Racial Mixtures in the Eastern United

States," *Annals of the Association of American Geographers* 43 (1953):138–55, is based on his Ph.D. dissertation, "Mixed Blood Populations of Eastern United States as to Origins, Localizations, and Persistence" (University of California, 1950). Several articles in *American Anthropologist*, vol. 74 (1972), offer more recent perspectives: Eugene Griessman, "The American Isolates," pp. 693–94; Calvin Beale, "An Overview of the Phenomenon of Mixed Racial Isolates in the United States," pp. 704–10; Edgar Thompson, "The Little Races," pp. 1295–1306; and William Pollitzer, "The Physical Anthropology and Genetics of Marginal People of the Southeastern United States," pp. 719–34. Other articles which pertain particularly to the genetic background of these groups are Calvin Beale, "American Tri-Racial Isolates, Their Status and Pertinence to Genetic Research," *Eugenics Quarterly* 4 (1957):187–96; C. Herion, "Factors in the Micro-Evolution of a Tri-Racial Isolate," *American Journal of Human Genetics* 18 (1966):26–38; R. C. Elston, "The Estimation of Admixture in Racial Hybrids," *Annals of Human Genetics* 35 (1971):9–17; and Thomas Harte, "Trends in Mate Selection in a Tri-Racial Isolate," *Social Forces* 37 (1959): 215–21. See also A. R. Dunlap and C. A. Weslanger, "Trends in the Naming of Tri-Racial Mixed-Blood Groups in the Eastern United States," *American Speech* 22 (1947):81–87, and Guy Johnson, "Personality in a White-Indian-Negro Community," *American Sociological Review* 4 (1939):516–18.

In view of the in-between status of the *mestizo* groups and the attempts of whites to pressure various Indian groups into a "colored" status, relations between Indians and blacks in the South is a crucial field of study. Yet, except for some pioneering work by James H. Johnston ("Documentary Evidence of the Relations of Negroes and Indians," *Journal of Negro History* 14 [1929]:21–43) and Kenneth W. Porter ("Relations between Negroes and Indians within the Present Limits of the United States," *Journal of Negro History* 17 (1932):287–367), there has been very little research on this topic for the South after 1840.

Local studies of groups not dealt with in this collection include J. K. Dane and Eugene Griessman, "The Collective Identity of Marginal Peoples: The North Carolina Experience," *American Anthropologist* 74 (1972):694–704, and the final chapter of Ruth Wetmore,

First on the Land: The North Carolina Indians (Winston-Salem, N.C.: Blair, 1975). For a fascinating study of a small remnant in Hyde County, North Carolina, which was forced to dissolve and acculturate, see Patrick Garrow, *The Mattamuskeet Documents: A Study in Social History* (Raleigh: North Carolina Division of Archives and History, 1975). This study corrects some inaccuracies in Frank Speck, "Remnants of the Machapunga Indians in North Carolina," *American Anthropologist* 18 (1916):271–76. For other states, see C. A. Weslanger, *Delaware's Forgotten Folk* (Philadelphia: University of Pennsylvania Press, 1943); Horace Mann Bond, "Two Racial Islands of Alabama," *American Journal of Sociology* 34 (1931):552–67; and James Howard, "The Yamasee: A Supposedly Extinct Southeastern Tribe Rediscovered," *American Anthropologist* 62 (1960):681–83. Lynwood Montell discusses an Appalachian group in *The Saga of Coe Ridge: A Study in Oral History* (Knoxville: University of Tennessee Press, 1970), which he updates in "The Coe Ridge Colony: A Racial Island Disappears," *American Anthropologist* 74 (1972):710–19. For a similar group, see Will Allen Drumgoole, "The Malungeons," *The Arena* 3 (1891): 470–79; Edward T. Price, "The Melungeons: A Mixed Blood Strain of the Southern Appalachians," *Geographical Review* 14 (1951): 256–71; and William Pollitzer and W. H. Brown, "Survey of Demography, Anthropometry, and Genetics in the Melungeons of Tennessee: An Isolate of Hybrid Origin in Process of Dissolution," *Human Biology* 41 (1969):388–400.

Indians in Virginia

Very little has been published on post-1840 Virginia Indians, and much material remains buried in local and state records. For the field notes of early anthropologists who visited Native peoples in the state, see the Mooney Papers in the National Anthropological Archives and the Speck Papers in the American Philosophical Society. Their publications are James Mooney, "The Powhatan Confederacy Past and Present," *American Anthropologist* 9 (1907):144; Frank Speck, *The Rappahannock Indians of Virginia*, Indian Notes and Monographs (New York: Heye Foundation, 1925), vol. 5; and

Frank Speck, *Chapters on the Ethnology of the Powhatan Tribes of Virginia*, Indian Notes and Monographs (New York: Heye Foundation, 1928), vol. 1. See also John Pollard, *The Pamunkey Indians of Virginia*, BAE Bulletin 17 (1894).

More recent studies include C. W. J. Blume, "Present Day Indians of Tidewater Virginia," *Quarterly Bulletin of the Archeological Society of Virginia* 6 (1950): 1–8; Theodore Stern, "Chickahominy," *Proceedings of the American Philosophical Society* 96 (1952): 206; and Patrick Garrow, "An Ethnohistorical Study of the Powhatan Tribes," *The Chesopiean, a Journal of North American Archaeology* 12 (1975): 2–78. The most extensive scholarship on these groups has been done by Helen Rountree, beginning with her Ph.D. dissertation "Indian Land Loss in Virginia: A Prototype of Federal Indian Policy" (University of Wisconsin–Milwaukee, 1973). See also her articles, "Powhatan's Descendants in the Modern World: Community Studies of the Two Virginia Indian Reservations, with Notes on Five Non-Reservation Enclaves," *The Chesopiean, a Journal of North American Archaeology* 10 (1972): 62–96, and "Change Came Slowly: The Case of the Powhatan Indians of Virginia," *Journal of Ethnic Studies* 3 (1975): 1–20.

Lumbee Indians

The best general history of the Lumbees, based on a comprehensive search of the literature as well as extensive oral interviews with Lumbee people, is Adolph Dial and David Eliades, *The Only Land I Know: A History of the Lumbee Indians* (San Francisco: Indian Historian Press, 1975). This book also has the best bibliography on the group. For a condensed view of the outline of Lumbee history, see Adolph Dial's essays and panel-discussion participation in Mahon, ed., *Indians of the Lower South.* An outstanding study of Lumbee reactions to white pressures on them in the 1860s and 1870s is W. McKee Evans, *To Die Game: The Story of the Lowry Band, Indian Guerrillas of Reconstruction* (Baton Rouge: Louisiana State University Press, 1971). For background on the area of North Carolina in which the Lumbees resided, see W. McKee Evans, *Ballots and Fence Rails: Reconstruction on the Lower Cape Fear*

(Chapel Hill: University of North Carolina Press, 1967). See also Lewis Barton, *The Most Ironical Story in American History: An Authoritative Documented History of the Lumbee Indians of North Carolina* (Charlotte, N.C.: Associated Printing, 1967).

Earlier investigations include Stephen Weeks, "The Lost Colony of Roanoke: Its Fate and Survival," *Papers of the American Historical Association* 5 (1891):441–80; James Mooney, "Croatan," in Frederick Hodge, ed., *Handbook*; Orlando McPherson, *Indians of North Carolina*, Senate Document No. 677, 63d Congress, 3d sess. (1915); George E. Butler, *The Croatan Indians of Sampson County* (Durham, N.C.: Seeman Printery, 1916); and John Swanton, *Probable Identity of the "Croatan" Indians* (Washington: U.S. Office of Indian Affairs, 1933).

Recently there have been a number of valuable Ph.D. dissertations on the Lumbees, including Gerald Sider, "The Political History of the Lumbee Indians of Robeson County, North Carolina: A Case Study of Ethnic Political Affiliations" (New School for Social Research [New York], 1971); Abraham Makosky, "Tradition and Change in the Lumbee Community of Baltimore" (Catholic University of America [Washington], 1971); John Gregory Peck, "Urban Station: Migration of the Lumbee Indians" (University of North Carolina at Chapel Hill, 1972); Vernon Thompson, "A History of the Education of the Lumbee Indians of Robeson County, North Carolina, from 1885 to 1970" (University of Miami, 1973); and Karen Blu, "'We People': Understanding Lumbee Indian Identity in a Tri-Racial Situation" (University of Chicago, 1972).

Indians of Louisiana and Eastern Texas

No major work provides a complete history of the related tribal remnants which occupy Louisiana and the neighboring Alabama-Coushatta reservation of eastern Texas, but background is contained in Swanton, *Indian Tribes of the Lower Mississippi* and *Indians of the Southwestern United States*, and in William H. Gilbert, "Surviving Indian Groups." A general survey is Fred Kniffen, *The Indians of Louisiana* (Baton Rouge: Louisiana State University Press, 1965). An excellent bibliography of scholarly works is contained in Robert Neuman and Lanier Simmons, *A Bibliography Relative to Indians of the State of Louisiana*, Anthropological Study No. 4 (Baton Rouge: Louisiana Department of Conservation, 1969). For a brief look at the educational problems facing Native peoples in the 1940s, see Willard Beatty, "Education of Louisiana Indians," *Louisiana Educational Survey* 4 (1942): 1–3.

Bobby H. Johnson analyzes the history of one group in *The Coushatta People* (Phoenix: Indian Tribal Series, 1976). See also Dan Flores, "The Red River Branch of the Alabama-Coushatta Indians: An Ethnohistory," *Southern Studies* 16 (1977, Northwestern State University at Natchitoches, La.): 55–72. Their kinsmen in eastern Texas are covered in W. W. Newcomb, *The Indians of Texas: From Prehistoric to Modern Times* (Austin: University of Texas Press, 1961); Aline Rothe, *Kalita's People: A History of the Alabama-Coushatta Indians of Texas* (Waco: Texian Press, 1963); and in an Indian Claims Commission report by Daniel Jacobson et al., *Alabama-Coushatta Indians . . .* (New York: Garland Publishing Co., 1974).

Jacobson, whose Ph.D. dissertation is "Koasati Culture Change" (Louisiana State University, 1954), published "The Origin of the Koasati Community of Louisiana," *Ethnohistory* 7 (1960): 97–120. Mary Haas wrote a fascinating article, discussing differences, in "Men and Women's Speech in Koasati," *Language* 20 (1944): 142–49. For a rare illustrated examination of the Coushattas, along with the Chitimachas and Houmas, in the early twentieth century, see M. Raymond Harrington, "Among Louisiana Indians," *Southern Workman* 37 (1908): 656–61.

The best summary of Chitimacha history is Herbert T. Hoover, *The Chitimacha People* (Phoenix: Indian Tribal Series, 1976). In the late nineteenth and early twentieth centuries, they received attention from anthropologists, beginning with Albert Gatschet, "The Shetimasha Indians of St. Mary's Parish, Southern Louisiana," *Transactions of the Anthropological Society of Washington* 2 (1883): 148–58. His field work was reported in *Bureau of American Ethnology Third Annual Report* (1885), pp. 22–23. He was followed by John Swanton, "Mythology of the Indians of Louisiana and the Texas Coast," *Journal of American Folklore* 20 (1907): 285–89, and "Some Chitimacha Myths and Beliefs," *Journal of American Folk-*

lore 30 (1917):474–78. David Bushnell wrote "The Chitimacha Indians of Bayou LaFourche, Louisiana," *Journal of the Washington Academy of Sciences* 7 (1917):301–7, and B. W. Merwin followed with "Basketry of the Chitimacha Indians," *The Museum Journal: University of Pennsylvania* 10 (1919):29–34. Frances Densmore, *A Search for Songs among the Chitimacha Indians of Louisiana,* Smithsonian Anthropological Papers No. 19 (Washington: Smithsonian Institution, 1943), includes remarks about tribal history, legends, and medical practices.

The Louisiana Houma Indians were not given much attention until the 1930s, but with Frank Speck, "A Social Reconnaissance of the Creole Houma Indian Trappers of the Louisiana Bayous" (*América Indígena* 3 [1943]:134–46, 212–20), outsiders began to show steady concern. Vernon Parenton and Roland Pellegrin, "The Sabines: A Study of Racial Hybrids in a Louisiana Coastal Parish," *Social Forces* 29 (1950):148–58, is not entirely trustworthy, but it was corrected by Edison Roy, "The Indians of Dulac: A Descriptive Study of a Racial Hybrid Community in Terrebonne Parish, Louisiana" (M.A. thesis, Louisiana State University, 1959). The best recent studies are Ann Fischer, "History and Current Status of the Houma Indians," in Levine and Lurie, eds., *The American Indian Today;* Max Stanton, "The Indians in the Grand Caillou-Dulac Community" (M.A. thesis, Louisiana State University, 1971); Max Stanton, "A Remnant Indian Community: The Houma of Southern Louisiana," in J. Kenneth Morland, ed., *The Not So Solid South* (Athens: University of Georgia Press, 1971); and Ernest C. Downs and Jenna Whitehead, "The Houma Indians: Two Decades in a History of Struggle," *American Indian Journal* 2 (1976):2–18.

Few printed materials deal extensively with the Tunicas, and anthropological linguistic works account for most of them. See John R. Swanton, *A Structural and Lexical Comparison of the Tunica, Chitimacha, and Attakapa Languages,* BAE Bulletin 68 (1919), and his "The Tunica Language," *International Journal of American Linguistics* 2 (1922):1–39. Mary Rosamond Haas published "A Grammar of the Tunica Language" in *Handbook of American Indian Languages,* ed. Frans Boaz (New York: J. J. Augustin, 1935), as well as "Tunica," *Handbook of American Indian Languages* 4 (1940): 1–143; "The Solar Deity of the Tunica," *Papers of the Michigan*

Academy of Science, Arts and Letters 28 (1942): 531–35; "A Grammatical Sketch of Tunica," in *Linguistic Structures of North America* ed. Harry Hoijer, Viking Fund Publications in Anthropology No. 6 (New York: Viking Fund, 1946), pp. 337–66; "French Loan-Words in Tunica," *Romance Philology* 1 (1947–48): 145–48; "Tunica Texts," *University of California Publications in Linguistics*, vol. 6 (1950): 1–174; and "Tunica Dictionary," *University of California Publications in Linguistics*, vol. 6 (1953): 175–332.

Frank G. Speck's work with the Tunicas is documented in the Speck Papers, American Philosophical Society. The papers of Caroline Dormon, an amateur anthropologist and personal friend of John R. Swanton, are in the Louisiana Room at Northwestern State University, Natchitoches, Louisiana. Notes and letters of Albert Gatschet, James Dorsey, and John R. Swanton relating to the tribe are in the National Anthropological Archives. Other useful documentation on the Tunicas is in the Avoyelles Parish Court House, Marksville, Louisiana; the library of the Supreme Court of Louisiana, New Orleans; the library of the School of Law, Louisiana State University, Baton Rouge; the State Land Office, Baton Rouge; and the Works Progress Administration's Survey of Federal Archives in the State of Louisiana, Louisiana State University, Baton Rouge. Beginning in December 1974, Ernest C. Downs, as director of the Southeastern Indian Project at the Institute for the Development of Indian Law, undertook a study of the legal history of the Tunicas. Twenty-four tapes, or approximately forty hours of recorded interviews with tribal members, were collected and transcribed as part of this study. Downs was the interviewer in the tapes, which were collected in 1975 and 1976.

An early account by James Dorsey is "The Biloxi Indians of Louisiana," *Proceedings of the American Association for the Advancement of Science* 42 (1893): 267–87, as is an anonymous 64-page handwritten book titled "Biloxi Vocabulary: An Essay on the Language of the Indians of Lower Louisiana," which is in the archives of the Thomas Gilcrease Institute of American History and Art, Tulsa.

Though most Choctaw Indians lived in Mississippi or Oklahoma, some bands of Choctaws resided in Louisiana by the early nineteenth century. They were first described in three articles by David Bushnell, *The Choctaw of Bayou Lacomb, St. Tammany Parish, Louisiana*, BAE Bulletin 48 (1909); "Myths of the Louisiana Choctaw," *American Anthropologist* 12 (1910): 526–35; and "The Choctaw of St. Tammany," *Louisiana Historical Quarterly* 1 (1917): 11–20. More recently, aspects of their history have been dealt with by John H. Peterson in an interesting reconstruction of past lifestyles, "Louisiana Choctaw Life at the End of the Nineteenth Century," in Hudson, ed., *Four Centuries of Southern Indians*, and by Hiram F. Gregory, "Jena Band of Louisiana Choctaw," *American Indian Journal* 3 (1977): 2–16.

Catawba Indians

The best summary of Catawba history is Charles Hudson, *The Catawba Nation* (Athens: University of Georgia Press, 1970). See also James Mooney, *The Siouan Tribes of the East*, BAE Bulletin 22 (1894); Frank Speck, "The Catawba Nation and Its Neighbors," *North Carolina Historical Review* 16 (1939): 404–17; Chapman Milling, *Red Carolinians* (Chapel Hill: University of North Carolina Press, 1940); Brewton Berry, "The Mestizos of South Carolina," *American Journal of Sociology* 5 (1945): 34–41, and *Almost White*; and Douglas Summers Brown, *The Catawba Indians: The People of the River* (Columbia: University of South Carolina Press, 1966).

For the story of how the Catawbas were caught up in, but ultimately survived, the removal era, see James Covington, "Proposed Catawba Indian Removal, 1848," *South Carolina Historical and Genealogical Magazine* 54 (1954): 42–47. There was hardly any documentation of Catawbas in the mid- to late nineteenth century, until the Office of the Indian Rights Association printed a manuscript by Lewis Scaife, *History and Condition of the Catawba Indians of South Carolina* (Philadelphia, 1896). This was followed a year later by a report to Congress, "The Catawba Tribe of Indians," Senate Document 144, 54th Congress, 2d sess. (3 February 1897).

After that, anthropologists began to take an interest in the modern Catawbas. See Albert Gatschet's two articles, "Grammatic Sketch of the Catawba Language," *American Anthropologist* 2 (1900): 527–49, and "Onomatology of the Catawba River Basin," *American Anthropologist* 4 (1902): 52–56. M. R. Harrington followed with "Catawba Potters and Their Work," *American Anthropologist* 10 (1908): 399–407. John Swanton published "Catawba Notes," *Journal of the Washington Academy of Science* 8 (1918): 623–29; see also his *Indians of the Southeastern United States.*

The largest amount of early ethnographic work was done by Frank Speck, the results of which are noted in the Speck Papers, American Philosophical Society, and in several of his publications: "Some Catawba Texts and Folklore," *Journal of American Folklore* 26 (1913): 319–30; *Catawba Texts* (New York: Columbia University Press, 1934); "Siouan Tribes of the Carolinas as Known from Catawba, Tutelo, and Documentary Sources," *American Anthropologist* 37 (1935): 201–25; "Catawba Medicines and Curative Practices," in *Twenty-fifth Anniversary Studies*, Philadelphia Anthropological Society, ed. D. S. Davidson (Pittsburgh: University of Pittsburgh Press, 1937); "Question of Matrilineal Descent in the Southeastern Siouan Area," *American Anthropologist* 40 (1938): 1–12; "The Cane Blowgun in Catawba and Southeastern Ethnology," *American Anthropologist* 40 (1938): 198–204; "Catawba Religious Beliefs, Mortuary Customs, and Dances," *Primitive Man* 12 (1939): 21–57; "Catawba Games and Amusements," *Primitive Man* 17 (1944): 19–28; "Catawba Herbals and Curative Practices," *Journal of American Folklore* 57 (1944): 37–50; *Catawba Hunting, Trapping, and Fishing* (Philadelphia: University of Pennsylvania Museum, 1946); "Catawba Texts," *International Journal of American Linguistics* 12 (1946): 64–67; "Ethnoherpetology of the Catawba and Cherokee Indians," *Journal of the Washington Academy of Science* 36 (1946): 355–60; and "Catawba Folk Tales from Chief Sam Blue," *Journal of American Folklore* 60 (1947): 79–84. Speck co-authored, with C. E. Schaeffer, "Catawba Kinship and Social Organization with a Resume of Tutelo Kinship Terms," *American Anthropologist* 44 (1924): 555–75.

Aspects of more recent Catawba life are dealt with in Vladimir Fewkes, "Catawba Pottery-Making, with Notes on Pamunkey Pottery-Making, Cherokee Pottery-Making, and Coiling," *Proceedings*

of the American Philosophical Society 88 (1944):69–124; George
Hicks, "Catawba Acculturation and the Ideology of Race," in *Symposium on New Approaches to the Study of Religion*, ed. Melford
Spiro (Seattle: University of Washington Press, 1964); and George
Hicks, "Cultural Persistence versus Local Adaptation: Frank G.
Speck's Catawba Indians," *Ethnohistory* 12 (1965):343–54.

Alabama Creek Indians

For cultural background on the Creeks, see two classics by John
Swanton, *Early History of the Creek Indians and Their Neighbors*
and *Social Organization and Social Usages of the Indians of the
Creek Confederacy*, both published as part of the BAE *Forty-second
Annual Report*, 1924–25 (1928). For background on the origins of
the remnant Alabama Creek community, see Angie Debo, *The
Road to Disappearance*, and Mary Young, *Redskins, Ruffleshirts,
and Rednecks: Indian Allotments in Alabama and Mississippi,
1830–1860* (Norman: University of Oklahoma Press, 1961).

The subsequent history of Alabama Creeks was ignored until
some initial publications by Frank Speck, "Notes on Social and
Economic Conditions among the Creek Indians of Alabama in
1941," *American Indigena* 7 (1947):195–98, and "The Road to Disappearance: Creek Indians Surviving in Alabama: A Mixed Culture
Community," *American Anthropologist* 51 (1949):681–82. Despite
Speck's beginnings, no other scholar devoted much attention to the
group until the work of J. Anthony Paredes appeared. His publications include "The Emergence of Contemporary Eastern Creek Indian Identity," in *Social and Cultural Identity*, ed. Thomas Fitzgerald (Athens: University of Georgia Press, 1974); "The Folk Culture of the Eastern Creek Indians: Synthesis and Change," in *Indians of the Lower South*, ed. John Mahon; "The Need for Cohesion
and American Isolates," *American Anthropologist* 78 (1976):335–
37; and "New Uses for Old Ethnography: A Brief Social History of a
Research Project with the Eastern Creek Indians, or How to Be an
Applied Anthropologist without Really Trying" *Human Organization* 35 (1976):315–20. Recently the Creeks compiled their own

history, *Creek Nation East of the Mississippi: Yesterday, Today and Tomorrow* (Atmore, Ala.: Creek Nation East of the Mississippi, Inc., 1975).

Choctaw Indians

The best studies of the Mississippi Choctaws in the 1820s and 1830s are Arthur DeRosier, *The Removal of the Choctaw Indians;* Mary Young, *Redskins, Ruffleshirts, and Rednecks;* Grant Foreman, *Indian Removal;* and Angie Debo, *The Rise and Fall of the Choctaw Republic.* For a survey of Choctaw history, which focuses on Oklahoma, see David Baird, *The Choctaw People* (Phoenix: Indian Tribal Series, 1976).

There is much less writing on the post-1830 history of those Choctaws who remained in Mississippi. An attempt at a survey is Thelma Bounds, *Children of Nanih Waiya* (San Antonio: Naylor, 1964), which is not trustworthy. One of the earliest documentary evidences of the Mississippi Choctaws after removal is J. F. H. Claiborne, "Choctaw Indians Memorial," U.S. House of Representatives, *House Documents,* 28th Congress, 1st sess. (1844). Some indication of Choctaw status and relations with black people is in Vernon Wharton, *The Negro in Mississippi, 1865–1890* (New York: Harper and Row, 1965); see also Wyatt Jeltz, "The Relations of Negroes and Choctaw and Chickasaw Indians," *Journal of Negro History* 33 (1948): 24–37. The unsettled land status of the Choctaws is reviewed in Franklin Riley, "Choctaw Land Claims," *Publications of the Mississippi Historical Society* 8 (1904): 345–50. The best short summary of nineteenth-century post-removal Mississippi Indians is John Peterson, "The Indian in the Old South," in Charles Hudson, ed., *Red, White, and Black.*

For the early twentieth century, John Swanton, *Source Material for the Social and Ceremonial Life of the Choctaw Indians,* BAE Bulletin 103 (1931), concentrates on aboriginal survivals among surviving Mississippi Choctaws. Other studies that focus on culture change during that era are Fred Eggan, "Historical Changes in the Choctaw Kinship System," *American Anthropologist* 39 (1937):

34–52, and Eugene Farr, "Religious Assimilation: A Case Study of the Adoption of Christianity by the Choctaw Indians of Mississippi" (Th.D. dissertation, New Orleans Baptist Theological Seminary, 1948).

More sociological analysis has been done of recent Choctaws, beginning with Joe Jennings, Vernon Beggs, and A. B. Caldwell, "A Study of the Social Economic Condition of the Choctaw Indians in Mississippi" (unpublished mimeograph, Bureau of Indian Affairs, 1945), and Charles Tolbert, "A Sociological Study of the Choctaw Indians in Mississippi" (Ph.D. dissertation, Louisiana State University, 1958). See also an undated mimeograph, "Mississippi Choctaw" (Philadelphia, Miss.: Choctaw Agency, Bureau of Indian Affairs, n.d.). For educational changes, see Etha Langford, "A Study of the Educational Development of the Choctaw Indians of Mississippi" (M.A. thesis, Mississippi Southern College, 1953); the unpublished manuscript of Charles Moore and Joseph Steve, "Survey of School Drop-Outs in the Seven Choctaw Communities in Mississippi" (Philadelphia, Miss.: Choctaw Agency, Bureau of Indian Affairs, 1963); and John Egerton, "The Other Philadelphia Story," *Southern Education Report* 2 (1966): 24–28.

The most extensive research on recent Choctaws has been done by John Peterson, beginning with his 1968–69 anthropological field work leading to his dissertation, "The Mississippi Band of Choctaw Indians: Their Recent History and Current Social Relations" (Ph.D. dissertation, University of Georgia, 1970). Peterson's publications on the Choctaw include "Assimilation, Separation, and Out-Migration in an American Indian Group," *American Anthropologist* 74 (1972): 1286–95; *Socio-Economic Characteristics of the Mississippi Choctaw Indians* (Mississippi State: Mississippi State University, Social Science Research Center, 1970); and *Reservation, Reservoir, and Self-Determination: A Case Study of Reservoir Planning as It Affects an Indian Reservation* (Mississippi State: Mississippi State University, Water Resources Research Institute, 1975). See also Barbara Spencer, John Peterson, and Choong Kim, *Choctaw Manpower and Demographic Survey, 1974* (Philadelphia, Miss.: Mississippi Band of Choctaw Indians, 1975), and Bobby Thompson and John Peterson, "Mississippi Choctaw Identity: Genesis and Change," in

The New Ethnicity, ed. John Bennett (Minneapolis: West Publishing Co., 1975), pp. 179–96.

For the tribal government's view of its past and present status, see Mississippi Band of Choctaw Indians, *An Era of Change* (Philadelphia, Miss., 1972).

Cherokee Indians

Pre-removal Cherokee history is covered in William Fenton and John Gulick, eds., *Symposium on Cherokee and Iroquois Culture*, BAE Bulletin 180 (1961); Fred Gearing, *Priests and Warriors: Social Structures for Cherokee Politics in the Eighteenth Century* (Washington, D.C.: American Anthropological Association [Memoir 93], 1962); Henry Malone, *Cherokees of the Old South* (Athens: University of Georgia Press, 1956); James Mooney, *Myths of the Cherokees*, BAE Nineteenth Annual Report (1900); and James O'Donnell, *Southern Indians in the Revolution* (Knoxville: University of Tennessee Press, 1973). Marion Starkey, *The Cherokee Nation* (New York: Knopf, 1946); Grace Steele Woodward, *The Cherokees* (Norman: University of Oklahoma Press, 1963); and Earl Pierce and Rennard Strickland, *The Cherokee People* (Phoenix: Indian Tribal Series, 1976), provide summaries of overall Cherokee history but focus on Western Cherokees after 1838. A fascinating study of Cherokee use of black slaves is Theda Perdue, *Slavery and the Evolution of Cherokee Society, 1540–1866* (Knoxville: University of Tennessee Press, in press).

Although there is considerably more scholarship on the Oklahoma Cherokees than on their North Carolina kinsmen, the Eastern Cherokees are better documented than any other group remaining in the Southeast. Part of this is because they were the earliest federally recognized group among the southern remnants, and had more attention from anthropologists. There are also more extensive manuscript collections relating to them. Major manuscript collections are at the Smithsonian Institution's National Anthropological Archives (James Mooney Papers, Inoli Papers, Eastern Cherokee Papers), Washington, D.C.; National Archives (Bureau of Indian Affairs Record Group 75), Washington, D.C.; Federal Regional Records

Center (Cherokee Agency Records), East Point, Georgia; North Carolina State Department of Archives and History (David Settle Reid Papers, William Stringfield Papers, William H. Thomas Papers, and various state and country government records), Raleigh, North Carolina; Duke University Library (William H. Thomas Papers, James W. Terrell Papers, and James Taylor Papers), Durham, North Carolina; Western Carolina University Library (William H. Thomas Papers and James W. Terrell Papers), Cullowhee, North Carolina; Guilford College Library (Quaker Collection), Greensboro, North Carolina; University of North Carolina Library (Southern Historical Collection, Duff Green Papers, and Jacob Silver Papers), Chapel Hill, North Carolina; Thomas Gilcrease Institute (Cherokee Eastern Band Papers, Will West Long Papers), Tulsa, Oklahoma; and Archives of the Museum of the Cherokee Indian, Cherokee, North Carolina.

The most valuable overview of Eastern Cherokee history to the 1890s is in Mooney, *Myths of the Cherokees*. More recent summaries are William R. L. Smith, *The Story of the Cherokees* (Cleveland, Tenn.: Church of God Publishing House, 1928); Horace Kephart, *The Cherokee of the Smoky Mountains* (Ithaca, N.Y.: Atkinson Press, 1936); Chapman Milling, *Red Carolinians* (Chapel Hill: University of North Carolina Press, 1940); Thelma Brown, *By Way of Cherokee* (Atlanta: Home Mission Board of the Southern Baptist Convention, 1944); Douglas Rights, *The American Indian in North Carolina* (Durham, N.C.: Duke University Press, 1947); Sonia Bleeker, *The Cherokee Indians of the Mountains* (New York: William Morrow Co., 1952); and most recently a chapter on the Eastern Cherokee in Wendell Oswalt, *This Land Was Theirs: A Study of the North American Indian* (3d ed.; New York: Wiley, 1978).

For the removal era, see G. D. Harmon, "The North Carolina Cherokees and the New Echota Treaty," *North Carolina Historical Review* 6 (1929):237–53; Denton Bedford, *Tsali* (San Francisco: Indian Historian Press, 1972); James Rand, *The Indians of North Carolina and Their Relations with Settlers* (Chapel Hill: University of North Carolina Press, 1913); Henry Malone, "Cherokee–White Relations on the Southern Frontier in the Early Nineteenth Century," *North Carolina Historical Review* 34 (1957):1–14; and Duane King, "The Origin of the Eastern Band of Cherokees as a

Social and Political Entity," in *The Cherokee Indian Nation: A Troubled History*, ed. Duane King (Knoxville: University of Tennessee Press, in press).

Not much research has been devoted to nineteenth-century post-removal Eastern Cherokees, but excellent Indian-authored writings have been edited and translated by Anna and Jack Kilpatrick, *The Shadow of Sequoyah: Social Documents of the Cherokees, 1862–1964* (Norman: University of Oklahoma Press, 1965); their companion volume is *Chronicles of Wolftown: Social Documents of the North Carolina Cherokees, 1850–1963*, BAE Bulletin 196 (1966). The struggle to gain clear title to their lands and the resulting confused legal status of the North Carolina Indians are dealt with in Charles Royce, *The Cherokee Nation of Indians*, BAE Fifth Annual Report (1887); Gaston Litton, "Enrollment Records of the Eastern Band of Cherokee Indians," *North Carolina Historical Review* 17 (1940): 199–231; H. G. Robertson, "The Eastern Band of Cherokee Indians, from 1835 to 1893," *North Carolina University Magazine* 31 (1901): 173–80; Mattie Russell, "William Holland Thomas, White Chief of the North Carolina Cherokees" (Ph.D. dissertation, Duke University, 1956); Mattie Russell, "Devil in the Smokies: The White Man's Nature and the Indian's Fate," *South Atlantic Quarterly* 73 (1974): 53–69; and Richard Iobst, "William Holland Thomas and the Cherokee Claims," in King, ed., *The Cherokee Indian Nation: A Troubled History*.

Nineteenth-century travel accounts relating to the Cherokees include Charles Lanman, *Letters from the Alleghany Mountains* (New York: G. P. Putnam, 1849); "Quallatown Indians," *Friends' Weekly Intelligencer* (Philadelphia) (Society of Friends), 1849, 6: 2–3; David Schenck, "The Cherokees in North Carolina," *At Home and Abroad* 2 (1882): 321–37; Wilbur Zeigler and Ben Grosscup, *The Heart of the Alleghanies, or Western North Carolina* (Raleigh, N.C.: Alfred Williams, 1883); Charles Pointer, *The Eastern Cherokees* (Philadelphia: Indian Rights Association, 1888); Thomas Donaldson, *The Eastern Band of Cherokees of North Carolina: Extra Census Bulletin* (Washington: Bureau of the Census, 1892); Virginia Young, "A Sketch of the Cherokee People on the Indian Reservation of North Carolina," *Woman's Progress* (1894), pp. 172–73; and

William Stringfield, "North Carolina Cherokee Indians," *North Carolina Booklet* 3 (1903): 5–24.

Analyses of late nineteenth-century social aspects are in several publications by the anthropologist James Mooney (besides his *Myths of the Cherokees*), including *Sacred Formulas of the Cherokees*, BAE Seventh Annual Report (1890); "Evolution in Cherokee Personal Names," *American Anthropologist* 2 (1889): 61–62; "The Cherokee Ball Play," *American Anthropologist* 3 (1890): 105–32; "Cherokee Theory and Practice of Medicine," *Journal of American Folklore* 3 (1890): 44–50; and—co-authored with Frans Olbrechts—*The Swimmer Manuscript: Cherokee Sacred Formulas and Medicinal Prescriptions*, BAE Bulletin 99 (1932). More recent writings on this era are Sharlotte Neely, "The Quaker Era of Cherokee Indian Education, 1880–1892," *Appalachian Journal* 2 (1975): 314–22, and Walter Williams, "The Merger of Apaches with Eastern Cherokees: Qualla in 1893," *Journal of Cherokee Studies* 2 (1977): 240–45.

For the early twentieth-century Eastern Cherokees, a valuable history was written by a member of the tribe, Henry Owl, "The Eastern Band of Cherokee Indians before and after the Removal" (M.A. thesis, University of North Carolina, 1929). Excellent research on the 1930s is contained in Charles Weeks, "The Eastern Cherokee and the New Deal," *North Carolina Historical Review* 53 (1976): 303–19. See also *The Eastern Cherokees: How They Live Today, Their History* (Knoxville: J. L. Caton, 1937); and John Brown, "Eastern Cherokee Chiefs," *Chronicles of Oklahoma* 16 (1938): 3–35.

The vast majority of writing for the twentieth century has been done by anthropologists. See Leonard Bloom, "The Acculturation of the Eastern Cherokee" (Ph.D. dissertation, Duke University, 1937); Gertrude Flanagan, "A Study of the Dietary Habits of Three Generations of the Eastern Cherokee Indians" (M.A. thesis, University of Oklahoma, 1938); Herbert Marshall, "The North Carolina Cherokees" (M.A. thesis, Oklahoma A&M University, 1940); Frank Speck and Claude Schaeffer, "The Mutual-Aid and Volunteer Company of the Eastern Cherokee," *Journal of the Washington Academy of Sciences* 35 (1945): 169–79; and three publications by William Harlan Gilbert: "Eastern Cherokee Social Organization," in

Social Anthropology of North American Tribes, ed. Fred Eggan
(Chicago: University of Chicago Press, 1937); *The Eastern Chero-*
kees, BAE Bulletin 133 (1943); and "The Cherokees of North Carolina: Living Memorials of the Past," *Smithsonian Institution An-*
nual Report for 1956 (Washington: Government Printing Office,
1956) pp. 529–55.

For an analysis of Cherokee acculturation, see John Witthoft,
"Observations on Social Change among the Eastern Cherokees," in
The Cherokee Indian Nation: A Troubled History. Another aspect
of acculturation is treated in William Wood, "The Eastern Cherokee
Veteran of World War II" (M.A. thesis, University of North Caro-
lina, 1950). There are a number of works relating to Cherokee educa-
tion, including Walter Thomas, "A Survey of Educational Facilities
in Cherokee County, North Carolina, with Recommendations"
(M.A. thesis, University of North Carolina, 1948); Myrtle Bonner,
"Education and Other Influences in the Cultural Assimilation of
the Cherokee Indians on the Qualla Reservation in North Carolina"
(M.A. thesis, Alabama Polytechnic Institute, 1950); Carrie Abbott,
"Pupil Progress in Swain County Elementary Schools" (M.A. thesis,
University of North Carolina, 1950); Lillian Thomasson, *Swain*
County: Early History and Educational Development (Bryson City,
N.C.: n.p., 1965); and Paul Kutsche, "Cherokee High School Drop-
outs," *Journal of American Indian Education* 3 (1964): 22–30. The
best overview of the topic is Sharlotte Neely Williams, "The Role
of Formal Education among the Eastern Cherokee Indians, 1880–
1971" (M.A. thesis, University of North Carolina, 1971).

Psychological anthropology approaches are contained in Paul
Kutsche, "The Rorschach Comparison of Adult Male Personality
in Big Cove, Cherokee, North Carolina, and Henry's Branch, Kentucky" (Ph.D. dissertation, University of Pennsylvania, 1961), and
Laura Hill King, "Synthesis of Cherokee Death Customs" (M.A.
thesis, University of Tennessee, 1976).

Cherokee arts are dealt with in Dorothy Arnold, "Some Recent
Contributions of the Cherokee Indians of North Carolina to the
Crafts of the Southern Highlands" (M.A. thesis, University of Ten-
nessee, 1952); Willard Carl, "Creative Adaptations of Mississippian
Culture Design Motifs as Sources for Modern Cherokee Crafts"
(M.A. thesis, University of Tennessee, 1966); and Rodney Leftwich,

Arts and Crafts of the Cherokee (Cullowhee, N.C.: Land of the Sky Press, 1970). Frank Speck and Leonard Broom analyze *Cherokee Dance and Drama* (Berkeley: University of California Press, 1951), and Wallace Umberger, "A History of *Unto These Hills*, 1941 to 1968" (Ph.D. dissertation, Tulane University, 1970), discusses the impact of tourism through the outdoor drama held in Cherokee.

Much of the anthropological writing of the last two decades has been coordinated by John Gulick. His publications include "The Acculturation of Eastern Cherokee Community Organization," *Social Forces* 36 (1958):246–50; "Language and Passive Resistance among the Eastern Cherokees," *Ethnohistory* 5 (1958):60–81; and *Cherokees at the Crossroads* (Chapel Hill: Institute for Research in Social Science at the University of North Carolina, 1960). Gulick's book was based in part on research by graduate students who worked with him, and several theses resulted: John Grant, "Behavioral Premises in the Culture of Conservative Eastern Cherokee Indians" (M.A. thesis, University of North Carolina, 1957); Hester Davis, "Social Interaction and Kinship in Big Cove Community, Cherokee, North Carolina" (M.A. thesis, University of North Carolina, 1957); Annie Gardner, "Social Organization and Community Solidarity in Painttown, Cherokee, N.C." (M.A. thesis, University of North Carolina, 1958); Raymond Fogelson, "A Study of the Conjuror in Eastern Cherokee Society" (M.A. thesis, University of Pennsylvania, 1958) and Raymond Fogelson, "The Cherokee Ball Game: A Study in Southeastern Ethnology" (Ph.D. dissertation, University of Pennsylvania, 1962). From her research, Harriet Kupferer, another Gulick student, published *The Principal People, 1960: A Study of Cultural and Social Groups of the Eastern Cherokee*, BAE Bulletin 196 (1966); "The Isolated Eastern Cherokee," in *The American Indian Today*, ed. Stuart Levine and Nancy Lurie (Deland, Fla.: Everett/Edwards, 1968); "Cherokee Change: A Departure from Lineal Models of Acculturation," *Anthropologica* 5 (1963):187–98; and "Health Practices and Educational Aspirations as Indicators of Acculturation and Social Class among the Eastern Cherokee," *Social Forces* 41 (1962):154–63. In 1973 a second edition of Gulick's *Cherokees at the Crossroads* was published, with an updated epilogue by Sharlotte Neely Williams that analyzed changes in the 1960s and 1970s. Her research concentrated on the Snowbird Community of Cherokees; see Sharlotte Neely Williams, "Ethnicity in a Native American Community" (Ph.D. dissertation, University of North Carolina, 1976).

For a recent overview from the tribal government's perspective, see Eastern Band of Cherokee Indians, *Cherokee Progress and Challenge* (Cherokee, N.C.: Eastern Band of Cherokee Indians, 1972). In 1976 the Museum of the Cherokee Indian began publishing the *Journal of Cherokee Studies*, which promises to become a major organ for research on Cherokee history and culture.

Florida Seminole and Miccosukee Indians

Unlike many southeastern Indians, the Florida Seminoles have had historical writings on each era of their history. A good summary of the entire history of the group, which focuses on Oklahoma after the Second Seminole War, is Edwin McReynolds, *The Seminoles* (Norman: University of Oklahoma Press, 1957). For more extensive discussion of the warfare which led to removal, see John Mahon, *History of the Second Seminole War, 1835–1842* (Gainesville: University of Florida Press, 1967). An extraordinary first-person account by an officer who served through the war is John Sprague, *The Origin, Progress, and Conclusion of the Florida War* (1848 reprint; Gainesville: University of Florida Press, 1964). For other primary sources, see John Bemrose, *Reminiscences of the Second Seminole War*, ed. John Mahon (Gainesville: University of Florida Press, 1966), and M. M. Cohen, *Notices of Florida and the Campaigns* (1836 reprint; Gainesville: University of Florida Press, 1964).

The post-removal period, leading to the Third Seminole War, is dealt with in Kenneth Porter, "Billy Bowlegs (Holata Micco) in the Seminole Wars," *Florida Historical Quarterly* 45 (1967):219–42; John Gifford, *Billy Bowlegs and the Seminole War* (Coconut Grove, Fla.: Triangle Co., 1925); U.S. Congress, *Report of the Secretary of War*, House Executive Document 2, 35th Congress, 2d sess., 1858; and several articles by James Covington: "The Florida Seminoles in 1847," *Tequesta* 24 (1964):49–59; "A Seminole Census: 1847," *Florida Anthropologist* 21 (1968):120–22; "The Indian Scare of

1849," *Tequesta* 21 (1961): 53–63; and "An Episode in the Third Seminole War," *Florida Historical Quarterly* 45 (1966): 45–59.

Government attention to the Florida Seminoles resumed after the turbulent Civil War era, and is summarized in other articles by James Covington: "White Control of Seminole Leadership," *Florida Anthropologist* 18 (1965): 137–46; "Apalachicola Seminole Leadership: 1820–1933," *Florida Anthropologist* 16 (1963): 57–62; and "Federal and State Relations with the Florida Seminoles, 1875–1901," *Tequesta* 32 (1966): 45–59. Federal reports include U.S. Senate, *Report of the Secretary of the Interior*, Executive Document 35, 40th Congress, 3d sess., 1869; U.S. House of Representatives, *Report of the Commissioner of Indian Affairs*, Executive Document 1, 42d Congress, 3d sess., 1872; William Sturtevant, ed., "R. H. Pratt's Report on the Seminole in 1879," *Florida Anthropologist* 9 (1956): 1–24; U.S. Senate, *Message from the President of the United States Transmitting a Letter of the Secretary of the Interior Relative to Land upon Which to Locate Seminole Indians*, Executive Document 139, 50th Congress, 1st sess., 1888; U.S. House of Representatives, *Report of the Commissioner of Indian Affairs*, Executive Document 1, 50th Congress, 2d sess., 1888; idem, Executive Document 1, 53d Congress, 2d sess., 1893; idem, Executive Document 5, 55th Congress, 2d sess., 1897. For the early twentieth century, see U.S. Senate, *Everglades of Florida*, Senate Document 89, 62d Congress, 1st sess., 1911; idem, *Seminole Indians in Florida*, Senate Document 42, 63d Congress, 1st sess., 1913; idem, *Special Report of the Florida Seminole Agency*, Senate Document 102, 67th Congress, 2d sess., 1921; and idem, *Survey of the Seminole Indians of Florida*, Senate Document 314, 71st Congress, 1st sess., 1931. The U.S. Department of the Interior compiled *Narrative Reports of the Superintendents of the Florida Seminole Agency and Special Commissioners, 1893–1940* (Washington: Government Printing Office, 1893–1940).

Much of the history of the Seminoles in the late nineteenth and early twentieth centuries is known through whites who traded for animal skins and plumage with the Indians. The best analysis of this form of cultural interaction is Harry Kersey, *Pelts, Plumes, and Hides: White Traders among the Seminole Indians, 1870–1930*

(Gainesville: University Presses of Florida, 1975), which relies heavily on interviews with surviving members of the trading families and their personal documents. Many taped interviews with these traders are on file at the Center for the Study of Southeastern Indians, Florida State Museum, Gainesville. See also Harry Kersey, "Pelts, Plumes, and Hides: White Traders among the Seminole Indians, 1890–1930," *Florida Historical Quarterly* 52 (1973):250–66, and Charlton Tebeau, *The Story of the Chokoloskee Bay Country* (Miami: University of Miami Press, 1955).

For the late nineteenth and early twentieth centuries, there are excellent photograph collections on the Seminoles in the Audiovisual Department of the National Archives, Bureau of Indian Affairs Record Group 75. Also excellent is the photograph collection of the National Anthropological Archives of the Smithsonian Institution, also in Washington, D.C. In Florida, the Historical Society of Fort Lauderdale, the Historical Association of Southern Florida (Miami), and the Collier County Historical Society (Naples) also have fine photograph collections.

White-authored accounts for this period include Mary Wintringham, ed., "North to South through the Glades in 1883: The Account of the First New Orleans *Times-Democrat* Exploring Expedition," *Tequesta* 23–24 (1963–64):33–93; Monroe Kirk, "Alligator Hunting with Seminoles," *Cosmopolitan* 13 (1892):576–81; Monroe Kirk, "A Forgotten Remnant," *Scribner's* 7 (1893):303–17; Minnie Moore-Willson, *The Seminoles of Florida* (New York: n.p., 1896); and Charles Coe, *Red Patriots: The Story of the Seminoles* (Cincinnati: n.p., 1898; reprinted, Gainesville: University of Florida Press, 1974).

Educational and missionary intrusions are covered in several articles by Harry Kersey: "Educating the Seminole Indians of Florida, 1879–1970," *Florida Historical Quarterly* 49 (1970):16–35; "The Ahfachkee Day School," *Teachers College Record* 72 (1970):93–103; "The 'Friends of the Florida Seminoles' Society, 1899–1926," *Tequesta* 34 (1974):3–20; "The Case of Tom Tiger's Horse: An Early Foray into Indian Rights," *Florida Historical Quarterly* 53 (1975):306–18; and "Private Societies and the Maintenance of Seminole Tribal Integrity, 1899–1957," *Florida Historical Quarterly* 61 (1978):297–316. An individual focus from the perspective of early white teachers and missionaries is contained in Emily Lagow Bell, *My Pioneer Days in Florida, 1876–1898* (Miami: McMurray, 1928); Harriet Randolph Parkhill, *Mission to the Seminoles* (Orlando: n.p., 1909); and Harry Kersey and Donald Pullease, "Bishop William Crane Gray's Mission to the Seminole Indians in Florida, 1893–1914," *Historical Magazine of the Protestant Episcopal Church* 42 (1973): 257–73.

For general studies of the early twentieth century, see James Covington, "Florida Seminoles, 1900–1920," *Florida Historical Quarterly* 53 (1974): 181–97; Alason Skinner, "The Florida Seminoles," *Southern Workman* 40 (1911): 154–63; Alason Skinner, "Notes on the Florida Seminole," *American Anthropologist* 15 (1913): 63–67; J. R. Henderson, "The Seminoles of Florida," *Wide World* (1926): 348–51; Walter Hough, "Seminoles of the Florida Swamps," *Home Geographic Monthly* 2 (1932): 7–12; and W. Huston, "Los Indios Seminolas," *Revista Geographica Espanola* 7 (1940): 49–58. William Webb, "The Indian As I Knew Him" *Ethnohistory* 1 (1954): 181–98, includes some reminiscences of the Seminoles in the early 1900s. See also two articles on demography by Wilton Krogman: "The Racial Composition of the Seminole Indians of Florida and Oklahoma," *Journal of Negro History* 19 (1934): 412–30, and "Vital Data on the Population of the Seminole Indians of Florida and Oklahoma," *Human Biology* 7 (1935): 335–49.

By the 1940s and 1950s, as Seminole culture began to change rapidly, anthropologists spent more time among these Indians, analyzing traditional lifestyles. Among the earliest were Alexander Spoehr, *Camp, Clan and Kin among the Cow Creek Seminoles of Florida*, Field Museum of Natural History Anthropological Series 33, No. 3 (Chicago: Field Museum, 1944); Robert Greenlee, "Ceremonial Practices of the Modern Seminoles," *Tequesta* 3 (1942): 25–33; idem, "Medicine and Curing Practices of the Modern Florida Seminoles," *American Anthropologist* 46 (1944): 317–28; idem, "Aspects of Social Organization and Material Culture of the Seminole of Big Cypress Swamp," *Florida Anthropologist* 5 (1952): 25–31; Ether Cutler Freeman, "Our Unique Indians, the Seminoles of Florida," *The American Indian* 2 (1944–45): 14–27; idem, "The Seminole Woman of the Big Cypress and Her Influence in Modern Life," *American Indigena* 4 (1944): 123–28; idem, "We Live with the Seminoles," *American Museum of Natural History* 49 (1942): 226–36; John Goggin, "Silver Work of the Florida Seminole," *El Palacio* 47 (1940): 25–32; idem, "The Present Condition of the Florida Seminoles," *New Mexico Anthropologist* 1 (1949): 37–39; idem, "Florida's Indians," University of Florida *Economic Leaflets*, vol. 10 (1951); idem, "Source Materials for the Study of the Florida Seminoles," in *Laboratory Notes, Anthropology Laboratory*, no. 3 (Gainesville: University of Florida Press, 1959); Ether Cutler Freeman, "Culture Stability and Change among the Seminoles of Florida," in *Men and Cultures*, ed. Anthony F. C. Wallace (Philadelphia: University of Pennsylvania Press, 1960); Ether Cutler Freeman, "Two Types of Cultural Response to External Pressures among the Florida Seminoles," *Anthropological Quarterly* 38 (1965): 55–61; Ira England, "The Florida Seminole: A Study in Acculturation, Culture Change and Curriculum," (Ed.D. dissertation, University of Florida, 1957); William Sturtevant, "Notes on Modern Seminole Traditions of Osceola," *Florida Historical Quarterly* 33 (1955): 206–17; M. R. Harrington, "Seminole Adventure," *The Masterkey* 20 (1946): 157–59; idem, "Seminole Oranges," *The Masterkey* 20 (1946): 112; idem, "Seminole Surgeon," *The Masterkey* 27 (1953): 122; Frances Densmore, "Three Parallels between the Seminole Indians and the Ancient Greeks," *The Masterkey* 25 (1951): 76–78; Frances Densmore, "The Seminole Indian Today," *Southern Folklore Quarterly* 18 (1954): 212–21; and Federal Writer's Project of the Works Progress Administration, *The Seminole Indians in Florida* (Tallahassee: Florida Anthropological Society, 1951).

Recent ethnographic studies have tended to be more specialized, such as Hilda Davis, "The History of Seminole Clothing and Its Multi-Colored Designs," *American Anthropologist* 52 (1955): 974–80. Frederick Sleight, "Kunti: A Food Staple of the Florida Indians," *Florida Anthropologist* 6 (1953): 46–52, built upon earlier research by John Small, "Seminole Bread—The Conti . . . ," *Journal of the New York Botanical Garden* 22 (1921): 212–37. Louis Capron published several studies: *The Medicine Bundles of the South Florida Seminole and Green Corn Dance*, BAE Bulletin 51 (1953); "Notes on the Hunting Dance of the Cow Creek Seminole," *Florida Anthropologist* 9 (1956): 48–67; "Florida's 'Wild' Indians, the Seminoles," *National Geographic* 90 (1956): 819–40; and "Florida's

Emerging Seminoles," *National Geographic* 126 (1969):716–34. William Sturtevant wrote "The Medicine Bundles and Busks of the Florida Seminoles," *Florida Anthropologist* 7 (1954):31–70; "A Seminole Personal Document," *Tequesta* 16 (1956):55–75; and "Accomplishments and Opportunities in Florida Indian Ethnology," in *Florida Anthropology*, ed. Charles Fairbanks (Tallahassee: Florida Anthropological Society, 1958).

An important overview by William Sturtevant, "Creek into Seminole," is in *North American Indians in Historical Perspective*, edited by Leacock and Lurie. Other recent general surveys include Wilfred Neill, *Florida's Seminole Indians* (Silver Springs, Fla.: Ross Allen, 1952); Irving Piethman, *The Unconquered Seminole Indians* (St. Petersburg: n.p., 1957); Wyatt Blassingame, *Seminoles of Florida* (Tallahassee: Florida Anthropological Society, 1959); Charlton Tebeau, *Florida's Last Frontier* (Miami: n.p., 1966); Merwyn Garbarino, "Seminole Girl," *Trans-Action* 7 (1970):40–46; Merwyn Garbarino, *Big Cypress, a Changing Seminole Community* (New York: Holt, Rinehart and Winston, 1972); R. T. King, "Clan Affiliation and Leadership among the Twentieth Century Florida Indians," *Florida Historical Quarterly* 55 (1976):138–152; and Charles Fairbanks, *The Seminole People* (Phoenix: Indian Tribal Series, 1976).

List of Contributors

List of Contributors

ADOLPH L. DIAL is associate professor and chairperson of the American Indian Studies Department at Pembroke State University, North Carolina. His book *The Only Land I Know: A History of the Lumbee Indians* is about his own people, focusing on his native Robeson County. He was recently appointed by Congress as a member of the American Indian Policy Review Commission, representing nonfederally recognized Indians.

ERNEST C. DOWNS served as director of the Southeastern Indian Project at the Institute for the Development of Indian Law, Washington, D.C. He also worked on the staff of the American Indian Policy Review Commission and on the Senate Select Committee on Indian Affairs, concentrating on nonfederally recognized Indians. He is now a consultant and freelance writer in Washington, D.C.

W. McKEE EVANS is professor of history at California State Polytechnic University, Pomona. He is best known for his books *Ballots and Fence Rails: Reconstruction on the Lower Cape Fear* and *To Die Game: The Story of the Lowry Band, Indian Guerrillas of Reconstruction*.

THOMAS FRENCH is assistant reference librarian at Xavier University, Cincinnati.

CHARLES HUDSON is professor of anthropology at the University of Georgia. He is a past president of the Southern Anthropological Society and the author of *The Catawba Nation* and *The Southeastern Indians*. He edited *Red, White, and Black: Symposium on Indians in the Old South* and *Four Centuries of Southern Indians*.

HARRY A. KERSEY JR. is professor of education at Florida Atlantic University. He is the author of *Pelts, Plumes, and Hides: White Traders among the Seminole Indians, 1870–1930.*

SHARLOTTE NEELY is assistant professor of anthropology at Northern Kentucky University. She has done field research in the Snowbird Community of the Eastern Cherokees.

J. ANTHONY PAREDES is associate professor of anthropology at Florida State University. In addition to his field work among the Eastern Creeks, he has done research with Ojibwa Indians in Minnesota. He is editor of *Anishinabe: Six Studies of Modern Ojibwa.*

JOHN H. PETERSON JR. is associate professor and head of the Department of Anthropology at Mississippi State University. His publications include several reports on Choctaw history and ethnography, and he served as the planner for the Choctaw tribal government.

HELEN C. ROUNTREE is assistant professor of anthropology at Old Dominion University. Her field-work experience has been among Shoshone Indians of Nevada, as well as with various Virginia Indians.

MAX E. STANTON is associate professor of anthropology at Brigham Young University, Hawaii Campus. His field research has been devoted not only to Houma Indians but also Crow Indians and to Samoan immigrants in Hawaii.

WALTER L. WILLIAMS has an interdisciplinary background in history and anthropology and is assistant professor of history at the University of Cincinnati. He has had field-work experience among Eastern Cherokees.

Index

Index

Jackson, Andrew, 17
Jefferson, Thomas, 72, 75
Jim Crow laws, effects on Indians. *See* Racism
Joligo, Cahura (Tunica chief), 73

Koasati. *See* Coushatta Indians
Ku Klux Klan, 65

Labor: wage labor employed by whites, 84, 118, 131, 168, 201, 205; Indian co-op labor, 105, 119. *See also* Sharecropping
Land claims cases. *See* Indian Claims Commission
Land expansion by whites over Indian lands, 10, 13, 16, 21–23, 50–51, 59, 62–63, 101, 113, 129–31, 136, 147, 151, 156–58, 165, 176, 181–82, 196–201, 204, 206–7
Land rights on reservations, 169
Langston, Tazewell (Pamunkey), 35, 42
Languages, 7–9, 98–99, 104, 116, 127, 129, 148, 160, 164, 167, 171, 175, 185, 204, 235
Lattanache (Tunica chief), 74
Long, "Speedy," 85
Louisiana, 72–109, 221–25. *See also* Bayogoula, Biloxi, Chawasha, Chitimacha, Choctaw, Coushatta, Houma, Natchez, Tunica, Washa
Lowry, Henry Berry, 51–52, 55–56, 65
Lumbee Indians, 49–71, 220–21

MacCauley, Clay, 177, 180
McGhee, Calvin W. (Creek chief), 123, 130, 136–38
McGhee, Houston (Creek chief), 138
McGhee, Lynn and Hettie (Creeks), 126, 127
Manac, Dixon and Betsy (Creeks), 127
Marshall, John, 17
Martin, Phillip (Choctaw), 150–51
Mattamuskeet Indians, 219
Mattaponi Indians, 28, 34–36, 39–40, 44. *See also* Upper Mattaponi
Medicine, 161
Meherrin Indians, 27
Melacon (Tunica chief), 78

Melungeons, 219
Mestizoes. *See* Tri-racial isolates
Meyer, Harvey, 98–99
Miccosukee Indians, 175, 186–87. *See also* Seminole
Migration, 12, 37, 45, 63, 66, 84, 103, 107, 119, 128, 139, 205. *See also* Urbanization
Missionaries to Indians. *See* Christianity
Mississippi, 228–30. *See also* Choctaw, Chickasaw
"Mixed-bloods," 14–15, 155, 166, 170, 202
Monacan Indians, 27
Montet, Numa F., 83
Mooney, James, 37, 39, 157, 162, 164–65
Moore-Willson, Minnie, 182
Moreau, Celestin, 78
Morgan, Washington, 161
Mormon converts, 116, 118

Nansemond Indians, 36, 40
Naquin, Victory (Houma chief), 99
Narragansett Indians, 30
Nash, Roy, 100
Natchez Indians, 73
Negroes. *See* Afro-Americans
New Deal, 167, 185, 233. *See also* John Collier
New Echota, 156
North Carolina, 157, 218–21. *See also* Catawba, Cherokee, Coharie, Haliwa, Lumbee, Mattamuskeet, Tuscarora, Waccamau-Siouan
Nottoway Indians, 27, 28, 30, 32–34

Oil on Houma lands, 101
Ojibwa Indians, 37
Oklahoma, 136, 148–49. *See also* Indian Territory, Removal
Osceola, Annie (Seminole), 183
Owl, Henry (Cherokee), 166

Pamunkey Indians, 28, 34–37, 39, 40, 42, 43, 115, 220, 226
Pan-Indian identity, 38, 46, 66, 68, 120, 130, 134, 137–39, 170–71, 206, 217
Parker, George, 31
Pembroke (N.C.), 58, 67